Group Genius

Group Genius

The Creative Power of Collaboration

KEITH SAWYER

BASIC BOOKS

A Member of the Perseus Books Group
New York

For Barb

Books published by Basic Books are available at special discounts for
bulk purchases in the United States by corporations, institutions, and
other organizations. For more information, please contact the Special
Markets Department at the Perseus Books Group, 2300 Chestnut Street,
Suite 200, Philadelphia, PA 19103, or call (800) 255-1514, or e-mail
special.markets@perseusbooks.com.

Designed by Brent Wilcox

Library of Congress Cataloging-in-Publication Data
Sawyer, R. Keith (Robert Keith)
    Group genius : the creative power of collaboration / by Keith Sawyer.
        p.   cm.
    Includes bibliographical references and index.
    ISBN-13: 978-0-465-07192-0; ISBN-10: 0-465-07192-9
    1. Group problem solving.   2. Creative thinking.   I. Title.
HD30.29.S29 2007
658.4'036—dc22

2007008007

PB: ISBN: 978-0-465-07193-7

10 9 8 7 6 5 4

CONTENTS

INTRODUCTION:
BEYOND THE LONE GENIUS

....

In 2006 CNN asked me to appear on a one-hour special about "genius" hosted by Sanjay Gupta, MD. The invitation presented a challenge: how to condense into a ten-minute segment my broad expertise and how to choose material that would be especially interesting to viewers. I had ten years of business experience as a management consultant, advising large companies like Citibank and U.S. West on innovation. I'd spent fifteen years studying the science of creativity, starting with my PhD in psychology at the University of Chicago. And through it all, I'd continued playing jazz piano just as I had back in high school and college.

But it didn't take me long to decide what to present on CNN—I took their crew to Chicago to film the onstage collaborations of iO, the influential improvisational theater that launched Mike Myers, Tina Fey, and the late Chris Farley. The reason? Both my research and my real-world experience had led me to the same conclusion: Collaboration is the secret to breakthrough creativity. I'd just finished a ten-year study of how Chicago actors improvise dialogue on stage, and I'd discovered that group improv was the purest form of collaboration. The rest of the CNN special was about individual genius—with segments on brain scanning and child prodigies—but when it came to creativity, the show focused on what I call "group genius."

Psychologists are taught to study the individual mind—indirectly, through ingenious experiments, or directly, using new technologies to photograph the brain in action. When I began to study creativity, I took the same approach, investigating what happened in the mind when people were being creative. I interviewed jazz musicians, and I developed theories to explain improvisation.

But I quickly became disappointed with this focus on the individual. My years of playing piano in jazz ensembles convinced me that what happened in any one person's mind could never explain what made one night's performance shine and another a dud. At any second during a performance, an almost invisible musical exchange could take the piece in a new direction; later, no one could remember who was responsible for what. In jazz, the group has the ideas, not the individual musicians.

In the business world, I'd seen many innovations emerge from a group's genius. In the early 1980s, at my first job after college, I designed video games for Atari. Each game benefited from constant collaboration; I talked to other game designers every day, and we held frequent brainstorming sessions to generate new game ideas. I worked with graphic designers who created the animation sequences that made the characters run, hop, and throw, and musicians who composed those memorable little beeps and boops. And in my next job, while advising Citibank on innovative new technologies, I learned about how John Reed, the CEO, put together a team of key executives to turn the cash machine and the credit card into everyday realities.

Because of these experiences in jazz and business, soon after I started graduate school I realized that the psychology of the individual mind couldn't explain group genius. So I began to search for an alternative approach to studying creativity. That's when I discovered "interaction analysis," a research tool that allows scientists to chart the minute-to-minute interactions that make collaboration so powerful. Applying this method to improvisational theater dialogues revealed how unexpected insights emerge from the group. And when I applied the method to everyday conversations, business meetings, and brainstorming sessions, I began to learn how collaboration drives innovation.

In recent years, I took this new perspective on collaboration and used it to better understand today's networked economy—for example, analyzing the way new ideas such as Google Earth's mash-ups emerged from Google's collaborative, improvisational culture, or how Cisco's innovative network technology brought its employees together electronically, dramatically expanding opportunities for collaboration. Everything I observed told me that each business success was based on collaboration—not only in trendy Silicon Valley companies such as the IDEO design firm or Apple Computer, but also in manufacturing firms such as 3M and W. L. Gore, and at highly technical research labs. The more I observed creativity in action the more I realized that the most radical breakthroughs—including television, the airplane, e-mail, and even the board game Monopoly—emerged from a collaborative web that can't be contained within any one company's walls.

Along the way, I collected stories of significant innovations—both historical, such as the airplane and the telegraph, and contemporary, such as e-mail and the mountain bike. And I made a fascinating discovery: Even though these products didn't result from a single conversation, their historical emergence followed the same process as an improvised conversation—with small sparks gathering together over time, multiple dead ends, and the reinterpretation of previous ideas.

These innovations all result from an invisible collaborative web, and in this book I draw on my research—including the lessons of improv theater—and the work of other social scientists to make this collaborative web visible. I begin in Part 1 by taking you on a journey through amazing examples of creative collaboration shown by earthquake and hurricane disaster response networks, military teams, and pickup basketball games. I use these to show that the most effective collaborations are improvisational—just like the work of the Chicago group iO that appeared on CNN's 2006 special.

I soon learned that only certain kinds of collaboration work in the real world—improvisations that are guided and planned, but in a way that doesn't kill the power of improvisation to generate unexpected insights. Brainstorming is a good example: Numerous studies have shown that this popular technique is usually a waste of time. The truth is that, despite the proliferation of advice in the business press, many companies don't know how to foster creative collaboration. Fortunately, today's research tells us how. For example, I show that improvised innovation is more likely to work when a group experiences *group flow*—the group equivalent of Mihaly Csikszentmihalyi's famous "flow" state, when we perform at our peak and lose track of time. And I show how to build brainstorming groups that realize their full creative potential.

By the end of Part 1, I hope to have convinced you of the creative power of collaboration. But you still might wonder: Isn't the individual mind the ultimate source of creativity? Doesn't each creative spark come from one person? In fact, researchers have discovered that the mind itself is filled with a kind of internal collaboration, that even the insights that emerge when you're completely alone can be traced back to previous collaborations.

In Part 2, I share the results of exciting new research on the collaborative nature of the mind. You'll have fun doing creativity games yourself—the same ones that top researchers use in their laboratories, games that tap into the brain processes that drive creative insight. I'll walk you through some classic "insight problems," those that require an "Aha!" experience to be solved. And you'll see that even though insight often feels like a solitary, private event, its roots are in collaboration.

When *Time* magazine interviewed me about creativity in 2006, I explained the key lesson of this research: There's no magic or mystery to the flash of insight. Indeed, using clever research designs, scientists have demonstrated how moments of insight can be traced back to previous dedication, hard work, and collaboration. And they've shown how we all can tap into the creative power of collaboration to make our own insights more frequent and more successful.

In Part 3, I move into the real world of earth-shattering innovation. I argue that most of what we've heard about famous inventions is wrong because it's based on the myth of the lone genius. I'll reveal the real stories behind famous inventions: the telegraph (not invented by Samuel Morse), the light bulb (not invented by Thomas Edison), and the airplane (not invented by the Wright brothers). Forget the myths about historical inventors; the truth is always a story of group genius. And today's innovations emerge from ever more complex organizations and many interacting teams. I'll show you how group genius creates today's cutting-edge products, including Motorola's Razr phone, Pringles Prints, and the Linux operating system.

Part 3 takes you inside some of today's most innovative companies and shows that they succeed by designing their organizations to maximize collaboration. I'll tell stories about innovative computer companies, such as Cisco and Apple; Web-based companies, such as YouTube and eBay; retailers, such as Whole Foods and Procter & Gamble; and manufacturers, such as Toyota and 3M.

Innovation is what drives today's economy, and our hopes for the future—as individuals and organizations—lie in finding creative solutions to pressing problems. My goal in this book is to reveal the unique power of collaboration to generate innovation. And it's my hope that you'll use these new insights about group genius to create more effective collaborations in your own life—at work, at home, and in your community.

PART I

The Collaborative Team

....

CHAPTER 1

The Power of Collaboration

ON DECEMBER 17, 1903, on a bitterly cold windswept beach in North Carolina, five men from the local lifeguard station stood in the sand and watched as Orville Wright took off in his handmade flyer into a twenty-seven-mile-per-hour wind. The twelve-horsepower engine kept him aloft for twelve seconds; he landed 100 feet away from the launch point. Orville and his brother, Wilbur, then took turns in making three more flights, the longest lasting fifty-nine seconds and covering 852 feet. No members of the press witnessed the event; Orville himself mounted his camera on a tripod and asked one of the lifeguards to snap the shutter. The resulting picture is the most famous image of innovation ever taken: The aircraft has just left its track and is 2 feet aloft; Wilbur, standing just off the wing, is leaning back as if astonished at their amazing feat.

How did these two bicycle mechanics from Dayton, Ohio, beat leading scientists, who had fortunes in funding, and win the international race to build the first airplane? The Wrights drew on the power of collaboration: They allowed their innovation to unfold from constant conversation and side-by-side work. Wilbur Wright later explained it this way: "From the time we were little children my brother Orville and myself lived together, played together, worked together and, in fact, thought together. We usually owned all of our toys in common, talked over our thoughts and aspirations so that nearly everything that was done in our lives has been the result of conversations, suggestions and discussions between us."

The Wrights kept detailed diaries of their transformative collaboration. These diaries show that the Wrights didn't experience a single moment of insight; rather, their collaboration resulted in a string of successive ideas, each spark lighting the next. In 1900, after four years of closely studying everything written on bird flight and glider designs, they took their first trip down to Kitty Hawk. After each practice flight, they modified the glider, and by the end of that first season, they had flown it safely, with several flights of more than 300 feet.

On their second trip to North Carolina in 1901, they realized that the wings weren't providing enough lift to carry the motor the craft would eventually need. Back in Dayton for the winter, they built a wind tunnel that was 6 feet long and, using a powerful fan hooked up to a gasoline engine, tested two hundred wing designs.

On their third trip to Kitty Hawk, in 1902, they were getting so good at flying their glider that they routinely made fifty or more flights each day. But they discovered an unexpected problem, known as "adverse yaw": When warping the wings to steer right or left, the glider lost control and leaned over too far, crashing the wing's tip into the ground (the Wrights called it "well digging"). Before they could fly safely, this problem had to be fixed. First, they added a vertical tail; this helped a bit, but the glider still crashed unpredictably. One day, Orville told Wilbur about a new idea: Modify the vertical tail so that it could be moved by the operator. Wilbur responded by suggesting that the new cable required to control the tail be tied into the wing-warping mechanism so that the operator could work both controls at once. This collaborative insight proved to be the final piece of the puzzle: By combining wing warping and a movable tail, they had mastered controlled gliding. Now they were ready for powered flight.

In 1903, they designed and built their own gasoline engine and propellers, and then scaled up the aircraft to support the extra weight. They refined the design further by adding a second vertical tail for better control. They arrived in North Carolina for the fourth time in September and worked through October and November fixing tiny problems that kept cropping up. Everything finally came together on that cold day in late December.

Invisible Collaboration

The Wright brothers lived together, ate together, and discussed their project every day. Their collaboration was visible to everyone around them, and it speaks from every page of their journals. But many creative collaborations are almost invisible—and it's these largely unseen and undocumented collaborations that hold the secrets of group genius.

The mountain bike provides a perfect example of what I call "invisible collaboration." No one knows exactly when and where that innovation originated, but it probably dates to the early 1970s in Marin County, California. In the early 1970s, road cycling was making a comeback in America, and Marin County was a cycling hotbed. In the off-season, some of these bicyclists started riding just for fun on the dirt trails of Mount Tamalpais, or Mount Tam as locals call it, which rises 2,571 feet above San Francisco Bay. The roots and rocks would have trashed their expensive road-racing bikes, so they went to yard sales and scrounged up old balloon-tire bikes from the 1930s and 1940s. The fat tires provided a little extra give on the rough terrain. The cyclists found the rush hard to beat as they flew down the trail named Repack

Road at breakneck speed, dropping 1,300 vertical feet in two miles, surrounded by oak and redwood pine trees.

But the old Schwinn frames weren't built for such rugged terrain, and many of them collapsed when they ran into an especially big rock. One trailside tree was dubbed "Vendetti's Face" after a local rider flew headfirst into the trunk. There were other problems, too. The old brakes, used constantly to control speed, would get so hot that the grease evaporated and left a trail of smoke behind each rider. Riders had to pack in new grease after almost every trip down the mountain (thus the trail name "Repack Road"). And because the old bikes didn't have shifters or gears, riding uphill was almost impossible.

On December 1, 1974, three riders from Cupertino, seventy-five miles to the south, showed up in Marin for an off-road race. They called themselves the Morrow Dirt Club. They were riding old balloon-tire bikes, but these machines were different: They'd been rigged up with shifters and multiple gears, and the handlebars were modified into today's familiar "longhorn" shape, providing better control. The Marin bikers had never seen anything like it before, and they quickly modified their own bikes with the new ideas. At about the same time, a third group of fat-tire riders had formed in Crested Butte, Colorado, a desirable location for scenic, rugged rides, such as the Pearl Pass road from Crested Butte to Aspen. A few years later, when five riders from Marin took their shifter-modified bikes to the Pearl Pass race, they not only left the local riders in the dust but also left behind their new ideas.

By the late 1970s, some of the more mechanically inclined riders were starting to make a living building custom mountain bikes, and business grew by word of mouth. When Gary Fisher and Charlie Kelly launched the first mountain bike company in 1979, they sold hand-made bikes costing $1,400. Even at that high price, buyers snatched them up. Within a few years, the big bike companies entered the business, and by 1986, mountain bike sales surpassed road bike sales. Ten years earlier, only a few hundred people had even heard of mountain biking; ten years later, in 1996, mountain biking was an Olympic sport.

The early riders in California and Colorado weren't trying to change biking forever and they weren't trying to start a new industry; they were just having fun. But then unexpected events followed their initial innovations. The Morrow Dirt Club designed the gear-shifter and the new handlebars; the Marin County riders devised brakes that wouldn't burn out; and several riders independently designed custom-made frames that wouldn't break on the big bumps. After that, still others created manufacturing techniques and marketing strategies, and gradually they modified the bike to appeal to mainstream America. Soon, all of us—buyers, riders, and commuters—did the rest. The mountain bike was the result of a largely invisible long-term collaboration that stretched from Marin to Colorado.

Although the Wright brothers will always hold a special place in history, today's airplanes also unfolded through invisible collaboration. The Wrights' most significant idea, to steer using wing warping and a moving vertical tail, was soon replaced by other aviators with a better invention: the aileron, a separate surface on the trailing edge of the wing that pivoted up and down. By the beginning of World War I, most of the Wrights' ideas had been replaced by better technologies.

We're drawn to the image of the lone genius whose mystical moment of insight changes the world. But the lone genius is a myth; instead, it's group genius that generates breakthrough innovation. When we collaborate, creativity unfolds across people; the sparks fly faster, and the whole is greater than the sum of its parts.

Collaboration drives creativity because innovation always emerges from a series of sparks—never a single flash of insight. The Wright brothers had lots of small ideas, each critical to the success of the first powered flight. The mountain bike wasn't commercially viable until many distinct ideas came together. These two stories show how the genius of the group emerges through the sanding and polishing of raw innovation.

Jazz Freddy

When scientists first began looking at creativity in the 1950s, they focused on the solitary creative person. Although this research provided important insights—for example, creative people are slightly above average in intelligence but aren't necessarily geniuses, and creative people are good at generating lots of ideas—by the early 1990s, those of us studying creativity had reached the limits of this approach. We were beginning to see that even the best creativity tests couldn't predict which children would become the most creative adults. Even the most enriched elementary school curricula seemed to have no significant impact on how creative students would be years later. My colleagues and I realized that we needed to find a new way to explain how innovation takes place and how to unleash each person's creative potential.

Psychologists are typically trained to focus on the individual, an approach firmly supported by our culture's belief that the solitary individual is the source of creativity. But to our surprise, beginning in the 1990s, our research began to point in the opposite direction. We began to see that innovations once believed to be the creation of a genius actually emerged from invisible collaborations, and that collaboration was responsible for famous creations throughout history.

Sigmund Freud is credited with creating psychoanalysis, but in fact these ideas emerged from a vast network of colleagues. The French impressionist painting associated with Claude Monet and Auguste Renoir emerged from a closely connected group of Parisian painters. Albert Einstein's contributions to modern physics were embedded in an international collaboration among many laboratories and many teams. Psychoanalysis, impressionism, and quantum physics emerged over many years of interactions, trial and error, and false starts—not in a single burst of insight.

As we moved beyond historical observation to the laboratory and to the everyday world, a new science of creativity began to form. My contribution has been to map the architecture of collaboration in two uniquely creative groups: the improvising ensembles of jazz and theater. These are the purest form of group genius; their creative performances emerge from everyone's equal participation.

In 1992, early in my research, I began to hear about an improvisational theater group called Jazz Freddy, which was performing at the Live Bait Theater in Wrigleyville—an urban neighborhood on the North Side of Chicago named for its central feature, the Chicago Cubs' Wrigley Field. The ten-member cast of Jazz Freddy chose the name to emphasize their links with jazz—their improvisations were free-flowing and unpredictable. I'd heard that the Live Bait had been sold out for every Jazz Freddy performance—pretty good for a type of theater that was off most people's radar at that time.

What made Jazz Freddy unique? After all, Chicago was the birthplace of modern improv theater, the city where the Compass Players and the Second City Theater created improv in the 1950s. By the early 1960s, Chicago improv was nationally known; it produced stars such as Mike Nichols and Elaine May as well as the legendary television program *Saturday Night Live,* which revolutionized small-screen comedy.

Through the 1980s, *Saturday Night Live* kept going strong. But back in Chicago, the improv scene had fallen into a rut. The famous Second City Theater had stopped improvising on stage, preferring instead to stick with scripted sketch comedy. Improv was risky; scripts were better at drawing in the large paying audiences of tourists who basically just wanted to see *Saturday Night Live,* live. It was a well-known secret among Chicago actors that during the break the cast worked furiously to weave the audience suggestions into the scripted material they were developing for the next season's show. Second City was undeniably funny and successful, but it didn't have the exciting edge that early improv had enjoyed.

Jazz Freddy was bringing back the excitement by doing something more radical, more free-form than Second City's sketch comedy. Jazz Freddy's goal was riskier than anything that had been tried before: Every night, they performed a fully improvised one-hour play in two acts, separated by an intermission.

On a Saturday night in April 1993, I made the forty-minute drive to Wrigleyville from my home at the University of Chicago. The rumors that I'd heard were true—the Live Bait was packed. I sat in a folding chair in the aisle about two feet from the stage, which was only a foot high, and barren except for ten wooden chairs. Right on schedule, the lights came up; the audience applauded as the cast members ran onto the stage and stood in an informal group facing the audience. Two cast members stepped to the front of the stage and asked the audience to supply an event and a location. "The Olympics," shouted one member of the audience. "A convent," yelled another.

The lights went down; in the dim glow cast by the aisle safety lights, we could see the ten cast members walking to the sides of the stage to sit in the wooden chairs. Two of the actors almost simultaneously decided to walk to the center of the stage; one of them, noticing that the other had started first, deferred and went back to his chair at stage left. The first actor, John, pulled a chair to the center of the stage and sat down, facing the audience, as the stage lights came up. He mimed working at a desk—he took a cap off of a pen, opened a book, and started to make underlining motions as he studied the page. He stopped to rub his eyes. He then turned the page and underlined some more. The other actors watched intently from the sides of the stage; the audience was completely quiet. After about twenty seconds, Mary stood up at the opposite side of the stage, and walked over to John, miming the act of carrying something in both hands held in front of her:

MARY: Here are those papers.
　　　 (*Mimes putting down the "papers" and remains standing.*
　　　 2 second pause.)
JOHN: Thanks.
　　　 (*Looks up to face* MARY. *2 second pause.*)
　　　 I really appreciate your doing those copies for me.

　　　 (BILL *approaches from stage left, also carrying "papers," and stops*
　　　 next to MARY.)

BILL: Here are those papers.
　　　 (*Puts down the papers.*)
JOHN: Thanks a lot,
　　　 (*Still facing the two*)
　　　 you guys have really been great.
　　　 (*2 second pause*)
　　　 I'm gonna stop booking for now.
　　　 (*Closes book on desk.*)
MARY: Okay.
BILL: Sure.
　　　 (*1 second pause*)
　　　 I'm gonna go get some more papers.
JOHN: Alright.
　　　 (*He stands up. 1 second pause*)
　　　 Thanks a lot, I appreciate it.
BILL: You're welcome.
　　　 (*1 second pause*)
　　　 We mean it.
　　　 (*As he says this,* BILL *touches* MARY's *arm;* MARY *reaches*
　　　 up her other hand to grasp his hand; they stand holding
　　　 hands.)
JOHN: Thanks for being in my corner.
BILL: We always will be.

Even these first thirty seconds of the one-hour performance demonstrate the key characteristics of improvisation. It's unpredictable; the actors don't even know who's going to speak next, much less what they're going to say. Even an offstage actor can walk on and take the next turn, as Bill does when he carries in more papers. The actors leave unusually long pauses between their turns of dialogue because they're just getting into the flow of the performance. And they choose ambiguous lines that open up possibilities.

After about ten minutes, the basic elements of the plot began to emerge, and the pace accelerated. By the intermission, Jazz Freddy had created two independent plotlines. The Olympics plot was about a baseball team training for the Olympics, and John has become an umpire who isn't very good and probably needs glasses. In the convent plot, the nuns are playing cards and spray-painting graffiti on the religious murals. One of the nuns has discovered that she's turned on by the janitor's boot fetish. The final scene in the first act takes place in heaven. God confers with Jesus and Saint Peter as they try to decide the best way to right things at the convent.

In the second act, the actors managed to weave these two plots together. The baseball games get ugly as the team members become filled with hatred for their opponents. Hoping to return the nuns to the straight and narrow, God sends Saint Peter to the convent disguised as a young girl. The play ends with several of the female baseball players quitting the sport to join the convent.

How can ten people go on stage and create such a complex and entertaining performance when they have absolutely no idea about what's going to happen? This is the question that I set out to answer. Armed with my video camera, I visited improv theaters all over Chicago; I ended up with a bookshelf full of videotapes—some of "long form" groups like Jazz Freddy, others of more traditional groups that did short skits and games. Then, back in the lab, I spent years analyzing the dialogues second by second, and I gradually began to understand how the performances emerged from the creative power of collaboration.

Inside the Black Box

It's not news to anyone in the corporate world that collaboration is powerful. Businesses everywhere are moving to team organizations, distributed leadership, and collaboration. The trend is so strong that even office furniture companies have been rethinking the cubicle-and-desk paradigm. James P. Hackett, chief executive officer of Steelcase, is leading the company in designing a new kind of furniture that will support group collaboration. Robyn Waters, Target's former vice president of trend, design, and product development, says that "collaboration is Target's secret sauce." Whole Foods Market attributes its success to its use of self-managed teams, which it calls the "Whole People" philosophy.

But the managers who have embraced the power of collaboration have largely taken a black-box approach: They look at overall team characteristics—such as members' personality traits—instead of investigating what goes on inside the box. My research strongly suggests that the secret to understanding what makes a collaboration successful lies inside the box, in moment-to-moment interactional dynamics.

Since the early 1990s, my colleagues and I have been using a variety of approaches to open up the black box of collaboration, to discover what happens when collaboration translates each person's creativity into group genius. My preferred approach is called *interaction analysis,* a time-consuming method of analyzing verbal gestures, body language, and conversation during collaboration. It requires about an hour of analysis for every minute of videotape to fully understand what's going on. I performed with many jazz and theater groups in the early 1990s, and because I was one of the group, they didn't mind when I set up my video camera and tripod. After two years of performing and collecting videotapes, I spent the next ten analyzing these collaborations, line by line and second by second. What I learned surprised me, and it changed the way I think about innovation.

In both an improv group and a successful work team, the members play off one another, each person's contributions providing the spark for the next. Together, the improvisational team creates a novel emergent product, one that's more responsive to the changing environment and better than what anyone could have developed alone. Improvisational teams are the building blocks of innovative organizations, and organizations that can successfully build improvisational teams will be more likely to innovate effectively.

On the basis of my research, I've identified seven key characteristics of effective creative teams.

1. Innovation Emerges over Time

No single actor comes up with the big picture, the whole plot. The play emerges bit by bit. Each actor, in each line of dialogue, contributes a small idea. In theater, we can see this process on stage; but with an innovative team, outsiders never see the long chain of small, incremental ideas that lead to the final innovation. Without scientific analysis, the collaboration remains invisible. Successful innovations happen when organizations combine just the right ideas in just the right structure.

2. Successful Collaborative Teams Practice Deep Listening

Trained improv actors listen for the new ideas that the other actors offer in their improvised lines, at the same time that they're coming up with their own ideas. This difficult balancing act is essential to group genius. Most people spend too much time planning their own actions and not enough time listening and observing others.

3. Team Members Build on Their
Collaborators' Ideas

When teams practice deep listening, each new idea is an extension of the ideas that have come before. The Wright brothers couldn't have thought of a moving vertical tail until after they discovered adverse yaw, and that discovery emerged from their experiments with wing warping.

Although a single person may get credit for a specific idea, it's hard to imagine that person having that idea apart from the hard work, in close quarters, of a dedicated team of like-minded individuals. Russ Mahon—one of the Morrow Dirt Club bikers from Cupertino—usually gets credit for putting the first derailleur on a fat-tired bike, but all ten members of the club played a role.

4. Only Afterwards Does the Meaning of
Each Idea Become Clear

Even a single idea can't be attributed to one person because ideas don't take on their full importance until they're taken up, reinterpreted, and applied by others. At the beginning of Jazz Freddy's performance, we don't know what John is doing: Is he studying for a test? Is he balancing the books of a criminal organization? Although he was the first actor to think of "studying," the others decided that he would be a struggling umpire, a man stubbornly refusing to admit that he needed glasses. Individual creative actions take on meaning only later, after they are woven into other ideas, created by other actors. In a creative collaboration, each person acts without knowing what his or her action means. Participants are willing to allow other people to give their action meaning by building on it later.

5. Surprising Questions Emerge

The most transformative creativity results when a group either thinks of a new way to frame a problem or finds a new problem that no one had noticed before. When teams work this way, ideas are often transformed into questions and problems. That's critical, because creativity researchers have discovered that the most creative groups are good at finding new problems rather than simply solving old ones.

6. Innovation Is Inefficient

In improvisation, actors have no time to evaluate new ideas before they speak. But without evaluation, how can they make sure it'll be good? Improvised innovation makes more mistakes, and has as many misses as hits. But the hits can be phenomenal; they'll make up for the inefficiency and the failures.

After the full hourlong Jazz Freddy performance, we never do learn why Bill and Mary are making copies for John—that idea doesn't go anywhere. In the second act, a brief subplot in which two actors are in the witness protection program also is never developed. Some ideas are just bad ideas; some of them are good in themselves, but the other ideas that would be necessary to turn them into an innovation just haven't happened yet. In a sixty-minute improvisation, many ideas are proposed that are never used. When we look at an innovation after the fact, all we remember is the chain of good ideas that made it into the innovation; we don't notice the many dead ends.

7. Innovation Emerges from the Bottom Up

Improvisational performances are *self-organizing*. With no director and no script, the performance emerges from the joint actions of the actors.

In the same way, the most innovative teams are those that can restructure themselves in response to unexpected shifts in the environment; they don't need a strong leader to tell them what to do. Moreover, they tend to form spontaneously; when like-minded people find each other, a group emerges.

The improvisational collaboration of the entire group translates moments of individual creativity into group innovation. Allowing the space for this self-organizing emergence to occur is difficult for many managers because the outcome is not controlled by the management team's agenda and is therefore less predictable. Most business executives like to start with the big picture and then work out the details. In improvisational innovation, teams start with the details and then work up to the big picture. It's riskier and less efficient, but when a successful innovation emerges, it's often so surprising and imaginative that no single individual could have thought of it.

Elixir

Today's most innovative companies are the ones that have successfully implemented the improvisational approach—from the award-winning Silicon Valley design firm IDEO to the manufacturing company W. L. Gore & Associates, tucked away in the countryside along the Delaware-Maryland border.

IDEO has contributed to more than three thousand products in at least forty industries, including Crest toothpaste tubes, toothbrushes, the original Apple computer mouse, an electric guitar, bike helmets, telephones, furniture, fishing equipment, and Nike sunglasses. IDEO succeeds because it has mastered improvisation—beginning with the classic collaboration technique known as brainstorming, which is designed so that each person's sparks of insight can be immediately built on by others. IDEO uses rapid prototyping so that shared ideas can prompt later ones. The company creates multiple teams to work on the same project independently so that different insights can cross-fertilize and blend; this strategy results in inefficient redundancies, and team members expect frequent failures. Employees aren't assigned to teams; each team forms spontaneously and then splits up when its task is done.

But a company doesn't have to be a trendy design firm to benefit from improvisational collaboration. In December 2004, *Fast Company* magazine went searching for the most innovative company in America—and they found W. L. Gore & Associates, maker of the famous GORE-TEX waterproof material. Most people don't know that Gore has created more than a thousand products—from Elixir, the top-selling acoustic guitar string, to Glide dental floss, to medical products such as heart patches and synthetic blood vessels.

Gore has succeeded by tapping into the power of collaboration. Bill Gore, the founder, created the company with hardly any hierarchy, few ranks and titles, and a minimum of structure, aside from such necessary support functions as human resources and IT. He organized the company into small task forces that constantly self-organize and regroup in response to changing needs. These self-managed teams don't have clear-cut roles and responsibilities: "Your team is your boss, because you don't want to let them down," one employee said. "Everyone's your boss, and no one's your boss." Teams form and manage themselves improvisationally, and employees define their own roles in the company improvisationally.

All employees reserve 10 percent of their time to pursue speculative new ideas (a practice also followed at innovation powerhouses such as 3M and Google). Ad-hoc teams form around these off-the-record ideas and operate for years before a new product is revealed to top management. The Elixir guitar strings started with a group of three employees who realized that the technology used in Gore's brand of Ride-On bike cables could be transferred to guitar strings. The Ride-On cables were coated with a thin film of plastic so that they'd slide through the cable housing with less friction; these engineers realized that by putting a similar coating on guitar strings they could prevent the dulling of sound that occurs when natural oils from the fingers corrode the strings. These three worked on the idea for 10 percent of their hours each week; once the idea had taken shape from this initial collaboration, they gradually persuaded six other colleagues to contribute their expertise. After three years of working without permission or oversight, the team was ready to start working on the project full-time, and they sought out the official support of the company. Soon after its release in 1997, Elixir quickly became the top-selling acoustic guitar string—a success that emerged from improvised innovation.

What do successful collaborations look like? Where do the most innovative ideas come from? Gore isn't unique; it turns out that the most innovative ideas emerge spontaneously, from the bottom up. To learn why, let's turn to the next chapter, where we'll examine the many different faces of improvised innovation.

....

CHAPTER 2

Improvising Innovation

IN NOVEMBER 1980, a violent earthquake hit southern Italy near Naples. Four thousand people were killed and 250,000 left homeless. Torrential rains caused mudslides and flooding. The mountainous region around Naples was a nightmare for relief groups. The rugged Apennine Mountains rise steeply from the coast, and one-lane roads snake through the valleys to hundreds of small towns. Mudslides blocked roads, bridges collapsed, and telephone and utility lines came down. It took days to organize an official response; the army didn't reach some mountain villages for three days.

Within a few hours, television reporters who had descended upon the disaster area reported horrible scenes, and they revealed to all Italy that there was no organized relief effort. Many people, frustrated and angry with the slow official response, decided that informal action was the only hope for the region. Almost six thousand volunteers rushed in to help. There were problems—these rescue groups caused traffic that blocked roads; some of them had no equipment; and a few hadn't even brought food for themselves. But soon a surprising thing happened: Without any management or leaders, the volunteers formed

themselves into unofficial organizations, emergent groups that saved hundreds of lives.

Students at a nearby university loaded a van and a couple of cars with whatever food and blankets they could find in their rooms and drove to a village that had been destroyed. They passed out the food and blankets and started search-and-rescue operations through the fallen buildings. The official response was still two days away; trapped survivors might well have died by that time.

The next day, friends of these students back at the university found a location where people could donate relief supplies or volunteer to go into the affected region. Soon, there emerged a complex system consisting of a collecting point on campus, a couple of trucks that went back and forth to the village, and a team in the village that distributed supplies and helped in search and rescue.

This system operated successfully for a few days until the army took over and restricted access. The students' efforts were thwarted because the military brass insisted that relief efforts go through official procedures. But paradoxically, the soldiers—although they enjoyed superior training in advance planning techniques—were initially less effective than the ad hoc group because they needed time to adapt their procedures to the unique features of the disaster. The surprising lesson from the 1980 Italian earthquake is that the planned and organized response was less effective than the improvised emergent response.

The Italian earthquake wasn't unique in benefiting from the improvisational wisdom of spontaneous response. After 2005's Hurricane Katrina, the biggest success story was the Coast Guard's search-and-rescue operation, and it succeeded because of improvisation. The Coast Guard rescued twice as many people after Katrina as it had in the previous fifty years—twenty-two thousand stranded in attics and on rooftops. Improvisation was a necessity because their main staging area in Gulfport, Mississippi, was destroyed. And the Coast Guard didn't do it alone; an emergent flotilla became available when civilian boaters came to help. Coast Guard commanders acted autonomously in the field and worked together with these emergent operations to multiply their effectiveness.

Most of us tend to believe that planning in advance makes groups more effective and that centralized control is especially important in a disaster. But studies repeatedly show the importance of these emergent groups. Strangers come together spontaneously in response to unexpected events and fade away once they're no longer needed. After decades of disaster research, we know that improvisational groups are often the fastest and most effective in the uncertain and rapidly changing conditions caused by a natural disaster.

Script-Think

We often fail to realize how important improvisation is to collaboration, even though companies such as IDEO and Gore appear frequently in the business press. A surprising number of people find it hard to believe that improvisation occurs at all. A friend whom I took to one of Jazz Freddy's one-hour improvised shows posed this question: "Which parts of it were improvised?" He was sure that most of the play had been decided ahead of time. In the following months, as I took others to see improv groups, I learned that this friend's reaction was typical; my other friends also thought that the performances were a kind of magic trick. I call this common reaction *script-think:* the tendency to think that events are more predictable than they really are. Psychologists believe this is a universal human tendency—think of how many conspiracy theories arise to explain complex and unplanned events.

Script-think isn't confined to the theater; even top business analysts can be fooled by it. For example, Honda's entry into the U.S. motorcycle market is one of the most successful improvisational innovation stories ever, and business experts had the story wrong for decades—and all because of script-think. In the 1950s, British companies sold almost half of all motorcycles purchased in the United States, right behind the market leader, Harley-Davidson. By 1973, that had dropped to less than 10 percent as Japanese manufacturers rapidly increased their U.S. market share. In Japan, the huge postwar demand for cheap transportation had resulted in a booming industry that produced small, inexpensive motorcycles. By 1959, Honda was the market leader; more than half of all motorcycles sold in Japan were Honda's tiny 50cc-engine Supercub. In spite of the company's success at home, in 1960 only 4 percent of Japanese motorcycles were exported. But six years later, Honda enjoyed more than 60 percent of the U.S. motorcycle market. How did the turnaround happen?

An in-depth 1975 case study by the Boston Consulting Group (BCG) concluded that Honda was successful because it had devised a great business plan. In BCG's analysis, Honda realized that the small motorcycles popular in Japan had no counterpart in the United States, and their plan was to occupy this niche. But although it's true that smaller motorcycles were responsible for Honda's success, the company didn't plan it that way: BCG had been misled by script-think. The real story is one of improvisational innovation.

Honda's original plan was to compete head-on with Harley in the large motorcycle segment. Mr. Honda himself believed that the 50cc Supercub wasn't suitable for the United States and that selling even a small number of them would hurt the company's image with the men who bought bigger motorcycles. Honda shifted to small motorcycles only as a result of two unexpected events. First, their big engines encountered terrible technical problems: Head gaskets would blow open and clutches would fail. Driving speeds and distances in the United States were much greater than in Japan, and the engines became stressed in a way that the Honda engineers hadn't foreseen. Honda had to withdraw them from the market immediately until the problems could be fixed. Second, the Japanese executives who were trying to sell these big motorcycles were using their own personal Supercubs to run errands around Los Angeles. Over and over, strangers would stop them in parking lots and ask where they could buy one. While the Honda executives were waiting for the big motorcycles to be redesigned, they asked their superiors back in Japan to let them try selling the small motorcycles. Honda was hesitant—the company didn't invest any money in marketing the small bikes—but decided it couldn't hurt to give it a try. The amazing result surprised everyone at Honda: Within four years, the company was selling one of every two motorcycles purchased in the United States.

Honda succeeded even though its advance planning failed—improvisation saved the day. It wasn't until 1963 that the company abandoned hopes of selling to the black-leather set and fully embraced the small-bike strategy by releasing the now-famous ad campaign: "You Meet the Nicest People on a Honda."

Innovation emerges from the bottom up, unpredictably and improvisationally, and it's often only after the innovation has occurred that everyone realizes what's happened. The paradox is that innovation can't be planned, it can't be predicted; it has to be allowed to emerge.

Taking a Fix

In 1985, the USS *Palau,* a navy helicopter carrier ship, was returning to its home port in San Diego. The approach to the harbor is notoriously tricky to navigate; the channel is narrow, it's filled with sailboats enjoying the year-round good weather, and over the course of several miles ships gradually end up turning almost 180 degrees to get around the island of Coronado and to their assigned berths at the navy base's pier. Changes in direction and speed have to be anticipated far in advance, and the crew has to know at all times exactly where the ship is located on the chart map of the harbor. Before the advent of the global positioning system (GPS), the quartermaster would determine the location of the ship by selecting three landmarks on shore. Crew members would first "take bearings" on these landmarks to find the line from the ship to the landmark and then use an electronic gyrocompass to determine the direction to the bearings with respect to true north. Then it's basic geometry that the ship has to be somewhere within the triangle formed by the three lines; the triangle would be calculated by two officers working at the chart table, and that calculation "fixed" the ship's location. When a ship is this close to shore, navy procedure demands that a fix be taken every few minutes.

As part of a study of group collaboration, Ed Hutchins, a professor of anthropology at the University of California in San Diego, had joined the navigation crew for their three-day voyage. He'd placed a tape recorder in the pilothouse to record the navigation team of eight officers and crew. As the staff was going about the tense business of navigating the entry to the harbor, the engineer's voice unexpectedly boomed over the intercom: "Bridge, Main Control. I am losing steam drum pressure. No apparent cause. I'm shutting my throttles." The ship's propulsion system had failed, shutting down the engines that drove the propeller, and simultaneously cutting off all electricity.

Everyone on the bridge knew that the ship would coast for miles before stopping, and the shoreline of downtown San Diego was less than half a mile away. With the electricity out, the navigator would have to steer the ship without the gyrocompass, an almost impossible task given the size of the ship and its slow response to shifts in the rudder.

The navigator eyeballed the familiar landmarks of San Diego harbor and estimated the ship's direction and position as best he could.

After estimating how much the rudder would have to be turned to stay within the narrow channel, he gave the first steering command to the helmsman. Then, unbelievably, things grew dramatically worse. The helmsman frantically replied, "Sir, I have no helm, sir!" A few seconds later, the rudder began working again, but the relief was temporary; for the next several minutes, control of the rudder came and went.

Sixteen minutes after the loss of power, the team's combined experience had allowed them to improvise a way to stay in the channel even without electricity and without a functioning rudder. But they weren't out of trouble yet; they still had to come to a stop and anchor the wounded vessel. If they dropped anchor too soon, the huge ship would block the channel, and if they dropped too late, they risked grounding the ship. They had to know exactly where the ship was, almost with second-to-second accuracy. How could they take a fix without their electronic instruments?

The ship's operation manuals described the exact division of labor involved in taking a fix, and responsibility for the task was distributed among six pilothouse crew members. Taking a fix without the gyrocompass requires five separate calculations involving six bearings and numbers, and a well-known formula tells how to use these numbers to calculate the exact location of the ship. But that formula is time consuming, and the navigator couldn't do it fast enough to take the frequent bearings he needed. The only solution was to rely on the whole team, but there was no time to plan a new division of labor; they had only minutes to reconfigure their group to handle the unexpected task. Instead of stopping to plan, the team improvised a response that saved the day.

When he analyzed his tapes later, Hutchins found that the team had explored at least thirteen organizational structures until, after about thirty fixes had been taken, a collaborative solution emerged: a way of dividing the five calculations between two men that turned out to be more efficient than the known formula—in fact, mathematically it was the most efficient solution possible. Hutchins was so impressed with the group that he concluded that "the solution was clearly discovered by the organization itself before it was discovered by any of the participants." The surprising lesson from the *Palau*'s near disaster is that when people improvise together, they develop innovative responses to unexpected events even though no one is consciously aware of exactly what the group is doing or why it works.

Planning for Improvisation

High-stakes situations such as the Naples earthquake and the *Palau* navigation are unusual. In most real-world situations, teams have more time. Researchers have discovered that if there's time, sometimes a small amount of advance planning can help make collaboration more effective. The key question, then, is this: What's the best balance of planning and improvisation?

In the early 1990s, Kathleen M. Eisenhardt and Behnam N. Tabrizi, of Stanford University's School of Business, surveyed seventy-two product development projects that took place in thirty-six computer companies in Europe, Asia, and the United States, each with annual sales of more than $50 million. They found that the most innovative teams were the ones that spent less time in the planning stage and more time executing—instead of planning, they improvised. Contrary to what many managers believe, the more time a group spent planning in advance, the slower project development was.

The improvisational teams didn't exactly wing it, either. They engaged in short bursts of planning that alternated with improvisation; in other words, they distributed design activities throughout the execution process. That's why the improvisational groups had better market success; because of the frequent design iterations, they could respond more quickly to shifts in the market and to feedback from customers. The improvisational teams were much more likely to finish on schedule, and because on-time projects earn 50 percent more than late ones, improvisation creates products that are more profitable for the company.

The key to innovation is always to manage a subtle balance of planning, structure, and improvisation. I've designed several workshop activities that demonstrate the power of improvisation. In one exercise, I put people into groups and I hand out sets of DUPLO LEGO blocks, various colored plastic playing pieces, dice, and decks of cards. I give each group twenty minutes to design a new game. They have to be able to explain how to play it in less than five minutes, and it must not take more than ten minutes to play. Then I let everyone play all the games, and I ask them to rate how creative and playable each game is. The most creative games (based on votes taken by other workshop participants who play each other's games) are always generated by a particular kind of collaboration, that is, when the members of the team start playing the game early in the twenty-minute period and improvisationally embellish and modify as they go along. The least creative games are the ones in which the team spends the entire twenty minutes carefully planning out the game but never actually play it themselves. The message that participants learn is that improvisation, interwoven with planning, is the key to successful innovation.

My idea for this workshop exercise came from David Bearison and Bruce Dorval—professors of psychology at the Graduate Center, City University of New York—who studied collaboration among children in elementary school by giving pairs of children twenty-five minutes to invent a new game that used a set of abstract game pieces and game boards. There were no rules, and there were no words or defining marks on the circular spaces on the boards. They videotaped eighty pairs of children, in first, third, and fifth grade, while they created a new game together. In the children's sessions, planning, negotiation, and collaboration all merged together in playful improvisation. They started playing "the game" almost right away, when only a couple of rules had been decided. Most of their game-designing negotiation occurred while they were playing; on average, only one-third of their game negotiation happened before they started playing. Once the children started playing, they didn't faithfully follow the rules they'd negotiated in advance; they embellished and modified those rules all along the way.

Children seem to improvise more naturally than adults. At the OC school in Salt Lake City, an innovative public school using an open-classroom philosophy, the teachers asked a group of second and third graders to develop a puppet play to perform for their parents. But the children weren't given a script, and the adults stayed in the background and didn't direct the rehearsals. The teachers didn't know what would happen. Would it be complete chaos, or could the children rise to the occasion?

One of the most interesting puppet plays was an improvised variation on the Snow White story called *Blue Night*. This title emerged from an improvisational discussion where one girl's idea—to invert everything about the original story and come up with a mirror version called *Black Night*—was merged with a second idea, *Blue Sky*. The *Blue Night* team worked out the story's theme and the main events before they started improvising. By the seventh rehearsal, they'd decided that the princess's trance would be caused by a poisonous banana, and that the dwarves would carry the princess to a glass coffin. During this seventh rehearsal, the group improvised the following dialogue:

CAROL: It's a banana! She's not breathing.
STACY: It looks a bit peculiar.

CAROL: She's not breathing! Come on let's carry her.

STACY: Try CPR!

CAROL: Let's carry her off.

The children improvised the dialogue by speaking it with their puppets during the rehearsals. Just like the product development teams studied at Stanford, these innovations were improvised.

On average, the groups started improvisationally negotiating in the fourth of their ten rehearsals. The children weren't taught to do it; these improvisational techniques emerged spontaneously. What's more, across the ten rehearsals, the percentage of time they spent improvising increased. As the basic form of the play fell into shape, as they became comfortable with each other and worked out ground rules for collaboration, they spent more time improvising.

In the adult world as well, maximum innovation comes from a careful balance between planning and improvisation. After all, there was never a plan to build a mountain bike, just enthusiasts who were trying to solve one problem at a time. But most of us, most of the time, have a tendency to spend too much time planning and never get to the improvisation. When teachers at the OC school asked adults to help some of the playcrafting groups, the adults acted as directors and told the children what to do. The children simply followed orders and didn't improvise at all. But if left to their own devices, children know how to improvise, and although we adults might need to relearn improvisation, it's well within our grasp. How can we use this basic human ability to be more creative in everyday activities?

In a landmark study of improvisational innovation, Anne S. Miner and her colleagues at the University of Wisconsin looked closely at the FastTrack company, which successfully developed and sold advanced technology products to industrial clients. By the 1990s, FastTrack was a well-established company with formalized structures and $2.4 billion in annual sales. Professor Miner's team taped more than twenty-five team meetings, over nine months, of a new product development project; interviewed all the team members and executives; and then spent more than four years analyzing the data.

Like many technology companies, FastTrack's highly formalized product development process required long, detailed written reports analyzing market potential and technical feasibility, and these reports had to be reviewed by senior committees before a project could begin. But Miner's team discovered that innovation often happened unofficially, below the radar of senior management, through three types of improvisational processes.

In the first, a new business process was improvised. To take an example, one product development team was charged with designing a software interface between its new product and one of the company's existing flagship products. But their job was difficult because the flagship software itself was often revised: The new product team had to keep changing its test schedules to correspond to the changes in the flagship software product. The frustrated team members decided to improvise. They waited until just before the next change, when the flagship team would have to test everything to make sure it still worked. Then they surreptitiously slipped in their own changes just before the testing began, essentially making the flagship team do their testing for them.

The second example was known informally within FastTrack as the "scientist special." This occurred when engineers designed and built products on their own, either in an interaction with a specific customer or as an unanticipated side-effect of their work on another project. For example, one team learned that a customer wanted to analyze samples very different from the ones that FastTrack's regular products could handle. Team members responded by designing and building a new detection device in their spare time; they used whatever parts were lying around, and frequently discussed among themselves how the new product would look. The new device worked so well that after management found out about it, they added it to the company's product line.

Improvisational innovation is particularly critical when companies are migrating from one product generation to the next, because it allows the company to move forward with the new product and not let problems with the old product get in the way. In markets with rapidly advancing technology, new product lines replace old ones with amazing speed, putting extreme pressures on design teams. Since there's not enough time to go through the approved design process in such a fast-changing environment, successful companies often handle these transitions improvisationally. One example of this occurred at FastTrack when a software upgrade on a research tool caused a moving arm to shift too frequently, making accurate measurement impossible. This would have taken a lot of time to fix properly, and the team knew that a major new product redesign in the works would get rid of the moving arm entirely. So instead of redesigning the arm or rewriting the software, the team improvised a fix: They found a small nylon washer in the lab that stopped the arm from shifting.

One of the most powerful abilities of innovative organizations is that they can improvise new uses for existing ideas. At FastTrack, one engineer discovered that when he fixed a bug in a program, he got an unexpected result: The time it took to do an information search dropped from twenty-two seconds to two seconds. During collaborative discussion, the team realized that the unexpectedly fast search could be used in marketing the product. It was only a bug fix until the team reframed its meaning.

Playing Without a Conductor

In the improvising teams we've encountered in this chapter, I haven't said a word about the team's leader. That's because the most effective improvisational groups are self-managing: They have a magical and mysterious ability to restructure and regroup in response to unexpected events without being directed by a leader. Self-managing groups are particularly effective at innovation in rapidly changing environments.

The paradox of innovation is that organizations emphasize order and control, and yet improvisation seems to be uncontrollable. The manager of a traditional team is responsible for breaking down the task, keeping everyone on schedule, and coordinating the team members. But the leader of a collaborative team couldn't be more different; this leader has to establish creative spaces within which group genius is more likely to happen. Because innovative teams are self-managing, the leader doesn't have as much direct managerial work to do. Instead, leaders of innovative groups are active participants in the work; they function more like a peer than a boss.

Since 1972, the Orpheus Chamber Orchestra of New York City has been doing something that most people thought was impossible: rehearsing and performing without a conductor. An orchestra with a conductor is an example of planned creativity—the conductor begins by studying the composer's score, refining his or her vision for the performance, and then going into the first rehearsal armed with a plan for how to achieve that vision with the musicians. In the absence of a single vision, how does a group rehearse a composition? How do the musicians arrive at a shared interpretation of the piece? Instead of the conductor, the twenty-seven members of Orpheus use the creative power of collaboration.

At one rehearsal, a musician stands up while the group is playing. Although this would be a breach of etiquette in most groups, the rest of the musicians continue to play. She carries her instrument out into the audience seats and listens for a few minutes while the rest of the musicians continue playing. Only after she returns to the stage does the ensemble stop playing and wait for her to speak. She tells them what the audience would have heard: The violas aren't loud enough. "Does anyone disagree?" she asks; no one does. She returns to her seat, and the violinist who is the acting concertmaster for this composition cues the group to try the passage again.

Orpheus was born when a group of Columbia University students formed a sort of musical commune in response to the 1960s dissatisfaction with authority figures and hierarchy. All decisions—about what pieces to perform, about which musicians to use—were made collectively. No one controlled the rehearsal; all musicians were free to say anything at any time. "We're always fighting with each other, but we're always fighting it *out,*" the musician Eric Bartlett says. This new approach appealed to some of the best young musicians in New York. By 1978, after only six years, the group performed at Carnegie Hall; today, Orpheus is formally based at Carnegie Hall, and its members are seasoned professionals who record for television and movies and teach at leading schools, including Juilliard and the New England Conservatory.

The Orpheus musicians talk about the importance of *listening,* with "listening" given a special, almost reverent emphasis, in the same way that jazz musicians talk about listening. Each musician has to listen to all the others with a degree of concentration and intensity that becomes almost like a Zen state of awareness—they have to listen closely to each other, to coordinate their voices and to negotiate a musical synergy nonverbally. Orpheus musicians talk about *trust* in each other: trusting each of the other musicians to listen to everyone—and to take responsibility for the entire piece, not only for their own parts. Soloists who have played with Orpheus can hear the difference in the way the orchestra follows them, even when they slow down or speed up.

Commercial success forced Orpheus to face some of the weaknesses of their improvisational system. Without a conductor to guide the rehearsals toward his vision, the musicians spent hours discussing details that a conductor would have dealt with in thirty seconds. Although the founding musicians were committed to their collaborative vision, they couldn't afford to pay musicians the going hourly rate for such long rehearsals, so they eventually worked out a compromise: They elected a concertmaster, from among the musicians, to lead each piece. Still, the concertmaster didn't stand in front of the orchestra and wave a baton; he was one of the musicians, and he sat in his usual chair during rehearsals of the piece. Even with this compromise, it still takes Orpheus three times as long to prepare for a concert as a conventional orchestra.

This inefficiency is one hallmark of improvised innovation. The southern Italian earthquake volunteer relief effort took far more people than the army's formal organization. At IDEO and Gore alike, many projects go nowhere. But the inefficiencies of the process are what results in unexpected innovation. With Orpheus, the result is a special synergy in the music that no conductor could ever duplicate. The critic James Traub says that at an Orpheus performance one has "the feeling that the musicians were playing as much for one another as for the audience." At an Orpheus concert, the listener hears the result of long hours of collective creativity and negotiation. Since the musicians are listening and interacting with each other *during* the performance, each performance is different, but in a different way than if they simply looked up at the conductor.

In an influential 1988 article, the legendary management guru Peter F. Drucker argued that the company of the future would be like a symphony orchestra. Yet Drucker realized that the scored symphonic work wasn't a perfect metaphor, because companies would have to be improvisational: "A business has no 'score' to play by except the score it writes as it plays." A few years later, John Kao, a Harvard Business School professor, in comparing business innovation to jazz performance, famously called collaborative creativity *jamming*. Jazz is a better model for innovation today than an orchestra because in organizations there is no script; individuals are often surprised by their collaborators; and creative solutions emerge unexpectedly.

As society changes more rapidly, and the business environment becomes more competitive and unpredictable, companies will increasingly have to rely on improvised innovation. In today's innovation economy, work is often done in small temporary teams, where the stakes are high, the meaning of the situation is uncertain, and the competitive and technological environment is rapidly changing. The organization of the future will run on group genius.

Each group will find its maximum creativity somewhere on the spectrum from the least improvisational to the most. Orpheus taps into the genius of the group, but they still perform from a score. Companies such as Gore and Google tell their employees to devote 10 to 20 percent of their time to unplanned new projects, but still that means 80 percent of the time they're working on official planned projects. Jazz and improv comedy are at the other extreme, where there's essentially no advance planning. This spectrum parallels the organizational contrast between incremental change and transformational change. If you want a radical innovation, you need your organization to be at the improvisational extreme.

From the southern Italian earthquake to the USS *Palau* in San Diego, people around the globe naturally form into improvisational groups. Even schoolchildren can do it. Why do people come together so readily? How can you create the conditions for group genius to emerge? To answer these questions in the next chapter, I borrow a famous concept from psychology—flow—and show what contexts cause group genius to emerge.

....

CHAPTER 3

Group Flow

Basketball is religion in Indiana, and one of its mega churches is Bloomington, home of the Big-Ten Indiana University Hoosiers, where larger-than-life coach Bobby Knight won three national championships between 1971 and 2000. But the Indiana tradition isn't just about famous coaches and national championships. In the legendary Old Fieldhouse on Seventh Street, there are sixteen indoor basketball courts in one cavernous space. The team doesn't use these courts anymore. Now, the Old Fieldhouse is called the HPER student rec center and it's one of the best places in the country for pickup basketball.

No coaches, no referees, and no championship: The players create their own teams, police their own behavior, and work out rules for who plays and when. Pickup basketball brings together people who would probably never meet off the court; for example, at a YMCA in Waukegan, Wisconsin, two of the regular players were Alan, a young black player just out of high school, and Pip, a middle-aged white judge. It turned out that Alan was a member of a gang. The others didn't know this until one of Alan's fellow gang members came up for trial in Pip's courtroom, and Alan was at the trial every day along with the rest of the gang. Pip said, "I looked up one day and he was in the courtroom, and Christ! It scared the hell out of me because I had been playing ball with him for a while and I gave this guy like twelve years." But they continued to play together, along with Sam, a thirty-year-old black man who worked with at-risk youth and with the police. Games at this YMCA brought together lawyers, police officers, a liquor store owner, a minister, factory workers, a flight attendant, and ex-cons.

The same thing happens every day and every week all over the country, from Lincoln Park in Santa Monica, California, to the legendary West Fourth Street basketball court in New York's Greenwich Village. Just like Bloomington and Waukegan, pickup ball brings together executives, professors, workers, and streetwise teenagers.

Why do these amateurs spend so much time and effort on basketball? There's no money in it, no admiring fans. When you win a pickup game, it earns you the right to play in the next game—nothing more. Many of the middle-aged men and women who play pickup basketball have suffered knee injuries; there's a real physical cost to the game.

They play because when you take away the referees, the clock, the rulebook, and the coaches, you're left with the pure, improvised essence of basketball. Basketball is one of the most improvised and team-oriented of all sports, the sports equivalent of group genius. In pickup games, everything that slows down the professional game has been taken away—there are no free throws in streetball, for example. There's nothing standing between the players and the deep feeling of peak experience that emerges when the team is in sync. Bill Russell, the famous center for the Boston Celtics, spoke frequently about this almost spiritual experience:

Every so often a Celtic game would heat up so that it became more than a physical or even mental game, and would be magical. That feeling is difficult to describe, and I certainly never talked about it when I was playing. When it happened I could feel my play rise to a new level. . . . The game would just take off, and there'd be a natural ebb and flow that reminded you of how rhythmic and musical basketball is supposed to be. . . . It was almost as if we were playing in slow motion.

Teams can win only by improvising and collaborating, changing constantly in response to the adjustments their opponents are making. One pickup player told this story of improvised innovation:

I was guarding Paul and sagging off him to help my teammates play defense. Our opponents collectively realized that I was leaving Paul to double-team whoever had the ball, so our foes began passing the ball to Paul. He caught the ball and scored a couple of shots. I adjusted by sticking close to Paul, but by then his teammates had realized that he was "hot," so they began to pick and pass. They set picks by getting in my way, freeing Paul. Then, they would pass him the ball and he would score again. My teammates grasped what Paul and his teammates were doing to me, so they began to help me guard Paul.

What's the magical chemistry that happens when a team improvises in response to every move by their opponents, without saying a word, and wins the game? The answer can't be found in the skill or creativity of any one player; the entire group makes it happen.

Peak Experience

I began to gain insight into this magical chemistry when I worked on my PhD at the University of Chicago with Mihaly Csikszentmihalyi, the famed psychologist who coined the term "flow" to describe a particular state of heightened consciousness. He discovered that extremely creative people are at their peak when they experience "a unified flowing from one moment to the next, in which we feel in control of our actions, and in which there is little distinction between self and environment; between stimulus and response; or between past, present, and future." Drawing on research with mountain climbers, club dancers, artists, and scientists, Csikszentmihalyi found that people are more likely to get into flow when their environment has four important characteristics. First, and most important, they're doing something where their skills match the challenge of the task. If the challenge is too great for their skills, they become frustrated; but if the task isn't challenging enough, they simply grow bored. Second, flow occurs when the goal is clear; and third, when there's constant and immediate feedback about how close you are to achieving that goal. Fourth, flow occurs when you're free to concentrate fully on the task. When you're lucky enough to work with these four features, you often enter the flow state—where people from all professions describe feeling a sense of competence and control, a loss of self-consciousness, and they get so absorbed in the task that they lose track of time.

Csikszentmihalyi has gathered years of data documenting that flow is the most essential ingredient in creativity. Creative people, in all professions and all walks of life, have their most significant insights while in a flow state. Even though most people say they enjoy time at home more than they enjoy working, Csikszentmihalyi's studies show that people are more likely to be in flow at work than when they're relaxing at home. Many other psychologists have confirmed the link between flow and creativity, especially at work. For example, when Teresa Amabile of Harvard University studied more than two hundred professionals at seven companies, she found that creative insights were associated with the flow state. Even the day after experiencing a flow state, people were more creative.

Flow researchers have spent a lot of time studying the individual creator, but people don't play pickup ball because of individual flow— dribbling the basketball or honing their shots—after all, you could do those things by yourself. They play because they love the high that comes from group genius. In fact, Csikszentmihalyi found that the most common place people experienced flow was in conversation with others. At work, conversation with colleagues is one of the most flow-inducing activities; managers, in particular, are most likely to be in flow when they're engaged in conversation.

Conversation leads to flow, and flow leads to creativity. What happens, I wondered, when flow emerges in a group activity? Does the group itself enter a flow state? Might there be something like "group flow"? And what happens when everything comes together to help a group be in flow? The answers tell us how to foster group genius.

The Ten Conditions for Group Flow

I began to explore these question by studying jazz ensembles. I was a jazz pianist throughout high school and college, and I've often sat in with professional groups. Basing my research on Csikszentmihalyi's seminal work, I discovered that, sure enough, improvising groups attain a collective state of mind that I call *group flow*. Group flow is a peak experience, a group performing at its top level of ability. In a study of over three hundred professionals at three companies—a strategy consulting firm, a government agency, and a petrochemical company—Rob Cross and Andrew Parker discovered that the people who participated in group flow were the highest performers. In situations of rapid change, it's more important than ever for a group to be able to merge action and awareness, to adjust immediately by improvising. In group flow, activity becomes spontaneous, and the group acts without thinking about it first.

To foster improvised innovation, the conditions for group flow must be created. Genius groups tend to emerge in contexts where ten key flow-enabling conditions are found.

1. The Group's Goal

Jazz and improv theater are relatively unstructured; the ensemble has no explicit goal. But the groups that we participate in during the workday—task forces, project groups, and committees—usually have a specific goal in mind. How can you apply the lessons from unstructured groups to more task-oriented ones? Jazz and improv theater groups are at one extreme of the spectrum of group types—the no-goal extreme. A basketball team, in contrast, has a very clear goal: to defeat the opponent. If group flow can occur in no-goal jazz groups and in focused basketball teams, what's the connection between goals and performance?

Business teams are expected to solve specific problems. They know that by the end of the meeting they have to come up with a resolution of the budget shortfall, or find a way to fix a software bug that threatens to spiral out of control. If the goal is well understood and can be explicitly stated, it's a *problem-solving* creative task. The group members then are more likely to be in flow while working toward such a goal if they've worked together before, if they share much of the same knowledge and assumptions, and when they have a compelling vision and a shared mission. One study of more than five hundred professionals and managers in thirty companies found that unclear objectives became the biggest barrier to effective team performance.

Jazz and improv groups are at the other extreme. The only goal is intrinsic to the performance itself—to perform well and to entertain the audience. This is *problem-finding creativity* because the group members have to "find" and define the problem as they're solving it. At first, this might seem very different from everyday business contexts. But many of the most radical innovations occur when the question or goal isn't known in advance.

The story of how 3M created the Post-it note is legendary in the annals of innovation: Spence Silver, a research scientist, was trying to improve the adhesive that was used in tape, and in 1968 he developed an adhesive that bonded very weakly and thus failed to achieve that goal. But Silver noticed something unusual about the adhesive: It formed itself into tiny balls that were just about the size of paper fiber. For five years, Silver told everyone who would listen about this new adhesive, and he tried to think of a way to use it in a product. One day, Art Fry, who worked in new-product development, attended a seminar where Silver described his adhesive. Fry sang in his church choir, and he had repeatedly been frustrated when paper bookmarks fell out of his hymnal. One Sunday morning, soon after the seminar, he realized that Silver's adhesive could be used to make a bookmark that wouldn't fall out, and the now-famous product was born.

The key to improvised innovation is managing a paradox: establishing a goal that provides a focus for the team—just enough of one so that team members can tell when they move closer to a solution—but one that's open-ended enough for problem-finding creativity to emerge, such as when the Gore engineer decided to pose himself the problem of creating a new guitar string. When the auto maker BMW decides to explore a new product possibility, executives outline a rough goal and then put several teams in competition; they work from studios in the Munich headquarters to DesignWorks in Los Angeles.

Competition, mixed with loosely specified goals, can be just the right recipe for group genius.

2. Close Listening

Listen to Jeffrey Sweet describing a great Chicago improv theater show:

> Tonight, things are going well. Tonight, watching them improvise is like watching an expert surfer. The surfer's incredible balance keeping him constantly poised on the crest of a wave; the cast, working from instinct rooted in hours of workshops and past improv sets, riding the crest of the moment. When they are on top, it is a sight to see. There is a thrill in watching them, a thrill born of the precariousness of their position and the ever-present threat that a misjudgment may send them hurtling into a wipeout.

Metaphors such as riding a wave, gliding across a ballroom with a dance partner, or lovemaking are common among actors and musicians when they talk about group flow. "When that's really happening in a band, the cohesiveness is unbelievable," said the jazz trombonist Curtis Fuller. "Those are the special, cherished moments. When those special moments occur, to me, it's like ecstasy. It's like a beautiful thing. It's like when things blossom." Even while contributing to the performance, each performer remains open and listens to the others.

Group flow is more likely to emerge when everyone is fully engaged—what improvisers call "deep listening," in which members of the group don't plan ahead what they're going to say, but their statements are genuinely unplanned responses to what they hear. Innovation is blocked when one (or more) of the participants already has a preconceived idea of how to reach the goal; improvisers frown on this practice, pejoratively calling it "writing the script in your head."

One consultant described a manager who fostered group flow: "She came into the meeting, and I know she had a thousand other things going on, but she was immediately there and with us. She was listening to what we had done and why, and throughout the interaction was asking good questions." People who listen closely are energizing, and people who energize others are proven to be higher performers.

3. Complete Concentration

Basketball's fast pace and the constant movement of players around each other demand that participants concentrate deeply and remain constantly aware of what their teammates and opponents are doing. "If you step back and think about why you are so hot all of a sudden you get creamed," said one of the basketball players Csikszentmihalyi interviewed. Time becomes warped, minutes seem like hours, and the basketball can appear to move in slow motion.

In musical ensembles, group flow is challenging to maintain; musicians can't relax their attention or else they'll fall behind. Musicians play nonstop, yet they also have to listen to what their fellow band members are playing and immediately respond: "You have to be able to divide your senses . . . so you still have that one thought running through your head of saying something, playing something, at the same time you've got to be listening to what the drummer is doing," one musician told me.

A high-pressure deadline might be seen as one of those challenges that increase flow for highly skilled people. But the research shows just the opposite: Group flow tends to fade in the presence of strict, high-pressure deadlines. Teresa Amabile of Harvard University has found that creativity is associated with low-pressure work environments—even though many people think they're more creative when they work under high pressure. In group flow, the group is focused on the natural progress emerging from members' work, not on meeting a deadline set by management. Flow is more likely to occur when attention is centered on the task. Small annoyances aren't noticed, and the external rewards that may or may not await at the end of the task are forgotten. A strict deadline is certainly a challenge, but not the right kind of challenge; the challenges that inspire flow are those that are intrinsic to the task itself.

Group flow is more likely when a group can draw a boundary, however temporary or virtual, between the group's activity and everything else. Companies should identify a special location for group flow, or engage in a brief rehearsal or warm-up period that demarcates the shift to performance. Many famous great groups have a strong feeling of group identity, of standing apart from the rest of the organization. IDEO's way of fostering group identity is practically a cliché today: Almost every group orders special baseball hats or T-shirts embroidered with a clever team name.

The downside of complete concentration is that other important priorities can be neglected. For example, Anne Miner and her colleagues watched as the Seefoods company put on hold the development of a salad line so that all energies were directed to the sandwich line—even though market research had already shown that the salad line would be successful. FastTrack scientist specials were often perceived by others to be distracting of the engineers from the original product plan because they drew resources from well-planned strategies enjoying proven market potential. In general, marketing and engineering saw the benefits of improvisation, but financial and manufacturing saw it as a source of potential inefficiency and error.

4. Being in Control

People get into flow when they're in control of their actions and their environment. This implies that groups won't be in flow unless they're granted autonomy by senior management. In 1995, Michael Crooke, the CEO of Patagonia, the outdoor clothing maker, read Csikszentmihalyi's influential book *Flow*; as a result, he has granted autonomy to his staff and given Patagonia a flow-oriented environment. Patagonia is located near the Pacific Ocean in Ventura, California; its entrance hallway is lined with employee surfboards. Yves Chouinard, the founder, a mountain climber like Csikszentmihalyi, instituted the policy "Let My People Go Surfing"—meaning that whenever the surf comes up, employees can go surfing. Crooke is building flow into Patagonia's teams; he says that flow is at "the center of everything" he's doing and compares the peak performance of Patagonia's teams to his own experiences at the age of nineteen, when he was part of a U.S. Navy SEAL team.

Group flow increases when people feel autonomy, competence, and relatedness. Many studies have found that team autonomy is the top predictor of team performance. But in group flow, unlike solo flow, control results in a paradox because participants must feel in control, yet at the same time they must remain flexible, listen closely, and always be willing to defer to the emergent flow of the group. The most innovative teams are the ones that can manage that paradox.

5. Blending Egos

Jazz musicians know that they need to control their egos; every jazz player can tell a story about a technically gifted young instrumentalist who was nonetheless a poor jazz musician. These musicians lack the ability to submerge their egos to the group mind, to balance their own voices with deep listening.

Group flow is the magical moment when it all comes together, when the group is in sync and the performers seem to be thinking with one mind. Said David Byrne of the Talking Heads: "You kind of subsume yourself and become part of the community of musicians." This is when audience members think they're reading from the same script—even though there's no script. Each performer is managing the paradoxes of improvisation by balancing deep listening with creative contribution.

In group flow, each person's idea builds on those just contributed by his or her colleagues. The improvisation appears to be guided by an invisible hand toward a peak, but small ideas build and an innovation emerges. In discussing a colleague who often participated in groups in flow, one executive had this to say: "He is animated and engaged with you. He is also listening and reacting to what you are saying with undivided attention."

6. Equal Participation

Group flow is more likely to occur when all participants play an equal role in the collective creation of the final performance. Group flow is blocked if anyone's skill level is below that of the rest of the group's members; all must have comparable skill levels. This is why professional athletes don't enjoy playing with amateurs; group flow can't emerge because the professionals will be bored and the amateurs will be frustrated. It's also blocked when one person dominates, is arrogant, or doesn't think anything can be learned from the conversation. One software developer described how his manager destroyed group flow: "We had been working like crazy on this project when he swooped in and just started telling us what we should do. He didn't take the time

to try to understand what we were telling him. . . . That really crashed
. . . the ideas that could have been developed in that session."

A recent social network analysis of a group of 101 engineers at a petrochemical organization found that supervisors generally sapped flow, but
a similar analysis of a government agency that reorganized after the September 11, 2001, terrorist attacks found that managers fostered group
flow. Managers can participate in groups in flow, but they have to participate in the same way as everyone else by listening closely and granting
autonomy and authority to the group's emergent decision processes.

7. Familiarity

One pickup player told the sociologist Jason Jimerson that "you gotta
know how to play with them"—group flow is more likely to happen
when players know the performance styles of their teammates and opponents. By studying many different work teams, psychologists have
found that familiarity increases productivity and decision-making effectiveness. When members of a group have been together for a while,
they share a common language and a common set of unspoken understandings. Psychologists call these shared understandings *tacit knowledge*—and because it's unspoken, people often don't even realize why
they are able to communicate effectively.

In improv, group flow happens only when all the players have mastered a body of tacit knowledge. Improv actors are taught a set of guiding principles that help make it work, rules such as "Don't deny" and
"Show, don't tell." Jazz musicians have to learn the basics of harmony,
melody, and the standard song forms such as twelve-bar blues and
sixteen-bar Broadway musical choruses. After they've learned that,
they have to master a dizzying array of conventions, customs, and unwritten rules—for example, it is customary that each soloist play just
about the same amount of time as the soloist before him.

Improv groups have three kinds of shared knowledge that can contribute to group flow: an overall flow or outline of the performance that all participants know in advance (although the length of each segment, and the timing of transitions, must still be improvised); a shared repertory of riffs, with a knowledge of how they typically sequence in order; and common agreement on the conventions—the set of tacit practices governing interaction in the group.

Group flow requires that the members share an understanding of the group's goals (because clear goals are so important to flow); they need to share enough communicational style to respond mutually to each other (because immediate feedback is critical to flow). But if group members are too similar, flow becomes less likely because the group interaction is no longer challenging. If everyone functions identically and shares the same habits of communicating, nothing new and unexpected will ever emerge because group members don't need to pay close attention to what the others are doing, and they don't continually have to update their understanding of what is going on.

After two or three years, members of groups can become too familiar with each other and their effectiveness starts to decrease. Close listening becomes less necessary because everything is shared; no surprises are left. When group flow fades away, the group usually breaks up because its members want to find new challenges elsewhere. Chicago improv ensembles rarely continue performing together for more than three months, and many shows last for much less than that before the members move on and form new combinations with actors likewise freed from other mature groups. Organizations should have mechanisms in place to smooth these natural transitions in the life span of creative groups.

Familiarity helps more for problem-solving creativity. If there's a specific goal and the participants don't share enough common knowledge, the group will have difficulty accomplishing its goal. Higher group cohesiveness has repeatedly been found to correlate with high performance, especially for larger groups (more than seven people).

But if a group needs to find and define a new problem, too much shared information becomes a problem. Problem-finding groups are more likely to be in group flow when there's more diversity; problem-solving groups are often more effective when more tacit knowledge is shared.

8. Communication

After Stefan Falk, the vice president of strategic business innovation at Ericsson, read *Flow* in 2002, he redesigned the company to make flow the core of its philosophy. Every manager was required to meet with each employee six times a year in elaborate feedback sessions lasting at least an hour. When Falk moved to Green Cargo, a large Scandinavian transport company, he went even further and required that managers and employees meet once a month for intensive sessions that are similar to executive coaching. In 2004, Green Cargo turned a profit for the first time in its 120-year government-owned history, and the CEO gives much of the credit to Falk's flow strategies.

Group flow requires constant communication. Everyone hates to go to useless meetings; but the kind of communication that leads to group flow often doesn't happen in the conference room. Instead, it's more likely to happen in freewheeling, spontaneous conversations in the hallway, or in social settings after work or at lunch.

9. Moving It Forward

In the last chapter, we learned about a FastTrack bug fix that, thanks to group genius, was reframed as a new "speedy reporting feature." Fixing the bug was important, but an even more significant innovation resulted because the team members kept moving the conversation forward.

What happened when a FastTrack team tried to figure out what to do about an unreliable part is another example of group flow. The part performed very well in some products but was not so great in others. One engineer explained that nothing could be done, and that the performance variability was the result of the part's unchangeable properties. The first idea would be simply to ignore the variability because even the poor-performing products met the minimum acceptable specifications. But other members of the team began to wonder whether customers who received a "hot" item first, then later an average or poor item, would feel ripped off. Suggestions came from everyone—test each part before making the product; ask the vendor to test the parts in exchange for a small fee—but all were too expensive.

Then one engineer said, "If you see a hot one, let me know. I can phone the customer and tell them we have this hot item and do they want it. Then they think, 'Oh yeah, FastTrack's really good guys. They look out for me.'" Rather than correct the variability, they ended up with an emergent, improvised solution—to use the variability to build customer relationships. Group flow flourishes when people follow the first rule of improvisational acting: "Yes, and . . ." Listen closely to what's being said; accept it fully; and then extend and build on it.

10. The Potential for Failure

During rehearsal, jazz ensembles rarely experience flow; it seems to require an audience and the accompanying risk of real, meaningful failure. Jazz musicians and improv theater ensembles alike never know how successful a performance will be. The pianist Franklin Gordon said, "It doesn't happen every single night . . . but at some point when the band is playing and everyone gets locked in together, it's special for the musicians and for the aware, conscientious listener. These are the magical moments, the best moments in jazz." Professional actors learn not to ignore the feeling of stage fright but to harness the feeling, to use it as a powerful force to push them toward the flow experience.

Many groups require a preliminary warm-up period to move into group flow. In Chicago blues bands, the ensemble plays the first set while the headlining lead singer, guitarist, or harmonica player remains backstage; this allows the ensemble to get in sync so that the band leader will have a fully warmed-up band when he comes on stage. "You just let them play to get the kinks out," said the jazz trumpeter Jimmy Robinson about the rhythm section. "After they'd got the feeling for one another and got themselves together, then the horns joined them." Similarly, improv theater groups typically perform group exercises in a separate room offstage while the audience members arrive and take their seats. Some of these exercises are high energy, and audience members occasionally hear strange shouts and pounding sounds from the back room as the ensemble works toward a state of group flow.

Of course, there's rarely time for "rehearsal" in the business world. The problem is that most businesses are designed to minimize risk, and most of them punish failure. But research shows us over and over again that the twin sibling of innovation is frequent failure. There's no creativity without failure, and there's no group flow without the risk of failure. Since group flow is often what produces the most significant innovations, these two common research findings go hand in hand.

There's a way to rehearse and improve, even in the business world. Psychological studies of expertise have shown that in every walk of life, from arts and science to business, the highest performers are those who engage in *deliberate practice*—as they're doing a task, they're constantly thinking about how they could be doing it better, and looking for lessons that they can use next time. The key is to treat every activity as a rehearsal for the next time. The best jazz bands engage in deliberate practice right in front of the paying audience.

Group flow happens when many tensions are in perfect balance: the tension between convention and novelty; between structure and improvisation; between the critical, analytic mind and the freewheeling, outside-the-box mind; between listening to the rest of the group and speaking out in individual voices. The paradox of improvisation is that it can happen only when there are rules and the players share tacit understandings, but with too many rules or too much cohesion, the potential for innovation is lost. The key question facing groups that have to innovate is finding just the right amount of structure to support improvisation, but not so much structure that it smothers creativity. Jazz and improv theater have important messages for all groups because they're unique in how successfully they balance all these tensions. These types of ensemble art forms embrace the tensions that drive group genius.

Live from New York

In 1949, the comedian Sid Caesar brought together a legendary group of comedy writers and created one of the biggest television hits of the 1950s, *Your Show of Shows,* ninety minutes broadcast live from New York every Saturday night. During the nine years the show was on the air, Caesar's writers included Mel Brooks, Carl Reiner, the M*A*S*H producer Larry Gelbart, Neil Simon, and Woody Allen. This was the first comedy show to move beyond the cream-pie and seltzer-bottle style of slapstick humor; his team developed challenging material that didn't insult the audience. Mel Brooks compared the group to a World Series baseball team, and many experts believe that this was the greatest writing staff in the history of television.

The writers developed the show in a small suite of rooms on the sixth floor of 130 West Fifty-sixth Street in Manhattan. Caesar created an improvisational environment focused on generating the funniest show possible. The team would bounce ideas constantly and keep moving forward. As Mel Brooks remembered it, "Jokes would be changed fifty times. We'd take an eight-minute sketch and rewrite it in eight minutes." Their writing followed a problem-finding style, where they rewrote the same scene until something great emerged from the group's genius. The writers felt as if they belonged to something greater than themselves—a classic result of group flow.

It's hard to find this kind of experience in a large corporation, which tends to reward closing up communication, narrowing the channels, and minimizing risk. That's why people who seek out group flow often avoid big companies and join small start-ups or work for themselves. Serial entrepreneurs keep starting new businesses as much for the flow experience as for additional success. In the global war for talent, organizations that need to innovate can't afford to let good improvisers go; they need to create the conditions for group flow and allow group genius to thrive.

Now we've learned that group genius comes from improvised collaboration, and we've learned where it's most likely to happen. But groups have a dark side, as well; we've all been in situations where the group made us all dumber. What's the difference between group genius and groupthink? How can a group be sure it's a smart one and not the dreaded "design by committee"? We'll answer that question in the next chapter.

CHAPTER 4

....

From Groupthink to
Group Genius

THE TERM "BRAINSTORMING" is so widely used that it's easy to
forget it was coined only in the 1950s by Alex Osborn, a founding partner of the legendary advertising firm BBDO. Osborn's key idea was that
the critical voice is the enemy of creativity; during a brainstorming session, ideas are kept flowing and critical analysis is put off for later. In the
1950s, Osborn funded the Creative Education Foundation at the University of Buffalo to teach his theory of "creative problem solving";
more than fifty years later, the annual Creative Problem Solving Institute is still going strong, and brainstorming is still practiced by corporations in every industry.

In a series of best-selling advice books, Osborn laid out the basic
principles of brainstorming still in use today. First, no criticism: Don't
evaluate any ideas until you've finished generating them. Second,
"freewheeling" is welcomed; the wilder the idea, the better. Third,

quantity is the goal; the more ideas you think up, the more likely you are to find the best ideas. Fourth, look for combinations of previous ideas, and for improvements on previous ideas.

IDEO has carried the banner of brainstorming more than any other company in recent years. Between 5 and 10 percent of each designer's time is devoted to brainstorming. IDEO has added a few rules to Osborn's original four: Stay focused on topic, stick to one conversation at a time, be visual, be physical, and use the space (white boards surround each room and Post-it notes are everywhere). To bring in ideas from employees who aren't team members, an IDEO brainstorm is scheduled in advance. A trained facilitator begins the planning by developing a list of potential participants; the goal is to make sure that all the necessary skills are represented in the group. Topics range from targeted, problem-solving tasks—"This tool is too noisy"—to vague, problem-finding tasks, such as "What can a computer be used for when it is off?" They last between forty-five minutes and two hours, and have between three and ten participants.

IDEO has special conference rooms designed for brainstorms; the brainstorming rules are displayed on signs around the room. Everyone gets butcher paper and pens. During the brainstorm, the facilitator enforces the rules and writes everyone's suggestions on the white board. Using a trained facilitator is essential to good brainstorming; research shows that groups led by a trained facilitator are twice as creative.

Brainstorming is the most popular creativity technique of all time. There's just one problem: It doesn't work as advertised. For every success story like IDEO's, you can find another company for which brainstorming has failed to deliver on its potential. This isn't surprising to psychologists; decades of research have consistently shown that brainstorming groups think of far fewer ideas than the same number of people who work alone and later pool their ideas.

The Perils of Design by Committee

We've all been in meetings that don't go anywhere. The wry phrase "design by committee" doesn't refer to group genius—Sir Alec Issigonis, the British designer of the original Mini car, used to say that a camel is a horse designed by a committee. The phrase captures a sad fact of life: In many organizations, the group ends up being dumber than the individual members. How do we make sure we have a genius group and not a stupid group? Fortunately, decades of research have shown us why brainstorming fails, and we can use this research to avoid the pitfalls of design by committee.

The first study of Osborn's technique was done at Yale University in 1958. Three psychologists recruited forty-eight people and put them into twelve four-man groups. They gave them Osborn's four basic rules of brainstorming, and then gave them twelve minutes each on three problems. Then for comparison, they recruited forty-eight more people to work alone on the same problems, for the same amount of time; the solo workers were also given Osborn's brainstorming rules. After the forty-eight solitary subjects had finished their tasks, the researchers randomly assigned them to twelve "groups" of four. The researchers chose to call these *nominal groups*.

The result surprised everyone: The nominal groups had generated almost twice as many ideas, for all three problems, as the brainstorming groups! The researchers then examined which groups had more original ideas—defined as any idea that came from one group or one person. Brainstorming lost again: The nominal groups generated about twice as many original ideas as the real groups. Finally, the researchers evaluated the quality of each idea by asking independent judges to rate all the ideas on three measures: feasibility, effectiveness, and generality. The nominal group had twice as many good ideas. The final score: nominal groups, 3; brainstorming groups, 0.

But just because nominal groups are more creative doesn't mean that the rules of brainstorming don't work—after all, the solo individuals were also using those rules. These studies just show that the rules work better when people use them alone than when they use them in groups. Several studies have shown that people who'd been through brainstorming training later had more ideas when they worked alone.

Researchers next looked for idea-generating rules that would work even better than Osborn's. They told their subjects: "The more *imaginative* or *creative* your ideas, the *higher* your score will be. Each idea will be scored in terms of (1) how *unique* or different it is—how much it differs from the common use and (2) how *valuable* it is—either socially, artistically, economically, etc." These instructions are very different from those given for classic brainstorming because people are being told to use specific directions in judging which ideas they come up with. Groups working with these instructions have fewer ideas than brainstorming groups, but they have more *good* ideas. What's most important is being explicitly told to be imaginative, unique, and valuable; then, it's okay if your critical faculties are still engaged. Osborn had one thing right: Most people use the wrong criteria to evaluate their ideas; they think about what will work, about what worked before, or about what is familiar to them.

This discovery—that when subjects are told they'll be evaluated for creativity, they're more creative than when they're told not to use any criteria at all—has been reproduced repeatedly in the laboratory. When groups are asked to suggest good, creative solutions, they have fewer ideas but those ideas are better than those generated by groups using the brainstorming rules. IDEO's brainstorming sessions are successful because their designers are implicitly guided by a drive to be creative and original, and because the sessions always conclude with a period of critical evaluation as the members of the group vote on their favorite ideas. The real challenge to creativity isn't only quantity; many managers are fond of saying that "ideas are cheap." Just as important is that, eventually, someone has to pick the best ideas, and that is accomplished by choosing for a combination of uniqueness and value.

An ingenious study at Purdue University in 1961 underscored the value of selection. The researchers asked students to invent brand names for three new products: a deodorant, an automobile, and a cigar. Half the groups were given the usual noncritical brainstorming instructions; the other half were given critical instructions: "No idea is ever worth anything unless it has been well thought out. . . . We want good, practical ideas. Let's try to avoid stupid or silly ones . . . the emphasis is on quality not on quantity." All the brand names were then judged by fifty other students as a measure of idea quality.

The noncritical groups generated about twice as many ideas as the critical groups, just as Osborn would have predicted. But the increase turned out to be an increase in *bad* ideas; both groups had about the same number of highly rated ideas, meaning that the critical group had a higher proportion of good ideas. In the real world, someone later has to evaluate the ideas and pick the good ones; that task would be more time-consuming for the longer list generated by the brainstorming group, and the end result would be the same number of good ideas anyway. Because there are more bad ideas to sift through with brainstorming, it's better to give the group members critical instructions because not only will they come up with just as many good ideas but they'll save others the work of weeding out more bad ideas later.

In addition to using groups to generate ideas, we should be using them to evaluate ideas. And that's another task where group genius wins out—it turns out that groups are better at evaluating ideas than a nominal group of solitary individuals.

Fixing Brainstorming

By about 1970, it was pretty clear that brainstorming wasn't supported by the research. Still, so many people were convinced that it was effective that researchers kept comparing real and nominal groups into the late 1970s, varying the situation a little bit each time; and every study confirmed the original 1958 findings. Although most of the studies were conducted in the lab, nominal groups have more and better ideas even when brainstorming is studied in a real company. For example, one study looked at a company that had a strong team culture; every employee had as many as three days of training in group dynamics, and trained facilitators led the groups. Existing company work teams were asked to generate ideas about ways their company could be improved. Even in this team-focused culture, nominal groups averaged twice as many ideas.

By the 1980s, even the skeptics were convinced: The original brainstorming design simply didn't work at generating the most original new ideas. But brainstorming groups are good at evaluating ideas, and they can be made more effective by altering the instructions (as IDEO has done). In the last few decades, psychologists have discovered how to reconfigure groups to make them maximally creative. They began by studying what was causing the productivity loss in brainstorming groups; if they could find out why brainstorming groups were less effective, they reasoned, then maybe they could show groups how to realize their full potential.

Researchers soon identified three possible reasons why brainstorming groups were less creative, and each cause suggests techniques to enhance group creativity. The first is *production blocking*. Group members have to listen closely to other people's ideas, which leaves individual members with less mental energy to think of new ideas. Also, individuals might be distracted from their own ideas by the flurry of idea generation around them. This is why productivity loss is greater with larger groups: Each person has less time to talk as the number of group members goes up.

One cause of production blocking is *topic fixation*—research shows that ideas in brainstorming groups tend to cluster in a few categories, which is less true of nominal groups. When compared with solo brainstormers, groups become fixated faster and stay in the same category for longer. The way to prevent topic fixation is by giving group members time periods to work alone, alternating with group interaction. For example, *electronic brainstorming*—where ideas are typed by each group member into a shared computer screen like a chat room—results in more creativity because topic fixation is reduced, and *brainwriting*—in which each member of the group takes five minutes to write out his or her ideas alone and then passes the list to the next person—is also much more effective than standard brainstorming. Electronic brainstorming and brainwriting groups both have just as many ideas as nominal groups.

Social inhibition is a second cause of productivity loss. This is when a group member holds back an idea for fear of what the others will think. When people are asked to brainstorm on a controversial political topic (such as how to reduce the number of immigrants in the country), they have fewer ideas than those who brainstorm about a noncontroversial topic (such as how life in the suburbs can be improved). And the same is true when there's an authority figure or an expert in the group, or when subjects are told that experts are watching and listening to them through a one-way mirror. If the boss is sitting in with the group, members are likely to be more worried about what he or she thinks than what their peers think. To reduce the negative effects of social inhibition, the first step is to make sure that the members of the group feel truly equal and that no authoritarian figure is present—one of the conditions of group flow. At IDEO, when Tom Kelley, the general manager, joins a brainstorming group, he defers to the group facilitator and follows the same rules as the other participants. A

second technique for reducing social inhibition is to use a trained facilitator to draw people out and to note who is holding back.

Social loafing is a third cause of productivity loss. When people are in
a group they don't feel as accountable for the outcome as they do when
they're working alone; the responsibility is distributed among the
group members, so individuals relax a little and perhaps don't work as
hard. In brainstorming groups, no one keeps track of who thought of
each idea. In laboratory studies, groups that expect each member to be
assessed separately come up with more and better ideas.

Groupthink

If brainstorming isn't the creativity panacea some people have thought it
to be, why does its popularity persist? It's because of the *illusion of group
effectiveness.* When researchers ask group members whether they think
their groups performed better than they did on the same task alone, they
always say that the group helped them—even though the researchers
have hard numbers that prove otherwise. When I create nominal groups
in my workshops, they're always more productive than the brainstorming groups, just as the research predicts. But the people in the solitary
condition find it boring to list ideas alone, whereas the brainstorming
groups enjoy high-energy conversation and laughter. Having a good
time makes people see the group as more effective than it really is.

A famous 1972 book by Irving Janis coined the term *groupthink* to describe those all-too-common situations where a team of smart people
ends up doing something dumber than they would have done if they
had been working on their own. Janis told a story about a group of
twelve smokers who were brought together by a health clinic to help
them reduce their smoking. At their second meeting, two of the most
dominant members argued that heavy smoking was an almost incurable

addiction. The majority of the others soon agreed that no smoker could be expected to cut down very much. But one heavy smoker, a middle-aged executive, disagreed; in fact, he said, by using willpower he'd stopped smoking completely since joining the group. The other eleven ganged up on him so fiercely that at the beginning of the next meeting, he announced, "I have gone back to smoking two packs a day and I will not make any effort to stop smoking again until after the last meeting." The other members of the group gave him a round of applause. Keep in mind that the whole point of the group was to reduce smoking!

The more esprit de corps in the group, the greater the likelihood that groupthink will result in bad decisions. When group cohesiveness is high, everyone gets along; they like each other and like being in the group. The group begins to share a little too much tacit knowledge; if a member challenges the others, he or she is ganged up on—just as the man who quit smoking was. The paradoxical finding is that even though everyone thinks collaboration is wonderful, only certain groups benefit from its power.

From Additive to Improvised Collaboration

How can we reconcile these studies of brainstorming and groupthink with the research that we've seen so far showing the power of collaboration? Perhaps the biggest problem with brainstorming studies is the simple fact that the tasks assigned to the group—coming up with a list of ideas or solutions—could, in theory, be performed by individuals. The creative activity of each person is *additive:* You can just add up the individuals to create a nominal group measure. But the most innovative groups engage in tasks that aren't additive.

Improvising groups are different from work teams that are brought together simply because there's too much work for one person, or because people equipped with different skill sets are needed. In those teams, a manager divides the labor and assigns the tasks. But with improvising teams, the set of subtasks isn't known at the beginning; the distribution of work emerges later. Some subtasks can never be broken up because they require the efforts of multiple team members. Division-of-labor teams aren't likely to generate true innovation, and even if they have status meetings once a week, innovations will rarely emerge.

In improvised innovation, a collective product emerges that could not even in theory be created by an individual. Think of a four-person jazz group as it improvises. Now, try to imagine a separate drummer, bassist, pianist, and saxophone player, each playing the same song but in separate rooms and unable to hear each other—this would be the nominal group. Imagine then using a recording studio to overlay their four performances to create a single recording; it would sound horrible. At every musical moment, there would be tiny but noticeable failures to sync up, and the "nominal band" could never get into a groove. The real jazz group would win, hands down. The creativity in improvised innovation isn't additive; it's exponential.

In brainstorming groups, one person's comment might inspire someone else to think of a new idea; but if the first person had been given enough time, he or she might have thought of that same idea. In a jazz group, there are so many different performance styles that no performer is capable of playing every phrase or rhythm. Jazz musicians play the same songs hundreds of times over the course of a career, and each time they play something new. Anyone asked to brainstorm "brand names for a deodorant" every Monday for a year would be hard-pressed to think of something new after the first few weeks. In group genius, the search space of possible solutions is much greater and much more complexly structured than the simple lists that are generated in lab studies. Groups need to be designed for genius, with the insights provided by the science of collaborative creativity—and science has come a long way since Osborn's cold-war fad.

Collaboration and Complexity

Up to now we've been talking about verbal creativity: coming up with words or sentences. What happens when a team's task is to develop something concrete or visual? IDEO, being a design firm, creates objects that have to look great, and their brainstorming rules include "be visual," "get physical," and "the space remembers." With visual creativity, researchers have found that groups beat out solo workers—a finding that group researchers did not discover until recently. Dan Schwartz, a Stanford psychologist, compared solitary problem solving with pairs solving the same problems. For example, Schwartz asked students to solve eight problems about gears that were all like this description except that the number of gears was different:

> Five meshing gears are arranged in a horizontal line much like a row of quarters on a table. If you turn the gear on the furthest left clockwise, what will the gear on the furthest right do?

Previous research has shown that individuals and groups can solve these problems easily. Both individuals and groups start out by twisting their hands in the air to simulate gear movement. But Schwartz discovered that in the process of solving eight gear problems, the collaborative pairs often discovered an underlying rule: If the gears add up to an odd number, the first and last gear will turn in the same direction (this is called the *abstract parity rule*). Once the pair discovered this rule, they stopped motioning with their hands and were able to solve the eighth and final problem, with 131 gears, in about one-tenth of the time.

Only 14 percent of the solo workers discovered the rule, but 58 percent of the pairs did: four times as many. Even if two of the individuals were pooled into a "nominal pair," mathematically they would be expected to discover the rule only 26 percent of the time. Because the pairs had to communicate to solve the problems, they developed collaborative representations that neither would have alone, and those representations had to be more abstract to accommodate the two perspectives that each student started out with.

These problems are very different from classic brainstorming, with its goal of generating long lists of ideas. First, the problem was something the students had never done before, so they didn't yet know how to talk about it. Second, all three tasks could be represented visually. Third, each task involved many different components and the task could be solved only by understanding the relations between those components.

Many innovations depend on visualization, abstract representation, and complex relations. Scientists often think about complex theories in visual and spatial ways; Albert Einstein solved advanced problems in physics by envisioning falling elevators and passing trains. And, of course, artistic endeavors such as painting and sculpture are deeply visual. Groups do worse at additive tasks, such as coming up with simple lists of ideas, but they often work better for the complexity of the real world—where new ideas are complex combinations of prior ideas, where the task is new and unfamiliar to the group members, and where new ideas often depend on visualization and abstraction.

Why Diversity Works

In the last chapter, we learned that before a group can move into flow, the members have to share tacit knowledge and demonstrate comparable skill levels. But we also learned that if the group members are too familiar with each other, interaction is no longer challenging, and group flow fades away. Only by introducing diversity can we avoid the groupthink that results from too much conformity.

A long research tradition shows that when solving complex, non-routine problems, groups are more effective when they're composed of people who have a variety of skills, knowledge, and perspective. Homogenous groups might work well if everything stays pretty much the same; they might even be more efficient. But the cost of short-term efficiency is eventual failure when the environment changes and innovation is required. For example, one study found that the most innovative banks—the ones that came up with the most new products and services—were led by teams that combined a wide range of expertise.

Diversity makes teams more creative because the friction that results from multiple opinions drives the team to more original and more complex work. As John Seely Brown, the legendary former head of Xerox PARC, puts it: "If you talk to film directors, you hear that the collision of ideas happens all the time in the filmmaking. . . . The breakthroughs often appear in the white space between crafts. . . . These crafts start to collide and in that collision radically new things start to happen." Conflict keeps the group from falling into the groupthink trap. But conflict is difficult to manage productively because it can easily spiral into destructive interpersonal attacks that interfere with creativity. Diversity enhances performance only when the group flow factors are present, including some degree of shared knowledge; a culture of close listening and open communication; a focus on well-defined goals; autonomy, fairness, and equal participation.

The most surprising creative insights always result from connections among different bodies of knowledge—this is the thesis of Frans Johanssen's book *The Medici Effect*. Says Paul Saffo, at the Institute for the Future, "An advance in a single field never triggers substantial change. Change is triggered by the cross impact of things operating together." The reason groups are so effective at generating innovation is that they bring together far more concepts and bodies of knowledge than any one person can. Group genius can happen only if the brains in the team don't contain all the same stuff.

Rewarding Group Genius

When groups work closely together, how do we know who's responsible for good work and good ideas? Who should be given the big raises and the promotions? If the members of the team know that their individual contributions can't be measured, there's always the risk of social loafing: Someone might sit back and let everyone else do the work. But rewarding each individual can easily interfere with the collaborative dynamic of the team. So what's a company to do?

Ruth Wageman spent four months studying more than eight hundred service technicians in 152 groups at Xerox Corporation. One-third of the groups had assignments that needed only one technician to solve, one-third worked on more complex tasks that required teamwork to solve, and one-third worked on assignments that required some solitary work and some teamwork. Wageman then manipulated the incentive structure: manager feedback on how well they were performing, merit pay increases, profit sharing. Sixty of the groups got group rewards, fifty-five got individual rewards, and seventy-seven got a hybrid combination of both.

The group reward condition resulted most consistently in high performance, although individual rewards worked just as well for the teams that were assigned solitary tasks. But when the task required teamwork, the group rewards resulted in the highest effectiveness. High levels of task interdependence, such as a basketball team, result in more communication, helping, and information sharing than solitary tasks. And there's no evidence of social loafing in interdependent teams—that's been observed only in temporary laboratory teams. Interdependent teams benefit the most from group rewards. These are also the teams that enter group flow and generate maximum innovation.

My research reveals the creative power of collaboration. But for well over a century, there's been an opposing belief that groups make people dumber. When the French sociologist Gustave Le Bon wrote an influential book about groups in the nineteenth century, he focused on mobs, riots, and panics. Janis's studies of groupthink remind us that there's always a potential dark side to collaboration.

Putting people into groups isn't a magical dust that makes everyone more creative. It has to be the right kind of group, and the group has to match the nature of the task. If the goal is creativity and innovation, then we can draw on the studies of this chapter to add a few more rules to the ten features of group flow:

- Don't use groups for additive tasks—tasks that people could do separately and then sum up. Instead, use them for complex and improvisational tasks.
- Keep groups to the minimum number of members required; this will reduce social loafing and production blocking.
- Use a facilitator who knows the research about what brainstorming formats work the best, and who knows how to help the group avoid production blocking and social inhibition.
- Because complex and unexpected innovations emerge from innovative groups as a whole, group rewards need to be in place.
- Allow the group to alternate work with frequent breaks, and switch constantly between group and individual activity.
- To take advantage of the increased innovation of diverse groups, compose groups with complementary skills.
- Keep in mind that group members who are low in social anxiety and who enjoy group interaction will perform better.

My final recommendation is the most important: Don't expect a rare and occasional brainstorming session to generate innovation. Brainstorming works best in an organization that enjoys a culture of innovation, an organization where brainstorm meetings are held so often that they're just a part of doing business. In IDEO's culture of frequent brainstorming, each year everyone attends many sessions composed of crosscutting groups of people; and the sessions are places where tacit knowledge is exchanged and developed, with combinations being made between different knowledge and project experiences. Group genius can't be bottled; it has to be spread throughout the organization and practiced every day.

After these first four chapters, you might be thinking that sure, collaboration helps, but the individual brain is the ultimate source of creativity. After all, aren't people more creative when they're alone? Many of us are familiar with stories about famous painters who paint alone in the studio—such as Jackson Pollock, who left the Manhattan art scene to paint in a barn out in the country. And although you've read my account of how the mountain bike emerged from invisible collaboration, you might still be thinking that one person is responsible for each new idea. For example, doesn't Russ Mahon of the Morrow Dirt Club get credit for the idea of putting gear shifters on those old bikes? Can collaboration really explain where creative ideas come from? The "Aha" moment, the flash of insight—that seems deeply solitary and individual. And if that's where creativity lies, then studying collaboration can touch on creativity only at the edges.

It's true that the individual mind plays a special role at the center of the creative process. But your own mind is more social than you realize. In the next three chapters I'll show the surprising connection between creative insight and group genius.

PART II

The Collaborative Mind

CHAPTER 5

··

Small Sparks

IN MAY 1926, in the English department at Oxford University, C. S. Lewis first met J. R. R. Tolkien. Lewis was twenty-eight, Tolkien thirty-four. Both felt like outsiders, in part for reasons of personality— Lewis was generally unimpressed with his colleagues and Tolkien was in a political struggle with them—but also because each man had a hobby that he hid from his illustrious colleagues: writing mythical fiction and poetry. Lewis and Tolkien formed a group with other local scholars, including Lewis's brother, Warner; Hugo Dyson; and Lewis's friends R. E. Havard and Owen Barfield. Lewis came up with the name for the group: the Inklings, a pun that described them not only as writers but also as people who were searching with "vague or half-formed intimations and ideas," as Tolkien wrote. Every Tuesday, they met at the Eagle and Child pub in Oxford to discuss Nordic myths and epics, and they read aloud from their own works in progress.

Another thing made Lewis and Tolkien different from their colleagues: At a time when most Oxford scholars were avowed atheists, they were Christians. Late on the night of September 19, 1931, Lewis, Tolkien, and Dyson walked around the quadrangles until three in the morning and talked about the fine points of the New Testament myth. Tolkien argued that although Christ's death and resurrection was structured as a myth, it had nonetheless happened because God intentionally made events easier for people to understand by causing them to unfold mythically. After this conversation, Lewis became a Christian believer.

Before the Inklings formed, Lewis had written a few unremarkable poems; Tolkien had been privately writing stories about elves and wizards since he was eighteen. Gradually, as trust built within the group, both men began to share their secret writing hobby. Tolkien sent Lewis one of his early unfinished epic poems, and Lewis gave him detailed comments on the stories of Beren and his gnomish allies, the orcs and the Narog. Other members of the group began experimenting with similar mythical fiction. For Lewis, his deepening Christian beliefs led him to explore the mythical nature of Christianity.

The themes that would later appear in each writer's books first emerged during the weekly discussions of the Inklings, and all the group members focused their shared visions in different ways. When a new idea emerged in discussion, the members would return home and draft a chapter capturing the idea; then they would take turns reading their drafts aloud at the next meeting, and listen to critical suggestions from the others. Tolkien's own lens on the circle resulted in *The Hobbit* and the three-volume *The Lord of the Rings,* an epic tale of elves, wizards, dragons, and hobbits. Lewis's lens resulted in *The Chronicles of Narnia.* Without the creative circle, these works might not exist, stories that today have been read by millions—and now, seen on the big screen.

Our image of the writer is one of solitude and inner inspiration. But *The Lord of the Rings* and *The Chronicles of Narnia* were not solo works, authored by lone geniuses; they unfolded in a collaborative circle. Tolkien and Lewis aren't the only writers who tap into the power of collaboration. T. S. Eliot's most famous poem, *The Waste Land,* was heavily edited by both Ezra Pound and Eliot's wife; both of them scratched out line after line and wrote in ideas for new text. The final published version was half the length of Eliot's original.

Even such a solitary act as writing has its origins in collaboration. How did the Inklings transform C. S. Lewis from a mediocre part-time poet into a famous novelist and channel Tolkien's mythical ideas into a coherent narrative? How did Eliot and Pound work together to produce what is now considered the most important modernist English poem? To answer these questions, we need to know more about what psychologists have learned about the creative process.

The First Cash Machine

In January 1976, John Reed was resting on a beach in the Caribbean. Reed was known as the boy wonder of banking, both because he had found success at such a young age—in 1970, when he was thirty-one, he was promoted to senior vice president, the youngest in Citibank's history—and because of his innocent, boyish face. When CEO Walt Wriston first promoted Reed, the directors at Citibank did not believe that this young man could run a $100 million division of eight thousand people. On the beach in 1976, only a few industry insiders would have recognized Reed. He had worked his way up in a distinctly unglamorous part of the bank, the computerized "back room" operations that took care of bookkeeping and customers' records. And the consumer bank—the division he was now in charge of—had always been a money loser and a career dead end; the hot shots worked in investment banking and mortgage lending, or on big deals with corporations and foreign governments. Reed brazenly predicted that within ten years the consumer bank would be Citibank's biggest moneymaker. Immediately after his 1970 promotion, Reed and his senior executives started to discuss the untapped potential of two new technologies:

automated teller machines and a credit card authorization system that could approve a purchase while the customer waited at the counter.

Reed had a habit of taking a notebook with him everywhere he went, even onto the Caribbean beach. On this day in 1976, it wasn't long before he felt compelled to pull out his notebook and start writing down ideas. As he described it to me in an interview:

> I was on a vacation, and I started out saying, "I'm sitting on a beach thinking about the business," and it went on for thirty pages. And it turned out to be the blueprint. I didn't sit down and say, "I'm gonna write a blueprint," I said, "I'm sitting on the beach thinking," and I sort of thought through the business in a systematic way.

What happened next is still legendary at Citibank: Reed took the notepad back to New York and circulated a memo on March 9, 1976, titled, simply, "From the Beach." These thirty pages turned out to be the blueprint for a new kind of bank, one based on a new technology: a network of street-level cash machines. Today, Reed is known as the person who transformed modern banking with the cash machine, with the idea to market credit cards nationally, and with many other ideas that are today a part of the everyday experience of the American consumer. When Citibank's network of cash machines came online in 1977, they were years ahead of every other New York bank. By 1981, Citibank's share of total New York deposits had doubled, and it took the other New York banks years to catch up.

Reed's spark came when he was alone, and nowhere near the office. What does this magical moment have to do with collaboration? To see the answer, let's look at Reed's spark a little more closely. First, the cash machine had been invented years before—by Docutel, an automated baggage-handling company, and their Dallas employee Don Wetzel. Second, Citibank wasn't even the first bank to install one: Chemical

Bank of New York opened the first cash machine on September 2, 1969, on Long Island, at the Rockville Centre branch at 10 North Village Avenue. Third, in the early 1970s, Citibank had already installed a network of Citicard I machines in all its branches—although these were behind the counters and could be used only by the tellers. Fourth, Reed's idea of a nationwide credit card network had been under discussion since his promotion in 1970. All these ideas occurred over time, and different people and groups contributed to each one. What made Reed's spark of insight so important was that he saw a way to bring many different ideas together—the cash machine, the credit card, the computer, the network—to create a new kind of bank.

Psychologists have discovered that creative sparks are always embedded in a collaborative process, with five basic stages:

1. *Preparation:* This involves a period of working hard, studying the problem, and talking to everyone else working on it.
2. *Time off:* The team member changes context and engages in other activities—often in conversation with others.
3. *The spark:* During the time off, a solution appears; but that solution is deeply embedded in the knowledge and social interactions of the preparation and time-off phases, and it builds on sparks that others have had.
4. *Selection:* An "Aha!" feeling doesn't always mean the idea is good. Creative people are very good at selecting the best ideas for follow-up, or they collaborate with others in selecting them.
5. *Elaboration:* Working out the idea typically requires a lot of additional ideas. Bringing them all together always requires social interaction and collaboration.

The vision captured in the memo from the beach would have meant nothing without the elaborate efforts of the entire organization; it took

$160 million for Citibank to blanket New York City with ATMs. At a time when credit cards were a high-end specialty product, it took yet more money to mass-market Visa cards. But the investments paid off: Citibank became the dominant consumer bank for the next decade, and Reed's brash 1970s prediction—that the consumer bank would be the profit leader—indeed came true. Reed wrote the memo, but hundreds of people collaborated, both before and after his 1976 vacation, to make it happen.

Bottema's Mirrors

The Hubble space telescope was carried into orbit by the shuttle *Discovery* on April 24, 1990. Hubble cost more than any other NASA spacecraft—even more than the Apollo mission that first put man on the moon. NASA decided to spend the money because every telescope on earth had a critical problem: The tiny molecules of oxygen, nitrogen, and carbon dioxide that make up our life-sustaining atmosphere also deflect light rays coming from distant stars and planets, and a telescope in the vacuum of space would provide a far clearer image. At its heart, the Hubble telescope contained a primary mirror that was less than eight feet across. The primary mirror gathered the light of distant stars and narrowed the image onto a secondary mirror that was one foot across, which then narrowed the image even further and sent it back through a tiny hole in the center of the primary mirror. Just behind the primary mirror was the brain of the telescope: a complex mechanism consisting of motors, electronics, and optics.

A few weeks after the launch, the team of twelve hundred men and women came to a horrible realization: The telescope, now orbiting Earth, had a fatal manufacturing flaw. Either the primary or the secondary mirror had been shaped to the wrong specifications; somehow, no one had noticed, in spite of years of testing. After a June 27 press

conference, Senator Barbara Mikulski—who had been one of the telescope's biggest supporters—called it a "technoturkey." The future of
NASA, and of all space exploration, was on the line, because Congress
wasn't going to waste billions of dollars again (at least, not on space exploration). NASA needed a creative solution—and to get it, its scientists and engineers followed the five stages of collaborative creativity.

First, the preparation stage. A team of top experts came together in
July for a last-ditch effort to fix the problem. In their discussions, they
quickly discovered that the flaw had occurred in the testing equipment
for the lenses; it had instructed the polishing machine to shape the mirror incorrectly. The good news was that the error was systematic because it had been driven by computers.

The NASA team came up with several ideas: mechanically deform-
ing the primary mirror, overcoating it to alter its shape, installing a corrective lens at the front of the telescope, replacing the secondary mirror.
But in the selection stage, the team soon discovered that none of the suggestions would work, each for different technical reasons.

Murk Bottema, an optical expert at Ball Aerospace, then had another spark of insight: to insert a set of ten coin-sized mirrors in the
light stream, just behind the tiny hole in the primary mirror. Each mirror would be deformed intentionally so that it became the exact reverse
of the deformities in the main mirror. That way, the image would be
corrected as the light was reflected to the five different scientific instruments at the edge of the big mirror. This time, in the selection stage,
the team ran the numbers and discovered that it was technically possible to shape each tiny mirror so that its reflection would correct for the
manufacturing flaw. But there was still one major problem: How could
they insert the ten mirrors just behind the main mirror? That spot was
a small empty space at the center of the contraption, and the original
designers had never thought anyone would ever need to go in there.

Jim Crocker, one of the engineers on the team, had flown to a meeting
in Germany, where the team was going to brainstorm about this new

problem. Like the other experts, Crocker had been studying the problem around the clock, on his own and in frequent meetings, gathering as much information as possible. On the morning of the meeting, Crocker stepped into the shower in his hotel room. The showerhead in the European-style fixture was mounted on an arrangement of adjustable rods. A tall man, Crocker had to adjust the showerhead, and at that moment the spark came: He realized that the tiny mirrors could be mounted on similar folding arms and then unfolded into the light stream from the side. He later said, "I could see Murk Bottema's mirrors on the showerhead."

But this wasn't the end of the story—after this insight, it still took a long elaboration stage to make it happen. The corrective device had only ten mirrors, but it needed 5,300 parts to make it work. Finally, success! When Hubble's repairs were fully tested in January 1994, it performed even better than expected.

Psychologists understand preparation, selection, and elaboration; those are conscious, rational activities. And they're always deeply social because collaborative groups do the work and make the decisions. But the spark of insight seems uniquely solitary. After all, Crocker had his idea in the shower! And Reed was far from Manhattan, all alone on the beach. As it turns out, even the moment of insight, this most private of moments, depends on creative collaboration. The brain itself is suffused with collaboration, and understanding how individual creativity combines with group genius is the key to realizing creative potential.

Thinking Outside the Box

In the first half of the last century, the Gestalt psychologists studied the "Aha!" moment using what are known as *insight problems*—thought puzzles that require a sudden spark of insight to solve. One of the most famous of these is the nine-dot problem. Take a minute or two to try to solve it before turning to the end of this chapter for the answer. Even if you remember seeing this problem long ago, you might have trouble remembering the solution.

● ● ●   **The Nine-Dots Problem: Connect**
● ● ●   **the nine dots with four connected**
● ● ●   **straight lines without lifting your**
● ● ●   **pencil from the paper.**

The Gestalt psychologists were known for the theory that some thoughts and perceptions can't be understood by analyzing their individual components, but have to be understood as complex wholes. These are the psychologists who created those famous illusions—the curvy goblet that suddenly turns into two faces in profile staring at each other, or the face of the haggard old woman who suddenly transforms into a young girl. No one can see both interpretations at the same time, and the transition from seeing one to the other is sudden.

Creative insight seemed to involve a similarly sudden reconfiguration. In 1926, the German Gestaltist Karl Duncker published the first study of creative insight. He began by criticizing the view of the famous American psychologist William James that sudden insights are the result of having a lot of information and being able to make connections between facts. Instead, Duncker pointed out that some problems are solved suddenly, so fast that no chain of connections can explain the discovery. To prove his argument, Duncker created a series of twenty ingenious puzzles that he claimed couldn't be solved by incremental reasoning. One of Duncker's most famous problems is the x-ray problem:

Suppose you are a doctor faced with a patient who has a malignant tumor in his stomach. It is impossible to operate on the patient, but unless the tumor is destroyed the patient will die. There is a kind of ray that can be used to destroy the tumor. If the rays reach the tumor all at once at a sufficiently high intensity, the tumor will be destroyed. Unfortunately, at this intensity the healthy tissue that the rays pass through on the way to the tumor will also be destroyed. At lower intensities the rays are harmless to healthy tissue, but they will not affect the tumor, either. What type of procedure might be used to destroy the tumor with the rays, and at the same time avoid destroying the healthy tissue?

If you can't solve this problem, don't feel bad about looking at the end of this chapter for the answer; of Duncker's forty-two subjects, only two found the solution, and even then only with hints from Duncker.

By asking his subjects to talk aloud as they tried to solve each problem, Duncker was able to identify a series of typical stages. First, you're drawn to an obvious solution, but you quickly realize that it can't work. Yet your mind is already fixated on that solution, and you're blocked from seeing the problem any other way. Prior experience is sometimes part of what leads you to fixate on the incorrect path. Then, suddenly, you overcome the fixation, you reformulate the problem and see the solution, and you experience a flash of insight.

Fixation, incubation, breakthrough. If you wanted evidence that creativity was an internal mental event, different from everyday thought, this is where you'd look. Duncker argued that prior experience doesn't help solve the problem, as it did with Reed and Crocker; it just gets in the way.

Duncker's research was suggestive, but it still couldn't tell us what was happening inside the mind, so we couldn't explore the role played by collaboration. That exploration would have to wait until the 1980s, when two research teams took very different approaches to creative insight, approaches that were not reconciled until just a few years ago.

The first approach was that of Janet Metcalfe, a Canadian psychologist who's now at Columbia University. Metcalfe is an expert in *metacognition*—how people think about their ongoing thoughts. In 1986 and 1987, she published the results of several studies that seemed to confirm the suddenness of insight solutions. First, for comparison, she collected problems that wouldn't require insight: trivia questions, simple algebra problems, and other problems that could be solved incrementally. Then she prepared another set of problems that seemed to require insight, including these two:

1. Imagine that you're a landscape gardener, and your client tells you to plant four trees. But the client wants each tree to be exactly the same distance from each of the other three. How will you do it?
2. Find ten coins. Arrange the ten coins so that you have five rows, with four coins in each row. How will you do it?

Metcalfe presented each of twenty-six volunteers with five insight problems and five noninsight problems. She pressed a mechanical clicker every fifteen seconds and asked participants to make a mark on a special sheet of paper that indicated how close they thought they were to the solution. A mark at the far left meant they were very cold, and a mark at the far right meant they were very hot. The sheet of paper had forty lines, exactly enough for the ten minutes they were allowed to work on the problem. For the algebra and trivia problems, it turned out the subjects felt warmer and warmer right up to the solution; but for the insight problems, they kept feeling cold until, suddenly, they found the solution. These studies strongly suggested that insight was different from more ordinary, incremental problem solving and the constant collaboration that accompanies it.

However, there were unexpected problems with Metcalfe's studies that the second approach would soon reveal. In 1981, Robert Weisberg and Joseph Alba, psychologists at Temple University in Philadelphia, published the first study that used the modern methods of cognitive psychology to analyze what was really going on while people solved

Duncker's insight problems. Weisberg was particularly interested in the Gestaltist idea that people have trouble solving these problems because they become fixated on an incorrect solution, or on an assumption that isn't warranted. For example, in the nine-dot problem, people typically assume that the lines have to stay within the box. The nine-dot problem is hard, as the saying goes, because you can't think outside the box.

A Gestaltist would expect that once the fixation is removed, the solution will occur quickly. The Gestaltist term for this is *restructuring*—viewing the situation in a new way that doesn't depend on past experience. In contrast, Weisberg started with the belief that past experience is always the way you solve problems—even insight problems. He believed that these were difficult not because you're blocked by fixation caused by prior experience but because you don't have enough of the right kind of prior experience; that is, experience with going-outside-the-dots puzzles. Most people have a lot of experience with connect-the-dots games, and that's why they start by going from dot to dot. They soon realize that this strategy can't solve the nine-dot problem, but they don't have any experience with other strategies.

Weisberg and Alba wondered what would happen if people were given a hint—if they were told to go outside the boundaries of the square. But when people were stumped, and the researchers gave them the hint, almost everyone stayed stuck. Then they got another hint: The researchers drew the first line of the solution. A few more people were able to get it. When the researchers showed the remaining people the second line of the solution, everyone solved the problem. They concluded that thinking outside the box isn't enough to be creative; you have to know *how* to think outside the box.

What's the best way to learn how to think outside the box? Showing people simple hints didn't help that much—they had to be shown almost half the solution before they could finish the task. Weisberg and Alba decided to try another approach: They trained people to connect the dots in triangles by going outside the triangles. Sure enough, after this training, they did much better on the nine-dot problem. These results bring us back to collaboration—because you always learn *how* to think in social interactions with teachers and peers.

Weisberg and Alba's study suggested that people are more creative later if, instead of just being told the answer, they actually solved a similar problem themselves. Mary Gick decided to test this hypothesis further with two colleagues, Robert Lockhart and Mary Lamon. Here's one of the fifteen insight problems they used:

A man who lived in a small town married twenty different women of the same town. All are still living and he never divorced a single one of them. Yet, he broke no law. Can you explain?

The solution is that the man is a clergyman. The researchers came up with two types of hints that corresponded to the two hypothesized possibilities. In the first one, the *declarative form,* they first gave subjects the sentence "It made the clergyman happy to marry several people each week." In the second one—the *puzzle form*—they gave the sentence "The man married several people each week because it made him happy"; then, a few seconds later, they presented the word "clergyman." The puzzle form at first causes the study subjects to form an inappropriate conception—that the man is marrying each woman himself—and then they are given the clue that allows them to reconceptualize. But with the declarative form, they never have to reconceptualize because they don't form an inappropriate conception.

The people who read the declarative form ahead of time didn't do any better than people who were not given a clue; they weren't able to transfer the clue to the new problem. But the people who were given the puzzle version did far better. This study explains Weisberg and Alba's finding; what's happening is, you store information in a different way when you solve a problem than when you passively receive information. If you've eaten only at fast food restaurants all your life, you'd go into any restaurant and seat yourself. But the first time you enter an upscale restaurant, this expectation will fail. The second time you enter a restaurant that has a hostess in attendance, you can easily access your memory of the earlier failure. But if a friend simply says, "Someday you'll learn that not all restaurants are like MacDonald's," that won't be stored in memory in the same way.

Experiments like these contradict several Gestaltist beliefs about creativity:

1. *We're blocked from creativity by our past experiences and our unwarranted assumptions.* To the contrary, Weisberg found that eliminating the false assumption only makes the problem slightly easier.
2. *When you break out of your fixation, the solution should come quickly and easily in a spark of insight.* That's not true, either. Instead, the "outside" hint opens up a new problem-solving domain, but that domain also requires expertise and prior experience.
3. *Insight solutions are independent of prior knowledge.* In reality, training in similar problems helps immensely.

Creativity isn't about rejecting convention and forgetting what we know. Instead, it's based on past experience and existing concepts. And the most important past experiences are in social groups filled with collaboration.

Confabulation

If insight isn't sudden—if it uses the same building blocks as other types of thought—how can we explain the many famous stories of significant artworks and ideas that seem to come out of nowhere? The English Romantic poet Samuel Taylor Coleridge said he had sparks of sudden insight all the time. He told the story of how he created his famous poem "Kubla Khan: Or, a Vision in a Dream" (referring to himself in the third person, a style common at that time):

> In the summer of 1797, the Author, then in ill health, had retired to a lonely farm-house between Porlock and Linton, on the Exmoor confines of Somerset and Devonshire. In consequence of a slight indisposition, an anodyne had been prescribed, from the effects of which he fell asleep in his chair at the moment that he was reading the following sentence, or words of the same substance, in "Purchas's Pilgrimage": "Here the Khan Kubla commanded a palace to be built . . ." On awaking he appeared to himself to have a distinct recollection of the whole [poem] and taking his pen, ink, and paper, instantly and eagerly wrote down the lines that are here preserved.

This is a classic version of a spark of insight, and books about creativity report stories like this all the time. The problem is that it's not true. Scholars who've examined Coleridge's notes have discovered that he read many different books that contributed material to the poem. Sometimes, word-for-word phrases from these books appear unmodified in his poem. And early drafts of the poem have been discovered among Coleridge's notes; further, these drafts contain versions of his insight story that describe the insight in very different ways.

Coleridge was known to be fascinated with dreams, and he was famous among his friends for making up stories about how he created his poems. A poem that he claimed to have written on "the Christmas Eve of 1794" in fact took two years to compose. Why would Coleridge lie about how he created his poems? And why does his lie so conveniently fit how we think insight works? If we can't trust what people say, the only way to understand the role of collaboration is to examine insight while it's happening.

In 1931, Norman Maier, a psychologist at the University of Michigan, revisited Duncker's insight problems. To analyze better what actually happened in the mind during the moment of insight, Maier decided to focus closely on one particular problem. In a large room filled with poles, clamps, pliers, extension cords, tables, and chairs, he hung two long ropes from the ceiling, long enough to touch the floor. With one rope next to the wall and the other in the center of the room, the ropes were far enough apart that you couldn't hold on to one and walk over to the other one. He asked each subject to come up with many different ways to tie the ropes together. The first thing they tried was to hold one rope and walk over to the other, but they quickly learned that wouldn't work.

Within ten minutes, most people came up with three solutions: (1) Stretch one rope as far toward the other as possible, tie it to one of the pieces of furniture, and then get the second rope and carry it back. (2) Take the extension cord and use it to lengthen one of the ropes. (3) Hold on to one rope and use the long pole to pull the other rope within reach. Only four in ten people also thought of a fourth solution: Tie something heavy to the end of the rope in the center of the room, such as the pair of pliers; start swinging it like a pendulum; and then grab the other rope, walk toward the first, and grab it when it swings within reach.

Maier gave a subtle hint to the 60 percent who didn't think of the fourth solution within ten minutes. He got up and walked over to one of the windows. On the way, he made sure he "accidentally" brushed one of the ropes so that it would start swinging. About a minute after he did that, another 40 percent of the students experienced a sudden spark of insight and came up with the fourth solution.

When Maier asked them later how they had come up with the pendulum idea, only one of them realized it had been Maier's accidental brush. All the rest said that they'd had a sudden moment of insight: "It just dawned on me." One person gave an incredibly elaborate explanation of the idea that had occurred to him: "I thought of the situation of swinging across a river. I had imagery of monkeys swinging from trees. This imagery appeared simultaneously with the solution." When Maier asked specifically whether they had seen the cord swaying when he walked to the window, they remembered his crossing the room, but no one remembered noticing the rope swinging. This is a perfect example of the phenomenon psychologists call *confabulation:* People have no trouble coming up with explanations for their behavior after the fact. They believe they had a solitary insight, but the real story is that a social encounter was responsible for the idea.

In 1996, the psychologists Christian Schunn and Kevin Dunbar performed a similar experiment. For two days, they had biology students come into their lab, and they split the students into two groups. The students in the first group were given a virus problem on the first day. While solving the problem, they learned that viruses are dormant because they're inhibited by controlling enzymes. Students in the second group were given a different problem, one that didn't involve inhibition. On the second day, the researchers gave all the students a genetics problem in which they had to discover how a certain set of genes is controlled, the answer being that the genes are controlled through inhibition.

You won't be surprised to learn that the students who were given the virus problem on the first day were more likely to solve the genetics problem. This phenomenon, in which an earlier stimulus causes related concepts and memories to be more readily accessible to consciousness, is called *priming*. But what you might not guess is that none of the students in the first group realized that the virus problem had helped them solve the genetics problem. When they described how they solved the second problem, only two of the eighty subjects mentioned the first problem. Even when they were asked directly, "Do you see any similarities between yesterday's and today's experiments, and what are they?" the subjects didn't realize they'd been primed to solve the problem. Just like Maier's subjects back in 1931, the students didn't realize that a previous social encounter was responsible for their spark of insight.

In Metcalfe's study, even just fifteen seconds before her subjects found the answer, they all felt very cold. But people often know more than they think they know. Maier's subjects didn't remember that he'd brushed the rope; Schunn and Dunbar's subjects didn't remember the virus problem. In both studies, the subjects' insights were inspired by previous social interaction—they just didn't remember the connection.

We're all a bit like Coleridge: We can't be trusted when we describe how our insights occur. The myth that insight emerges suddenly and unpredictably persists because most people aren't consciously aware of the social and collaborative encounters that lead to their insights.

How Insights Emerge

The studies described above were groundbreaking because for the first time they demonstrated that Gestaltist ideas about creative insight are wrong. Insight isn't different from everyday thought; it moves forward, step by step, and even when we're not consciously aware of what our minds are doing, we're still using everyday brain processes. And even when we feel a solitary, sudden inspiration, the origin can often be found in collaboration—that's what happened with John Reed and Jim Crocker. The next challenge for psychologists was to delve deeper into what goes on in the mind when we have an insight. In the real world, insight is unpredictable; we needed a way to re-create reliably the "Aha!" moment in the laboratory.

One of the simplest ways to re-create insight in the laboratory is by using what's called the Remote Associates Test, with its unfortunate acronym RAT. The RAT asks you to find a fourth "target" word that's related to each of the three test words. About half of the time, people say they get an "Aha!" feeling when they finally discover the target word. Try finding the target word for each of these five rows:

CREAM.........SKATE ....WATER
SHOW..........LIFE............ROW
CRACKER......FLY.............FIGHTER
DREAM ...,....BREAK.........LIGHT
HOUND........PRESSURE......SHOT

The RAT was originally developed in the 1960s by the psychologist Sarnoff Mednick, and it was based on his theory that creative insights were the result of forming unusual associations between mental concepts. These triplets are designed to be difficult: Although two of the three words have a similar relation to the target word, the third word has a completely different association. For example, "fire fighter" and "fire cracker" both involve combustion, but a "fire fly" isn't a fly that's on fire. "Blood pressure" and "blood shot" both refer to vessels in the body, but a "blood hound" has nothing to do with one's body. To solve RAT problems, one must bring together words from two remote *associative clusters* by finding a link between them. Mednick's theory was that people who can do this faster than others have a more intricate network in their minds that allows them to make connections between ideas that are farther apart.

The RAT seems to support our belief in a special moment of insight: You start by getting stuck as you search through one associative cluster;

then you give up and start searching your brain for another associative cluster, and you suddenly see a spark. But the way you feel while you're solving the triplets isn't the way it's really happening.

Here's an experiment, designed by the psychologist Kenneth Bowers and three of his colleagues, demonstrating that your mind is always working closer to a solution, even when you feel blocked. Bowers first chose a target word, and then created a list of fifteen words that were all remote associates of that word. For example, for the word "square" the fifteen words were these: times, inch, deal, corner, peg, head, foot, dance, person, town, math, four, block, table, box. Now, read the following list slowly and see whether you can identify the one word that is associated with all these words. As you proceed through the list, pause just after you read each word, make your best guess about what the target word is, and write it in the blank before continuing. Even if you're sure it can't be right, make sure to write something in every blank:

RED_____

NUT_____

BOWL_____

LOOM_____

CUP_____

BASKET_____

JELLY_____

FRESH_____

COCKTAIL_____

CANDY_____

PIE_____

BAKING_____

SALAD_____

TREE_____

FLY_____

Bowers found that the average person had a first hunch after ten words and were pretty sure after twelve words. But here's the really fascinating result. Bowers had everyone write down a guess after every word, just as I instructed you to do. Then he came up with a computer program that measured how closely associated each guess was to "fruit" (the answer to the above problem). Even before people knew they were getting closer, their guesses came closer and closer to fruit, and in a strikingly linear pattern. Whether it took a person five words or fifteen words, they showed the same incremental, linear pattern of getting closer and closer up to the end. But these same people often said the answer had come to them in a sudden flash of insight—even though the researchers had just gathered data showing it didn't happen that way.

If creativity is based in everyday thought—if there's no magical moment of insight, no mysterious subconscious incubation working on these problems—why did Jim Crocker and John Reed have to take time off from the problems they were working on? And if creativity is always collaborative, why did they have their sparks of insight when they were far away from the office? Stories such as theirs are what make us believe that we need distance from a problem to gain a significant insight, and that we need to get away from the group to be creative. If creativity is so collaborative, why does taking time off help the sparks fly?

The answer lies in understanding exactly what's happening in the mind when you're being creative. In the next chapter, we'll examine what psychologists have learned about the everyday mental processes that make up creativity—and how those processes are deeply collaborative. Successful creators know how to keep their sparks coming by tapping into a collaborative process that unfolds over time. In the next chapter, you'll learn how to use group genius to transform your sparks of insight into significant innovations.

Solutions

**Solution to the
Nine-Dots Problem**

The x-ray problem: Mount ten separate radiation guns around the patient's body, each of them set to deliver one-tenth the necessary radiation. Focus all ten on the tumor so that only at that point will the total radiation be high enough to destroy tissue.

The landscape gardener problem: One of the four trees must be planted on a hill (or in a deep pit) and the other three at the base, so that the four trees form the vertices of a pyramid.

The ten coins problem: Use the ten coins to form a five-pointed star shape; five coins form the five points and the other five form the pentagon at the center of the star.

The RAT triplet solutions: ICE, BOAT, FIRE, DAY, BLOOD.

CHAPTER 6

....

Collaboration over Time

IN 1829, Samuel F. B. Morse, having built a distinguished career as a portrait painter, embarked on a three-year tour of Italy, Switzerland, and France to improve his painting skills. On his way home in 1832, he had an encounter that would change his life forever.

Sailing back to the United States on the *Sully,* he met Dr. Charles Jackson of Boston. Jackson was entertaining the small group of wealthy passengers by talking about the new science of electromagnetism. How fast could electricity travel down a wire, one of the passengers asked. Jackson's response—that scientists thought electricity passed through any length of wire instantaneously—made a strong impression on Morse. Even though Morse had no prior knowledge of electricity, he had always been an inveterate tinkerer, and somehow he immediately realized that electricity could be used to send messages. He left the group, pulled out a notebook, and started drawing up plans to build an electric telegraph. When the *Sully* arrived in New York six weeks later, Morse was raring to transform his idea into reality.

This story sounds like a classic moment of startling creativity. An outsider with no prior knowledge or expertise hears the same information as other people; suddenly he has a leap of insight that changes the world. But because Morse didn't know anything about electricity, he didn't know that his idea wasn't new at all. The first suggestion that electricity could be used to send messages over long distances came in an unsigned letter published in *Scot's Magazine* on February 17, 1753—almost eighty years before Morse met Johnson. This anonymous inventor had the idea of stringing twenty-six wires, each wire corresponding to one letter. Between 1753 and 1830, at least sixty experimental electrical telegraphs were built. The most challenging task was coming up with a way to detect when electricity was in the wire; solutions included bubbling chemicals and sparks, but all these mechanisms were complicated and unreliable.

In 1820, the Danish physicist Hans Christian Oersted made a critical discovery: He noticed that when electric current flows through a wire, it creates a magnetic field. A subsequent spark of insight was the invention of the galvanometer, which reveals the flow of current by turning a needle. This led to another spark of insight, the electromagnet—a coil of wire that multiplies the electricity's magnetic field. These three insights together solved the problem of how to detect the presence of current in the wire—no more bubbling chemicals. But even after this long sequence of sparks, no one's telegraph worked. All the inventors ran into the same problem: The longer the wire they used, the weaker the electric signal became. Even one mile was too long to transmit a message.

Morse was ignorant of all this history when he had his "Aha!" experience in the middle of the Atlantic. Back in his cabin on the *Sully,* he thought of using short and long bursts of current to communicate information. He then figured out a way to use these bursts to send the numbers 0 to 9; to send words, the operator would use a special dictionary, with a four-digit number corresponding to each word. As they steamed toward home, Morse and Jackson worked together and came

up with a way to record incoming signals onto paper automatically—
an electromagnet moved a pencil that made marks on a paper tape.

Soon after he arrived home and began work on his telegraph, Morse
ran into the same problem that everyone else already knew about: The
signal weakened rapidly in long wires. Four years later, in 1836, Morse
was still stuck. What he didn't know was that the problem had been
solved years before, while he was studying painting in Europe. In 1830,
the American physicist Joseph Henry had discovered that if he used
many small batteries in a row rather than one large battery, these, together with the right kind of electromagnet, would keep the signal
strong. Henry wasn't working on telegraphy; for him, this was a purely
scientific matter. The first successful telegraph was built by Morse's
competitors across the Atlantic—the Englishmen William Fothergill
Cooke and Charles Wheatstone—because Wheatstone knew about
Henry's discovery.

In 1836, Morse was stumped, and he was also running out of money.
To pay the bills, he taught literature at New York University; while
there, he met Leonard Gale, a chemistry professor who happened to be
a personal friend of Henry's. Gale helped Morse redesign the battery
and the electromagnet according to Henry's ideas. Finally, after years
of collaboration and conversation, Morse had all the pieces in place,
and he was able to interest a wealthy investor, Alfred Vail. Together,
they replaced Morse's original numeric code with a new system in
which each letter got its own combination of dots and dashes. Morse
and Vail invented the code by counting the number of copies of each
letter in a typesetter's box; this way, the most common letters were the
easiest ones to tap out. "E" was a single dot.

Even after these important sparks of insight, it would be another
eight years before Morse constructed the first working telegraph line,
between Washington, D.C., and Baltimore. In 1844, the first message
was sent from the U.S. Supreme Court chamber to Vail in Baltimore:

"WHAT HATH GOD WROUGHT." And even then, almost every-
one thought it was just a clever novelty. The government and the military were already using an extensive network of semaphore towers for
long-distance communication, so they weren't interested. But after a
slow start, the new telegraph took off: In two years, there were two
thousand miles of wire; by 1850, there were twelve thousand; in 1852,
Scientific American wrote: "No invention of modern times has extended
its influence so rapidly as that of the electric telegraph." In October
1861, the first transcontinental telegraph put the Pony Express out of
business forever.

Morse didn't invent the telegraph in a sudden, solitary flash of insight. His 1844 telegraph line depended on many insights contributed
over time by many people. At every stage, Morse worked with others—Jackson, Gale, Vail—drawing on their expertise and collaboratively developing the next link in the chain. What made Morse
successful was the twelve years of hard work required to iron out the
technical problems, and the many small subsequent ideas that made
the original idea possible. Significantly too, a lot of new ideas were
eventually dropped; Morse's original four-digit code was never used.
Like Morse, creators usually don't know which sparks are important
until they start to collaborate; in their conversation with others, earlier
sparks start to make a new kind of sense. In the Jazz Freddy scene in
chapter 1, when the first actor sat down and started highlighting, only
later did it turn out that two other characters were helping him and
that some sort of high-stakes team activity was under way. Similarly,
Maier's subjects didn't realize that the experimenter's intervention gave
them the idea for the two-rope problem. All great inventions emerge
from a long sequence of small sparks; the first idea often isn't all that
good, but thanks to collaboration it later sparks another idea, or it's
reinterpreted in an unexpected way. Collaboration brings small sparks
together to generate breakthrough innovation.

The Origin of Species

Morse's story is an example of business invention. But the same process of innovation occurs in the arts and sciences. Writers don't sit down at the keyboard and spew out a novel; they compose in bits and pieces, and then later bring these pieces together. The novelist Anne Lamott is typical: She takes index cards everywhere because she knows that at any time she might find small but useful bits and pieces of dialogue, character traits, or events.

Science works the same way. In the nineteenth century, studying nature was something of a fad among wealthy gentlemen because of the romanticism of the era—the belief that God was found in nature, and that experiencing nature led to sublime emotions. In his youth, Charles Darwin was fascinated with geology; he also hunted birds and stuffed them for mounting, collected beetles, and closely studied the anatomical structures of flowers. When he graduated from Cambridge University, he had given up his original plans to become a minister, deciding instead to become a scientist.

The perfect opportunity presented itself when Robert FitzRoy, the captain of the *Beagle,* invited Darwin to join him on a voyage to map out the South American coast. They sailed in December 1831, and they returned to Falmouth, England, in October 1836. Darwin sent back many letters to colleagues during the expedition, and he returned with thousands of pages of scientific notes. None of his letters and notes contained even a hint of his later theory of evolution; most of these writings were about geology.

But Darwin's geological discoveries led him to formulate the question that would eventually drive his work on evolution: If the geology of the earth is always changing, wouldn't animals need to change in response? Darwin spent years pondering this question. Six years later, in 1842, he'd come up with the first outline of his theory of evolution by natural selection. In 1844, thirteen years after the *Beagle* left England, he wrote a paper outlining his theory. But rather than share it with colleagues, he set it aside, showed his wife where it was, and told her to publish it after his death. And then he moved on—to study barnacles. Between 1846 and 1854, he wrote four books about barnacles.

We know how Darwin's theory unfolded because he kept detailed notes that are still in storage at the University of Cambridge—six leather-bound notebooks, each about four inches by six inches, and each with about 125 pages, filled on both sides. Darwin had posed himself the task of developing a complete theory of evolution; and in the notebooks, we have a window into the constant role played by collaboration.

Darwin's creative process was surprisingly similar to Morse's. Morse took twelve years; Darwin took thirteen. Morse drew on the ideas of many other people; so did Darwin. In 1830, Charles Lyell, Darwin's Cambridge professor, had already convinced scientists that the biblical account of creation couldn't be true for geology. Even the idea of natural selection wasn't Darwin's; Lyell had already written that natural selection contributed to evolution. And Thomas Malthus, in his famous *Essay on Population,* had argued that all animals, including humans, produce far more offspring than could ever survive.

But Lyell and Malthus thought of natural selection as a conservative force that weeded out maladaptive variants through war, predators, and disease, and selected for offspring that were the same, only better. Darwin transformed this idea to solve the puzzle that he left the *Beagle* with—that if geography is always changing, organisms must change as well—and added an important new twist. He realized that if organisms produce far more offspring than can survive, if each one is slightly different, and if the natural world is slowly changing, then natural selection could result in change over time. This was the first theory of natural selection as an evolutionary force rather than as a conservative one, and it emerged from a long sequence of collaborations.

Learning from Failure

Successful innovators, like Morse and Darwin, don't succeed by getting lucky and being blessed with a rare good idea. They succeed by way of many small sparks, and by drawing on collaboration over time to build those sparks into something tremendous. Many of the ideas turn out to be wildly off the mark, but it turns out many not-so-good ideas are needed on the way to that rare great idea. Anne Lamott never uses most of her index cards. The original Morse code never would have worked—a system that sent only the numbers zero through nine, and then had operators use a special code book to match up multidigit numbers with words, would have been a nightmare to use. But Vail and Morse together later came up with a better code, the one known today as the "Morse code."

Morse's first idea for a way to detect the signals was a pencil that was deflected by an electromagnet, causing it to draw zigzag lines on a paper tape. Later, he and Vail replaced the pencil with an ink pen that drew a row of dots and dashes by lifting on and off the paper as it scrolled by. But even this system turned out to be unnecessary—soon after the telegraph began to take off, the first operators quickly learned how to distinguish the dots and dashes just by listening to the pen's scratches, and they never bothered to look at the tape.

Part of the reason Cooke and Wheatstone beat Morse to the invention is that Morse spent almost five years working on an absurdly complicated mechanism for sending messages. The basic idea was to have a long piece of thin metal with tiny teeth protruding from the top, the spaces between the teeth being either long or short. As the piece of metal was cranked through the device, it would create short and long pulses of electricity, depending on where the teeth were placed.

These bad ideas might sound like modest mistakes, but many of Morse's ideas were crazy schemes. In 1817, he invented a new kind of water pump that interested the local fire department but never went anywhere. In 1823, he began years of experimentation with a marble-cutting machine that would make copies of famous sculptures (his plan was to sell these to the public). It never worked. During his three years in Europe, he painted miniature copies of thirty-eight paintings hanging in the Louvre on a single canvas, six feet by nine feet; his plan this time was to exhibit the canvas in the United States and charge admission. When he met Charles Jackson during the voyage, his unfinished painting was rolled up in his luggage.

Perhaps Morse was just a lucky eccentric; surely Darwin, a scientist of great stature, was more consistent? No; just like Morse, Darwin's notebooks show that he reached many dead ends and produced a lot of ideas that scientists now consider weird:

The theory of monads. Darwin invented the word "monad" to describe a hypothetical tiny life-form that appeared spontaneously from inanimate matter. He spent years trying to make the monad theory work; later he revised it and argued that a species could survive only if it gave rise to other species—another wrong idea.

Pangenesis. Even though the theory—which included mysterious invisible particles that Darwin called "gemmules"—was incorrect, it influenced the new science of statistics through Darwin's cousin Francis Galton and his biometric approach to heredity. The incorrect spark of pangenesis inspired Galton with several later sparks that were correct.

Hybridization. Darwin spent a lot of time working on the now largely discredited theory that new species emerge from hybridization. (Gregor Mendel, known today as the father of modern genetics, also spent years working on this theory.)

Successful innovators learn from their failures. Even Darwin's dead ends provided critical links in the chain; the monad theory was wrong, but it led to Darwin's branching model of evolution. His work on hybridization led nowhere, but as a side-effect he learned about artificial selection, which he later realized was a man-made version of natural selection. His theory of coral reef formation, developed years before he'd even thought about evolution, had the same formal structure as the theory of evolution. Darwin had many key ideas before he realized how they would all fit together.

Successful innovators keep having ideas. They know that most of their ideas won't work out, and they're quick to cut their losses and pursue those few good ideas that resonate with their collaborators. If Morse had stuck with his sculpture machine, or Darwin with his gemmules, today few would remember them. But they used these bad ideas to spark new ideas that would change the world.

Historiometry

Perhaps Morse and Darwin are unique; perhaps other creators are on target more consistently. A branch of creativity science called *historiometry* has emerged recently to test that claim. Dean Keith Simonton, a professor at the University of California at Davis, pioneered this approach; he has developed a large database of illustrious, historical creators—people such as Isaac Newton, Leo Tolstoy, Leonardo da Vinci, and Ludwig van Beethoven. He then identified every creative product generated during the creator's lifetime and recorded how old the creator was at the time. Simonton's database provides a valuable portal into the origins of innovation.

Using this type of data, we now know that in every creative domain most people are somewhat unproductive, and a small minority are super productive. For example, 10 percent of the scientists write 50 percent of the scientific articles. The following figure shows the kind of analysis that Simonton's database makes possible. The horizontal axis shows the number of articles published in a career, and the vertical axis shows the number of scientists who published that number of articles. The huge hump at the left means that a lot of scientists publish only one article, and the long flat line at the right means that only a few scientists publish ten or more articles. Simonton has created graphs like this for every creative domain, from science to painting to poetry, and the graphs always have this same basic shape.

Distribution of Scientific Productivity

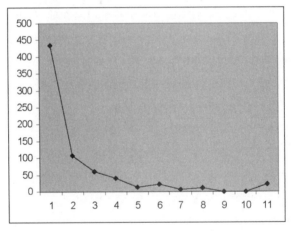

Looking at the graph, we'd be tempted to conclude that the most creative scientists are on the left. After all, the best ideas ought to emerge when people focus all their efforts, for a long time, on that one special idea. The scientists at the right seem to be spreading their energies a little too thin for any one article to be truly significant. But Simonton's database shows that the sheer productivity of a person—the raw output of creative products—is correlated with the creative success of that person. The most creative scientists are the ones at the right in the figure—that's where Darwin would be. Moreover, it turns out that for any given creator, the most creative product tends to appear during the time of most productivity. Paradoxically, slowing down and focusing on one work makes a person less creative.

Statistical research such as Simonton's is an important complement to more detailed biographic research; it shows that Darwin and Morse were typical. Darwin had a lot of ideas; famously, one really good idea. Morse's crazy ideas never went anywhere. Galileo was so convinced that planets moved in circular motion that he denied the existence of comets. Newton spent many years on alchemy, now known to be as incorrect as astrology and numerology. Einstein was so convinced that a deterministic unified field theory existed that he downplayed the important insights of the Copenhagen school of quantum mechanics.

The testimony of innovators across domains amply supports the idea that creativity emerges from high productivity. Linus Pauling, the Nobel Laureate, famously said, "I am constantly asked by students how I get good ideas. My answer is simple: First, have a lot of ideas. Then, throw away the bad ones." The chemist Sir Harold Kroto, also a Nobel Laureate, said, "Nine out of ten of my experiments fail, and that is considered a pretty good record amongst scientists." Intel's director of IT strategy and technology, Mary Murphy-Hoye, proclaimed, "If we're not failing ten times more than we're succeeding, it means that we're not taking enough risks." A 2004 survey by the Product Development and Management Association found that for every ten innovative project ideas, three entered development, two were launched, and only one succeeded.

Alberto Alessi, the famous Italian product designer, gets nervous if the company goes for a year without at least one major product failure. Alessi proudly admits that one major failure was the stylish Aldo Rossi Conical Kettle; it looks great sitting on the stove, but no one ever uses it because when the water boils, the handle gets so hot that the kettle can't be picked up. Alessi created a private company museum to display the company's failed products; weekly staff meetings are held in this space, where employees are surrounded by the flops. But in spite of its failures, the company is a success; it employs nearly a thousand workers and enjoys more than $100 million in annual sales.

Connecting the Sparks

Taking time off helps the sparks to fly, but only when that time off is embedded in a long process of collaboration over time. How do small sparks build on each other, and how are they driven by collaboration over time? Psychologists have made great strides toward understanding how new ideas build on previous ones. This new research shows how collaboration connects together the small sparks of individual minds, even when those sparks sometimes happen to a solitary creator. This research focuses on four everyday mental processes that are at the core of creativity: conceptual transfer, conceptual combination, conceptual elaboration, and concept creation.

The Fortress and the Tumor

Thomas Edison's original light bulb sockets were just wooden holes with two strips of wire at the side; the light bulbs all had to be mounted straight up or else they would fall out. Edison's lab team had been trying to think of a better way to secure bulbs in their sockets because some of their first installations were in ocean-cruising vessels. We screw in light bulbs today because one of Edison's lab assistants saw Edison cleaning his hands with turpentine; when the inventor unscrewed the metal top of the metal can, the assistant had the idea of a screw-in lamp base.

James Fitch made the first commercial steamboat, which he demonstrated at the Constitutional Convention in Philadelphia on August 22, 1787. It would turn out to be a brilliant idea, but it had an ungainly design that today seems crazy: Instead of a paddle wheel or a propeller, the engine drove six oars; the oars were suspended from a special beam that ran the length of the ship, over the heads of the passengers. By the summer of 1790, Fitch was running the nation's first steam passenger service, on the Delaware River—doing the thirty-eight-mile run from Philadelphia to Trenton in ninety minutes, at eight miles an hour. It was propelled by twelve oars, six on each side, and the passengers could see the oars swinging around as they looked at the countryside. It wouldn't be until 1809 that Robert Fulton patented his design for a steamboat propelled by a rear paddle wheel.

New ideas—those that last, and those that are later replaced—often come from *conceptual transfer,* also known as analogical thinking. The psychologists Mary L. Gick and Keith J. Holyoak are famous for their studies of analogical thinking. In 1980, to study Duncker's original x-ray problem, they first gave subjects an analogous story to see whether they could "transfer" the solution to the x-ray problem:

> A fortress was located in the center of the country. Many roads radiated out from the fortress. A general wanted to capture the fortress with his army. The general wanted to prevent mines on the roads from destroying his army and neighboring villages. As a result, the entire army could not attack the fortress along one road. However, the entire army was needed to capture the fortress. So an attack by one small group would not succeed. The general therefore divided his army into several small groups. He positioned the small groups at the heads of different roads. The small groups simultaneously converged on the fortress. In this way the army captured the fortress.

If you've already looked up the answer to the x-ray problem that appeared in the previous chapter, you might spot the parallels. (If not, take a look now at the answer at the end of that chapter.) The researchers first gave the subjects this story, and then gave them the x-ray problem and told them to use the fortress solution to help them solve it. Seven of them got the answer right away; for the other three, the researchers told them again to think back to the fortress story, and after that hint, those three got it, too. In contrast, none of those who didn't hear the fortress story were able to solve the x-ray problem. Gick and Holyoak told everyone to talk out loud into a microphone while they thought about the problem; when they later studied the tapes, they found a process of gradual, incremental work toward the solution—not a sudden insight.

Another group of fifteen people heard the fortress story, but they weren't told to use it to help solve the x-ray problem. This time, only three solved the problem, and only one of those three had noticed the analogy with the fortress story. Remembering the right analogy isn't enough to be creative; the key to creativity involves *noticing* the right analogy. Weisberg and Alba's research on the nine-dot problem showed that training on similar problems makes insight more likely; the fortress/x-ray study gives us an even better understanding of how to train for creativity. To be creative, you need to be aware of as many potential analogies as possible; and when faced with a problem, you should try as many different analogies as possible.

Rubber Army

Many successful products are created from conceptual combination. Combo snacks—cheddar cheese and pretzel. Reese's candies—peanut butter and chocolate. You can combine concepts just like famous product designers, and I'll prove it to you.

Pick a number between one and ten. Now, pick a second number between one and ten. You'll use these two numbers to try an experiment. In the table on page 113 are two columns of words. Use your first number to pick a word from column A, and the second number to pick a word from column B. Now, put these two words together to create a new object. For example, if both words are from row 1, your object would be PANCAKE BOAT. Imagine what your new object looks like, what kinds of things it can do, and what it can be used for. Maybe a pancake boat is a very flat boat, with a low profile that allows it to go under low-lying bridges. Or, it could be a new kind of restaurant that serves breakfast while touring the harbor.

	A	B
1	PANCAKE	BOAT
2	SNAKE	BOOK
3	CITY	DINNER
4	RUBBER	ARMY
5	ROCKET	SPONGE
6	BASEMENT	FRUIT
7	SOFA	FLASHLIGHT
8	COMPUTER	DOG
9	PONY	BOX
10	STONE	PAPER

Now reverse the order of the two words, so that the word from column B comes first: BOAT PANCAKE. Notice that this combination doesn't mean the same thing at all; for example, a boat pancake could be a pancake folded into a boat shape to hold extra syrup.

Even when you're not creating a new concept, you have to be creative just to understand a conceptual combination you've never heard before. In the experiment you just did with the table above, your combination probably had properties that were not held by the word in column A or the one in column B. To take the words in row 4, a *rubber army* might have the property "makes a good toy for a boy," but most people don't think of "good toy" when they hear the words army or rubber. These are *emergent attributes,* attributes that are not true of either base concept. People are incredibly creative in coming up with emergent attributes for noun combinations. When the psychologist James Hampton asked people to imagine nine different new concept pairs, such as "a piece of furniture that is also a fruit" and "a bird that is also a kind of kitchen utensil," they came up with 170 properties—an average of 19 for each pair. For "a piece of furniture that is also a fruit," emergent attributes included "regenerates itself" and "grows slowly." For "a bird that is also a kitchen utensil," attributes included "serrated beak" and "strong jaw."

Edward Wisniewski and Dedre Gentner used these types of pairs, but gave them an interesting twist: Some of the words they used were relatively similar, others were very different. They did this by identifying important dimensions that apply to all nouns, such as "artifact" versus "natural"; and "count noun" (nouns that can be preceded with numbers, such as "five chairs") versus "mass noun" (nouns that cannot be numbered, such as "sand" or "paper"). Then they gave subjects some pairs of concepts that varied on these dimensions and others that did not. For example, a "pony chair" combines a natural concept and an artifact concept, both count nouns; "snake paper" combines two concepts that are different in two ways: One is natural, the other an artifact; and one is a count noun, the other a mass noun. They discovered a fascinating result: The further apart two concepts are, the more likely it is that a truly creative idea will result.

Group 1: Count nouns		Group 2: Mass nouns		Group 3: Count nouns	
Natural	*Artifact*	*Natural*	*Artifact*	*Natural*	*Artifact*
Frog	Box	Clay	Candy	Elephant	Book
Moose	Chair	Copper	Chocolate	Fish	Car
Robin	Pan	Sand	Glass	Pony	Clock
Skunk	Rake	Stone	Paper	Snake	Ladder
Tiger	Vase	Sugar	Plastic	Squirrel	Pencil

To understand why, it helps to know a bit about how the mind represents concepts. Each concept is stored in the mind as a set of *properties* and the *values* of each property. For example, the concept "spoon" has properties and values "shape: long and thin," "function: holds liquid," "size: (large or small)," and "material: (wood or metal)." For many concepts, the properties interact with each other; most of us think that wooden spoons are large spoons and that metal spoons are smaller.

In the simplest type of conceptual combination, the properties for both concepts are joined together. Properties that are true of one concept but incompatible with the other are discarded; a pet shark cannot be "warm and cuddly," as most pets are. For two properties that are incompatible, you have to choose one; a pet "lives in a domestic environment," but a shark "lives in the ocean," and a pet shark can live only in one place. When combining, you'll pick the one that's most compatible with all the other properties of the new concept. If you said a "pony chair" is a chair that's furry and cute—but not alive—this is what you're doing.

In a second form of combination, *property mapping,* just one value is taken from one concept and merged with the second concept. If you think a "pony chair" is a brown and white chair, this is what you're doing: taking the "color: brown and white" value of "pony" and setting the color property of "chair" to the same value.

In a third, more complex, form of combination, the two concepts are brought together through a relationship. When imagining a "book box," you might think of the relationship of "containing"; "box" is the container and "book" is what is contained. If you think a "pony chair" is a chair that a pony sits in, or a chair that you sit in while taking care of a pony, this is what you're doing.

But the most creative combinations result from a fourth process, known as *structure mapping,* in which the complex structure of one concept is used to restructure the second concept. There are two kinds of structure mapping: internal structure and external structure. If your pony chair is a chair shaped like a pony, that's internal structure mapping—you took the internal structure of a pony and applied it to the chair. If you think a "pony chair" is a small chair, that's external structure mapping. What you're thinking of is not a chair that's smaller than a pony but a chair that's smaller than other chairs—in the same way that a pony is smaller than other horses.

The more similar two concepts are, the easier it is to use the simpler strategies of combining properties and values. That's the kind of innovation that results in Reese's candies—a combination of two snack foods. Concepts that are very different require more complex strategies of property mapping or structure mapping, and these strategies result in the most novel and innovative combinations. What happens when you combine a potato chip and a magazine? Who knows; but it might be Pringles Prints—potato chips printed with fun facts, trivia questions, and jokes.

Familiar Aliens

The third fundamental cognitive process that brings sparks together over time is *conceptual elaboration*—taking an existing concept and modifying it to create something new.

The first people to make baking soda in the United States were John Dwight, a farmer, and his brother-in-law, Austin Church, a physician. In 1846, they made the new product in the kitchen of the Dwight home, packing it into paper bags by hand. The product was so successful that Church's son, James Church, joined the business in 1867, and they renamed the product "Arm & Hammer Baking Soda." Today, the Arm & Hammer logo is one of the oldest and most recognized in American product history.

But by 1970, the Church & Dwight Company had run into a problem. Everyone was either buying box mix or not baking at all, and people no longer needed baking soda. The old box of baking soda was so useless that people had started putting the box in their refrigerators: Word of mouth had it that the powder absorbed odors. The company did some research and discovered that the claim wasn't just an old wives' tale—it actually worked! Church & Dwight decided to market the odor-absorbing qualities of baking soda. In 1972, they unveiled a new television ad campaign: Use Arm & Hammer in the fridge to "keep food tasting fresh." Within a year, more than half of American refrigerators contained an open box. Church & Dwight have now extended the product to new brands of deodorant, toothpaste, cat litter deodorizer, and laundry detergent.

Arm & Hammer Baking Soda owes its continued success to conceptual elaboration. The easiest way to elaborate a concept is to modify one of its property values while keeping the other properties the same. Popular songs are often small variations of existing songs; architects design new buildings that are only slightly different from existing buildings; chefs create recipes that are subtle variations of old favorites. In 1972, Church & Dwight changed a key property of their product, the "function" property, and kept everything else the same. But that insight was rarer and more difficult than creating yet another chicken and pasta dish because the "function" property of baking soda was one of its core properties, and core properties are resistant to change. The psychologist Thomas Ward showed this by asking people to imagine, draw, and describe animals that might exist on other planets. People assume certain core properties of animals: They all have eyes, ears, legs, and all have symmetrical bodies. And like a wooden spoon being large, some properties are linked together: Feathered animals also tend to have wings; scaled animals tend to have fins. On another planet, all these things might, of course, be different. But Ward's subjects didn't usually imagine them so. The property values they modified were predictable: more than two eyes, eyes in different locations, variations on limbs such as legs featuring wheels at the end.

It doesn't take much creativity to make a small conceptual elaboration, for example, changing the number of legs or eyes. What Church & Dwight did sounds simple, but baking soda's "function" property—set to "baking"—was perhaps the last you'd think of changing. To be more creative, you need to make sure you consider changing *all* properties and values.

Morphological Analysis Example

New invention category: A board game		
Property 1: Theme	*Property 2: Audience*	*Property 3: Materials*
Food	Seniors	Invisible ink
Family reunion	Couples only	Nylon
Laughter	College age	Bouncing balls
Best/Worst	Roseanne	Sponge rubber
Gossip	Yuppies	Kites/Gliders
Sex and Rock & Roll	Teens	Masking tape

One popular creativity technique, *morphological analysis,* does just that. It's usually done in a collaborative group, but it can be tried alone. Think of a product category for which you'd like to create a new invention, for example, a board game (see the table above). Then, start by breaking down that category into as many properties as possible. Don't leave anything off the list; put down even the most obvious, taken-for-granted properties. Once that's done, the group begins suggesting possible values for each property—and, as in brainstorming, the group is instructed to think outside the box and come up with crazy and apparently implausible values. The final step is evaluation and selection: Consider every combination of values, discard the ones that exist already or that aren't useful, and then begin a serious discussion about the remaining combinations.

Good Birthday Presents

The three mental processes we've been discussing—*conceptual transfer, conceptual combination,* and *conceptual elaboration*—build on existing concepts. But wouldn't it be even more creative to invent a completely new concept? Aren't genius creators different from the rest of us because they have a special ability to create concepts from whole cloth?

No, they're not. Psychologists have shown that by using a fourth cognitive process that brings sparks together, everyone can create new concepts. For example, even people who live in disaster-prone areas rarely have evacuation lists prepared and ready to go. But, interestingly, many of them—as in New Orleans' Katrina disaster—are quickly able to create a list of items for the category "Things to take with you when evacuating": children, blankets, food, important papers, expensive electronics, and pets. The psychologist Larry Barsalou calls this an *ad-hoc concept* because it's creatively, spontaneously produced. Other ad-hoc concepts include *things not to eat on a diet, good birthday presents, things to take on a camping trip,* and *heavy objects with which to prop open a door.* Barsalou's experiments show that everyone can create new concepts quickly.

Here's one story that Barsalou used to study this creative everyday ability:

Roy was in big trouble. The Mafia had a contract out on him for double-crossing them. He knew he couldn't continue living in Las Vegas or he'd be dead in a week. So he started thinking quickly about alternatives.

The ad-hoc category is *ways to escape being killed by the Mafia.* Included are items such as "change your identity and move to the mountains of South America." Barsalou's surprising finding is that right after you create a category, you're almost as good at thinking with it as you are with categories you've known about all your life, such as *bird* and *furniture*. For example, he found that ad-hoc categories have a "graded structure," just like common categories—meaning that not only can you quickly tell whether a new item is a member of the category, you can also tell how good an example of the category it is. For the ad-hoc category "things to take with you when evacuating," "children" and "food" are better examples than "expensive electronics." A tent is a more important item to take on a camping trip than a folding chair, even though both are useful. We are all able to create these ad-hoc categories quickly; in a flash, anyone can create a new conceptual structure to organize objects.

The Power of Visual Imagery

The four types of creativity I've discussed are examples of a type of thinking known as *propositional* or *linguistic*. Since the 1970s, psychologists have known that our minds have another deep-rooted mode of thinking: the spatial, or visual, mode. And as we saw in our exploration of brainstorming, it's even more creative than working with words or concepts. When we combine visual images, we can't help but create new objects with surprising and unexpected emergent properties.

Imagine a sphere, a cylinder, and a flat square. Now, pick a number between one and eight. Go to the Invention Categories table on page 121—the number you chose will tell you a product category. Your task is to combine the sphere, cylinder, and the flat square to invent a new product within that category. The parts can be combined in any way, they can be any size, and they can be made of any material. Close your eyes, and give yourself two minutes to come up with a name for your invention and a description of how it works.

Invention Categories

1 FURNITURE

2 PERSONAL ITEMS

3 TRANSPORTATION

4 SCIENTIFIC INSTRUMENTS

5 APPLIANCES

6 TOOLS AND UTENSILS

7 WEAPONS

8 TOYS AND GAMES

You've just done what the creativity researcher Ronald Finke had hundreds of college students do at Texas A & M University. Finke gave these students three simple parts, chosen randomly from the fifteen in the Invention Exercise below. He hired independent judges to rate the creativity of every student's invention. Amazingly, more than one-third of the students came up with new inventions that a team of independent judges rated as both practical and original.

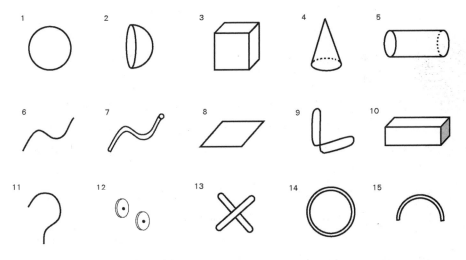

Invention Exercise. Give yourself one minute to use your three shapes to make an interesting, potentially useful object (from Finke, 1990, p. 41).

What's most interesting is how the students came up with these new ideas. When they started, they had no idea about what they were going to create. But as they began to experiment, putting the parts together in various ways, what unfolded was unpredictable and surprising, even to the creators and even to Finke, who designed the experiment.

Before looking at the drawings, the researchers came up with three inventions that they thought were particularly obvious for every one of the many combinations that appeared in their experiments; the subjects came up with those less than 15 percent of the time. When the students were asked to make three predictions about the images they would create just before they closed their eyes to begin, they predicted less than 19 percent of their emergent patterns—not much more than Finke had. Visual imagery is a powerful creativity technique because new combinations often appear suddenly, unpredictably, and unplanned.

Here's a second experiment. Pick three numbers from one to fifteen, and write them down. Using those three numbers, go to the Invention Exercise on page 121 and use your three numbers to pick three shapes. Now, give yourself one minute to put those shapes together to make an interesting, potentially useful object. You can combine the parts in any way as well as vary their sizes. You could put some of the parts inside others, and the parts can be made of any material. The only rule is that you can't deform any of the shapes (except for the wire and the tube, which can be bent and stretched any way you like), and you have to use all three parts in your design.

When you've got it, pick a number from one to eight, and use that number to pick an invention category from the Invention Exercise on page 121. Then take the new design and interpret it as a member of that invention category. Give yourself one minute to think about it.

It's not easy to fit your creation into a category when you don't know ahead of time what the category is. Only half of Finke's subjects were able to come up with an interesting and potentially useful object. And only one-third of those were able to complete the second step, interpreting their creation as a member of the invention category. This means that only one out of six people could complete both steps. But when independent judges rated the creativity of those inventions, they were more likely to be creative than in the first task—when people knew their category ahead of time. When people knew their category first, only one-third were judged creative, but for this second task, more than 50 percent of those who completed the task generated inventions that were judged to be creative. That means that you're more creative when you don't know ahead of time what category your invention will belong to.

Finke tried the experiment once more, but this time instead of giving the students three shapes and a category, he let them choose any three of the fifteen shapes as well as pick the category they wanted. You might think that reducing the constraints would make the students more creative, but just the opposite happened—the students were less creative. With so many choices, it was too easy to start with a fixed idea of what they wanted to create and then just pick and choose the objects and category that best realized their preexisting concepts. The original task, with more constraints, forced them to start creating before they knew what they were doing, thus allowing unexpected insights to emerge.

These experiments are another demonstration of the creative power of problem finding. In Finke's third experiment, the task allowed people to use a problem-solving style: They quickly decided what they wanted to invent, and then spent their time selecting the three shapes that would allow them to do that. But in his first two experiments—and especially in the one in which subjects didn't know the category—people had no choice but to do problem finding.

Problem-finding creativity sometimes goes unnoticed because when it's over it appears more predictable than it actually was—another example of script-think. The inventions that emerged in Finke's extreme problem-finding condition—when subjects had to design an invention and only later were told the category—seem as if they were originally designed with the knowledge of the category they would belong to. The researchers themselves had this reaction for.the most creative inventions, even though they knew that couldn't be so. Script-think is common with problem-finding creativity; after it's happened, it seems as if it must have been planned that way.

These studies of the creative mind show that hard work, collaboration, and deep familiarity with an area make you more creative. When you have more information about the creative domain, taking time off from a problem helps you to have a spark of insight because it frees your mind to play around in other conceptual spaces and to notice more potential analogies. When you're working hard on a problem, your mind is fully absorbed with one associative cluster; the others are forced into the background. Sometimes, you need to take a break and free your mind to allow the right analogy to emerge. But it won't happen if you haven't worked with those analogies and solved those problems yourself. One of the most solid findings in creativity research is the ten-year rule: It takes a minimum of ten years of hard work and practice before attaining the high level of performance that results in great creativity.

Collaboration makes the mind more creative because working with others gives you new and unexpected concepts and makes it more likely that your mind will engage in the most creative types of conceptual creativity—combining distant concepts, elaborating concepts by modifying their core features, and creating new concepts. Many new ideas are bad ones; collaboration over time is the best way to select the good ones. And although each single spark of insight is small, collaboration brings them all together and results in breakthrough innovation. Morse had the idea for dots and dashes, but he used them to send four-digit word codes; it was in collaboration with Vail that the idea of sending each letter with its own distinctive dot-dash pattern emerged. Lyell and Malthus had the idea of natural selection, but Darwin rejected their conservative interpretation of that process and came up with a new idea, a way that natural selection could drive the evolution of new species. Collaboration brings distant concepts together; it makes each individual more creative; and, most important of all, the emergent results of group genius are greater than those any one individual could think of alone.

Now that we understand the connections between the individual mind and collaboration over time, we're prepared to turn to an analysis of conversation—the driver of group genius.

CHAPTER 7

Conversation and the Mind

THE LABORATORY MEETING is a good example of an organizational design that speeds up the innovation process by bringing sparks together. At regular meetings, a scientist or a postdoctoral fellow reveals new findings from the latest experiments. The other members of the lab team ask questions about the findings, propose new interpretations of them, and suggest new experiments. At the end of many of these meetings, the group collectively comes up with a key scientific insight. The psychologist Kevin Dunbar took his video camera into biology labs to observe scientists thinking out loud.

In one session, a postdoctoral fellow was describing his experiments on how B-cells cause an autoimmune disease. He used analogies with other cells to explain what was happening. He then reported an unexpected finding: Heart B-cells and bone joint B-cells were found in both the heart and the joints. Since it's difficult for invading cells to penetrate the heart and the joints, they usually specialize. Everyone in this lab knew, for example, that in rabbits, CVX B-cells and colmenia B-cells can enter their corresponding body part only. By analogy, everyone expected

the different types of B-cells to be found only in the matching body part—but this analogy was misleading.

The lab director asked how it could be that both cells could enter the heart and the joint in the human body; the postdoc didn't know. The director then asked what properties were common to the two B-cells that would allow them both to enter the human heart. The postdoc responded by making an analogy to other experiments that suggested a common mechanism. In the discussion that unfolded, the group members developed a possible explanation for the unexpected finding.

Suddenly, they had a spark of collective insight. They realized that there might be two separate special properties: one that allowed the cell to enter the organ, and another that caused the disease. In the ensuing discussion, the group made several analogies between the two rabbit diseases and a human autoimmune disease they were studying in a separate project. Everyone immediately recognized a significant breakthrough—the analogy had unexpected and powerful implications for many other human autoimmune diseases. Their brainstorming became more intense, and other analogies led to suggestions for new experiments.

This kind of collaborative conversation accelerates the innovation process because the sparks happen in real time. Four times over the next nine months, Dunbar asked the presenting postdoc how this discovery had been made. And given what we've learned about confabulation, it's not surprising that the postdoc didn't remember the spontaneous analogies or how the insight had emerged from the group's conversation. We often forget where our own ideas come from, but it is abundantly clear from Dunbar's observations, as well as those of other researchers, that collaborative teams are the incubators of innovation.

A century ago, this wasn't as obvious. Even though Darwin's ideas built on the work of many other scientists and Morse depended on collaborations with Gale, Vail, and others, the lack of telephone, e-mail, and air travel made the pace of innovation incredibly slow. Today's pervasive and high-bandwidth communication and social networks give us the potential to be far more creative than humans have been at any time in history. Reaching our full creative potential is now possible for us all through the science of group genius.

The Horse's Ass

In the last chapter, we learned that analogies are often the source of creative sparks. But analogies aren't just mental processes; everyday conversation is filled with collaborative analogies. Over the years, businesses have tried to create unique conversational formats to enhance the power of collaboration, and one of the most famous is William J. Gordon's *synectics,* a group creativity technique designed to foster collaborative analogies. Synectics has been used in the largest companies, including Kimberly-Clark, Singer Sewing Machine, and RCA. What makes Gordon's approach so powerful is that it brings people together in collaborative teams to create new analogies through conversation.

One synectics group was trying to invent a liquid dispenser that could be used with sticky liquids—such as glue and nail polish—that dry out when they're exposed to air. Their one constraint was that the dispenser couldn't have a cover; the mouth had to open to release liquid and then close tightly afterward to prevent the liquid from drying out. And the mouth of the dispenser had to remain clean so that it wouldn't become clogged with dried glue. Here's how the discussion unfolded:

A   A clam sticks its neck out of its shell . . . brings the neck back in and closes the shell again.

B   Yeah, but the clam's shell is an exoskeleton. The real part, the real anatomy of the clam is inside.

C What difference does that make?

A Well, the neck of the clam doesn't clean itself . . . it just drags itself back into the protection of the shell.

D What other analogies are there to our problem?

E How about the human mouth?

B What does it dispense?

E Spit . . . the mouth propels spit out whenever it wants . . . oh, oh.
   It isn't really self cleaning . . . you know, dribbling on the chin.

A Couldn't there be a mouth which was trained so that it wouldn't
   dribble?

E Maybe, but it would be contrived as hell . . . and if the human mouth
   can't keep itself clean with all the feedback in the human system . . .

D When I was a kid I grew up on a farm. I used to drive a hayrack
   behind a pair of draft horses. When a horse would take a crap,
   first his outer . . . I guess you'd call it a kind of mouth, would
   open. Then the anal sphincter would dilate and a horse ball
   would come out. Afterwards, everything would close up again.
   The whole picture would be as clean as a whistle.

E What if the horse had diarrhea?

D That happened when they got too much grain . . . but the horse
   would kind of wink a couple of times while the anal mouth was
   drawn back . . . the winking would squeeze out the liquid . . .
   then the outer mouth would cover the whole thing up again.

B You're describing a plastic motion.

D I guess so . . . could we simulate the horse's ass in plastic?

This emergent insight was successful because of the way it brought
analogies together; the group went on to build a dispenser that operated just like the horse's ass.

Analogies are essential to collaborative creativity, and they're more
likely to emerge when participants bring their various experiences to the

table. This is borne out by Dunbar's studies of four science labs. Of the four, the one that didn't use analogies made no important discoveries. Dunbar dug a little deeper and learned that all the scientists in that group came from the same background and thus were able to communicate directly through their shared specialized language. Because they all shared the same definitions for each word, their communication remained direct and explicit; there was no place for the problem-finding reinterpretation that leads to unexpected innovation. When an experiment didn't work, they all knew exactly what they were supposed to do. But true innovation didn't happen because the group lacked different sources of knowledge to draw on to form analogies.

In the other three groups, the scientists came from a wide range of backgrounds, and because they didn't share a common language, they were forced to use analogies to develop new conceptual combinations. Gordon discovered the same thing with his synectics groups—better ideas emerged when people from different backgrounds came together. These discoveries reinforce a message that we've already learned from studies of group flow and brainstorming—if your group is too homogeneous, it will be less creative.

Integrative Collaboration

Even the mental concepts used to form analogies are deeply collaborative; conversation is the source of the mind's concepts. The psychologist Art Markman demonstrated this in an intriguing series of experiments. He assembled pairs of people in his lab and had them build LEGO spaceship models together; they used the required fifty-two pieces, along with the picture of the finished product on the box. The twist was that one of the two people was forbidden to touch the pieces, and the other wasn't allowed to see the picture. So they had to talk constantly to finish the spaceship. After finishing, each person was asked to sort the pieces into groups and then label each group. They created categories such as *bar* (for a thin brick), *tile* (for a flat brick), and *prism* (an odd shaped piece that was triangular). They also grouped the bricks according to their function in the model, for example, *rocket* for a piece that went at the back of the spaceship.

Markman then did a separate study with another group: He brought in one person at a time and had each person build the model alone. When these people were later asked to sort the pieces, they just piled them according to color. Talking about building the spaceship had caused the first group to create categories that were richer and more complex than those created by the solitary workers in the second group. Even the categories and concepts that you use to form your own thoughts are shot through with the collaborations from which they originated.

Even the most seemingly solitary creative activities, such as thinking by using one's own very private concepts, originate in collaboration. Vera John-Steiner, a creativity researcher at the University of New Mexico, analyzed many successful collaborations in her book *Creative Collaboration*. She quotes the feminist literary critics Carey Kaplan and Ellen C. Rose, who collaborated in writing books:

> Our minds meet in the air between us and we achieve, at our best, an unfettered, creative, generous reciprocity. . . . "She" and "I" metamorphose into "we," hypothetical, invisible, yet nonetheless articulate. . . . We learned first that we could sit together before a computer and write sentences that worked even better than did sentences we wrote alone.

The famous anthropologists Elinor Ochs and Bambi Schieffelin have engaged in a lifelong collaboration. They talked constantly, took notes together, and analyzed transcripts of children talking together:

We would always have the typewriter right there and we would switch off writing and talking. . . . We did not ever allocate parts of the paper to one person or another person but we actually [discussed] . . . every single sentence. . . . We would both kind of think of the next thing to say and then . . . paraphrase one another.

Claude Monet spoke of the famous creative circle of fellow impressionist painters—Alfred Sisley, Auguste Renoir, Paul Cézanne, Edgar Degas, Camille Pissarro—who supported each other in Paris during their early years of rejection:

Your mind was held in suspense all the time, you spurred the others on to sincere, disinterested inquiry and were spurred on yourself, you laid in a stock of enthusiasm that kept you going for weeks on end until you could give final form to the idea you had in mind. You always went home afterwards better steeled for the fray, with a new sense of purpose and a clearer head.

This wasn't just a matter of talking at the café while taking time off from the studio; these painters often went to the countryside together. Renoir and Monet painted together frequently in the summer of 1869, setting up their canvases side by side, monitoring each other's paintings, and discussing what they were doing. When you look closely at a pair of paintings, you can tell which one was painted by the artist standing on the left and which by the one at the right. But the styles are so similar that it's not always obvious who painted which one. Looking back, neither could say who was responsible for a given innovation.

Painters and poets were often members of the same circles; in Paris early in the twentieth century, the poet Guillaume Apollinaire was a member of the *bande à Picasso*. Pablo Picasso's biographer wrote: "So similar is their imagery that sometimes it seems as if the painter and the

poet had access to the same imagination." In 1907, Apollinaire introduced Picasso to Georges Braque. Both painters were then working
out the influence of Cézanne. "Almost every evening I went to
Braque's studio or Braque came to mine," Picasso said of their collaboration. "Each of us *had* to see what the other had done during the day.
We criticized each other's work. A canvas was not finished until both
of us felt it was." During one period of extremely close collaboration,
they both decided to sign their names on the back of each canvas, sig-
nifying that the individual identity of the painter was less important
than the collaboration that had actually created the work. John-Steiner
called it an *integrative collaboration,* a profound bonding that creates a
shared vision, and her research finds that these intimate collaborations
are the most radically innovative, the ones that have the potential of
transforming ways of seeing to create a completely new vision.

Conversational Insight

Stories such as these inspired me to begin my studies of creativity by listening to ordinary people's conversations. I videotaped these conversations, transcribed them, and then applied interaction analysis, the same
technique I used to study improv theater. This work—and that of colleagues around the world—provided a clear view of how creativity
emerges from collaborative conversation. Ronald Carter, a professor of
linguistics at the University of Nottingham in England and the leader
of the CANCODE corpus, one of the largest conversational taping
projects in the world, found thousands of examples of creativity in his
five-million-word database. For example, Carter captured the freewheeling conversation of three art school students. Mary was wearing
dangly earrings that were falling apart, and the various pieces were
swinging around.

MARY: It's my earring.

BETH: Oh. Lovely. Oh. Lovely.

MARY: It's fallen apart a bit.

BETH: It looks quite nice like that actually. I like that. I bet, is that supposed to be straight?

MARY: Yeah.

BETH: I reckon it looks better like that.

MARY: And it was another bit as well, was another dangly bit. Separate.

BETH: What attached to that one?

MARY: The top bit. Yeah. So it was even.

STACY: Mobile earrings.

BETH: Oh.

MARY: [Laughs]

BETH: I like it like that. It looks better like that.

MARY: Oh, what did I see. What did I see. Stained glass. There was . . . I went to a craft fair, um, Bristol. And they had this stained glass stall and it was all mobiles made out of stained glass.

STACY: Oh, wow.

Stacy joked that they were "mobile earrings," a conceptual combination of earrings and the mobile—a type of art sculpture that hangs from the ceiling and moves in the breeze. At the same time, she was making a pun on the noun "mobile" and the adjective "mobile," meaning something that moves around. It's like PANCAKE BOAT, but it emerged from the group.

These women aren't just being creative to score conversational points and impress their friends—they use these moments to reinforce their common bonds. Building on the "mobile earrings" creation, Mary next told a story about visiting a craft fair and seeing an artist who'd created mobiles made from stained glass. She took the new concept of "mobile earrings" and built on it to take the conversation in a different, creative direction—again, one that reinforced their shared experience.

Since 1990, I've been studying what goes on in collaborative teams, and I've found that conversation is wonderfully improvisational as long as we open ourselves up and let it happen. Here's an example of an improvisational conversation between a manager, Theresa, and an interface designer, Tony, at a software company. Tony has just realized that to make the interface more user-friendly, the software will have to be changed. But he's not sure which changes to make and he doesn't have the authority to order them to be made. As they improvise together, an unexpectedly creative solution emerges.

TONY: Theresa, when you get a minute could you come here?

THERESA: Sure. Just a sec.

THERESA: What's the problem?

TONY: The problem is that some of the files need to go on the Web server, and some on the video server. On the Web, these files [draws on white board], on the video, these files.

THERESA: It used to be on one server.

TONY: Yeah, but how do you make it simple for the users? This has to go on this server [points], this on that server [points].

THERESA: But even here [points] you may have these types of files.

TONY: Well, we may at some point, for tech support purposes, have to allow them to have this list [points], or separate GIF and HTML folders.

[Pause; both of them stare at the white board.]

TONY: Here is the problem I see: The folders have to have different names, but you need a folder for each presentation to not override other types of files.

THERESA: We need to have it ask the user to give the presentation a name—we need to have Jim add some code that gives it a name. Devin [turns to Devin]—does it make it easier for you if it has the same or separate folders?

DEVIN: Separate.

THERESA: [Looking at Tony, pointing at Devin] So there's your answer.

TONY: Okay. Then here are the folders [pointing at white board].

THERESA: Is index.html your Javascript?

TONY: No.

THERESA: I've got it! Make two starts! This will create two folders.

TONY: So that loads start and that loads index?

THERESA: You may want to not make it index, because that's the default presentation.

TONY: Having it up here screws you up either way.

THERESA: The problem is if you're doing many presentations . . . [pauses]. I'm not sure I understand the main issue any more.

TONY: There's a lot of naming issues and overriding issues that have to be addressed.

THERESA: Let's name the issues. Folders need titles for the name of presentation to reduce erroneous overrides.

TONY: Plus ease of use for uploading stuff. So, rather than have fifteen folders . . . [draws on the white board].

THERESA: The options for multiple presentations are . . . [she adds to Tony's drawing].

TONY: Okay. So that would have a link to the presentations and to the images!

THERESA: Great. Then Devin could point users here [points], and Jim could add the code that names the presentation.

TONY: Cool.

This conversation generates innovation because Tony and Theresa are doing what good improv groups do—following the "Yes, and" rule of accepting the partner's suggestion and then building on it further. When they were interviewed later, they said they were in group flow during this conversation. That's because neither Tony nor Theresa started the discussion with a preconceived idea, and neither attempted to drive the flow of the conversation.

Conversational insights occur all the time in business. Computer Motion's AESOP is a case in point. AESOP, the world's first commercial surgical robot, holds the internal or "endoscopic" camera during laparoscopic surgery. Before it was invented, a surgical assistant had to hold the endoscopic camera and minor hand tremors always caused problems. AESOP can understand the surgeon's verbal commands, and it has been used in more than a hundred thousand surgeries. The idea for AESOP was born in a conversation between the founder of Computer Motion, Yulun Wang, and the surgeon Ron Lattimer. Like the founders of other robotics companies, Wang had intended to focus on the military and automobile industries, but those sectors were both in an economic slump in the early 1990s. One of the few growth industries was health care, so Wang decided to talk to doctors.

During their conversation, Lattimer told him about laparoscopic surgery, noting that if a robot could hold the scope and the camera, the problem of the inevitable small hand movements would be solved. "If I can have direct control of that camera, that would be very helpful for me," he noted. Wang later said, "That was a significant moment, the very first time the concept of AESOP came into being."

Lattimer couldn't have thought of the idea by himself because he was unfamiliar with robotics technology. Wang couldn't have thought of it either because he knew little about surgery. Together in conversation, they devised a way of improving health care for thousands of patients.

Many of today's most creative products emerge from collaborative conversation. Here's a transcript of a story meeting of the artists working on the Cartoon Network's cartoon *Samurai Jack*. The meeting was led by the creator, Genndy Tartakovsky (the creator of *Dexter's Laboratory*). Andy has the seed of an idea for a new episode and submits it to the group's creative process. There are about ten people in the room; other than Andy and Tartakovsky, whenever one of the others speaks up, I've simply indicated "artist":

ANDY: We're looking to do the story we talked about, where Jack gets infected with a virus and it takes over his arm. Then it would slowly take over his whole body. Then half of him becomes evil, and he's going to fight himself.

TARTAKOVSKY: How do we set it up?

ARTIST: Could he have battled Aku, and Aku has a cold, and he sneezes on him?

TARTAKOVSKY: [Nods]: It's almost like we're at the end of another show with a great fight. Except this one starts with a battle. And he's fighting these robots, and Aku's commanding them. It's cold and drafty, and Aku starts sneezing, and says, "Oy, I've got to get some chicken soup."

ARTIST: Oy?

ARTIST: How do we get it out that he's infected?

ARTIST: We had talked about him showing a guy his face. And it's half in shadow.

ARTIST: He becomes Aku.

ARTIST: He becomes *Jaku*.

ARTIST: The more evil he becomes, the more erratic his body is.

ARTIST: Maybe somebody's getting robbed, he saves him, and the guy thanks him, and he's walking away, and in Jack's other hand is the guy's watch.

ARTIST: Do we need to find somebody to summon him? Is there a psychic battle with himself?

ARTIST: Or a fight in his head? I was thinking, he knows a place to cleanse himself—a monastery. And the monks help him.

ARTIST: The B story is no one's trusting Jack—they see him and they run.

TARTAKOVSKY: It's always stronger if Jack can help himself. I like the image of Jack as Aku with one eye. I like it half and half. The more I think about it, the body of the show is him fighting himself.

ARTIST: He realizes he'd better get out of the city before he hurts someone, so he travels to a village.

TARTAKOVSKY: I still want to keep it real simple, though.

ARTIST: At the monastery, they tie him up so he can't do any harm.

TARTAKOVSKY: Does Aku know that Jack has what he has?

ARTIST: No, he's too sick.

In this collaboration no one is in charge, and no one creates any more than anyone else; they practice the equal participation that leads to group flow. Even though the discussion started with Andy's idea, he said nothing after getting it started. And even though Tartakovsky is the group leader, he doesn't dominate the group. The cartoon, a collective creation of ten people, emerges from group genius.

Indexicality

Because I believed the engine that drives collaboration is conversation, I chose to do graduate study at the University of Chicago; the distinguished faculty included not only the famous creativity researcher Mihaly Csikszentmihalyi but also many legendary conversation scientists in linguistics, psychology, and anthropology, led by MacArthur genius grantee Michael Silverstein. This combination allowed me to bring together the sciences of creativity and of conversation for the first time, enabling a deeper understanding of collaboration than either science could develop alone.

One warm spring day in Chicago, I took a break after lunch and walked across campus to the coffee shop. I'd had a meeting that morning and was wearing a business suit and tie. As I was walking back to my office across the broad quadrangle, I was approached by a group of high school boys carrying duffel bags. Because they were followed by three adult men, I guessed that they were a visiting sports team with their chaperones. Seeing the coffee cup in my hand, one of the boys said, "The coffeehouse that way?" in an abrupt and slightly rude tone of voice, nodding back to the building I'd just come from. I politely said yes, it's that way, and down the stairs in the basement. The three men had been close enough to hear the exchange, and as they passed by seconds later, one of them asked, a bit loudly but with exaggerated deference, "Is the coffeehouse this way, Sir?"

We both knew that he'd already overheard the directions I gave to the high school kid. So why did he ask me the question again? He was doing several things at once. First, he was apologizing for the boy's rudeness, letting me know that he thought the tone was disrespectful. Second, by asking the question loudly and distinctly, he made sure that the boy could overhear him, letting the boy know he'd been out of line. Third, he made it clear to me that he was reprimanding the boy. I was amazed at the creativity of his question—apologizing and reprimanding, with a simple question that didn't actually sound like either an apology or a reprimand.

Scholars who study conversation explore the relationship between each participant's actions and the conversation that emerges from the entire group. Conversation analysis gives us the tools to study how individual sparks of insight combine during collaboration. Among these scientists, the chaperone's apology is known as *indirect speech.* Indirect speech, unlike explicit speech, is impossible to understand out of context. If the man had said, "I'm very sorry that my boy here wasn't more polite to you," anyone could have guessed what he meant. But "Is the coffeehouse this way, Sir?" can't be understood unless a lot about the situation is known. This context-dependence is called *indexicality;* the most creative speech is highly indexical—deeply embedded in the immediate social context.

Linguists have found that more than 50 percent of all speech is indexical—some estimate that 90 percent of what we say is indexical. The pronouns "he" and "it" are indexical because there's no way of knowing what they refer to outside the preceding conversational context. During a conversation, and depending on the context, "here" might mean any of the following: in this room, in this neighborhood, in this city, in the United States, at this company. And which room, which neighborhood, and which company will change with every conversational group.

Researchers have shown that even using single indexical words provides opportunities for creativity. The conversation scientists Michael Silverstein and Starkey Duncan brought two strangers into their lab and simply asked them to "get to know each other." A few minutes into one conversation between two graduate students, the pronouns "here" and "there" each had at least three possible meanings—with "there" referring either to their hometowns, their undergraduate institutions, or the cities of those institutions, and "here" referring to Chicago, or the university, or the research laboratory. Simple questions such as "Did you like it there?" or "How did you end up here?" could be answered in many different ways, and could lead down many different conversational paths. The most creative conversations are like improvisational theater dialogues; each speaker reinterprets what was said before and builds on it in a new direction so that unexpected creativity emerges from the group.

A second characteristic of indirect speech is that it opens itself to more potential interpretations; it invites the listener to participate creatively. For such a statement to communicate successfully, the speaker and the listener have to collaborate in determining what it means. Americans tend to think it's the speaker's responsibility to communicate clearly and unambiguously, and that the listener shouldn't have to do any real work. But in other cultures—from Japan to the Caribbean and many in between—indirect speech and creative listening are highly valued. In Japan, the cultural value of *sasshi* emphasizes the concentration on the listener, and the assumption that he or she will be able to guess the speaker's meaning even if it's not explicitly stated. For example, if a Western student misses a class and wants to borrow a friend's notes, the student will usually just ask outright: "I missed last week's class, and I'd really like to get your notes." In contrast, here's a typical Japanese student's approach:

STUDENT: Hi.

CLASSMATE: Hi.

STUDENT: How are you?

CLASSMATE: I am all right.

STUDENT: Is your class going OK?

CLASSMATE: Yeah. It is a lot of work.

STUDENT: I agree.

CLASSMATE: You think so, too?

STUDENT: It is a little demanding, isn't it?

CLASSMATE: Yeah.

STUDENT: But for me, I was absent last week and it became even tougher I feel.

CLASSMATE: Yeah. Is that so?

STUDENT: Yes. And I would like to borrow your notes. Is that possible?

Indirect statements open up more possibilities for the listener, and the resulting conversation becomes more of a collaborative creation. The indirection of the chaperone's apology allowed the boy to behave as if he didn't hear or understand the comment. With Silverstein's grad students, "How did you end up here?" can be answered in many different ways: "I saw a poster advertising the research study" (here = the laboratory); "I wanted to study with a famous professor" (here = University of Chicago); "I rented a U-Haul" (here = city/neighborhood). The questioner could then say, "No, I meant . . ."; but a creative conversationalist will often simply let the conversation unfold in the unexpected new direction.

Equivocality

The indexicality of creative speech might seem far removed from innovation in the real world. But today's most innovative companies have made a science of indirectness, and they've discovered that it results in greater innovation.

A three-year study of eight innovative organizations—including the design consulting firm IDEO and the airplane manufacturer Boeing—conducted by Andrew Hargadon of the University of California, Davis, drew important conclusions about how innovative companies use indirect communication to drive creativity. Each of the firms had tried to capture and centralize the collective knowledge of their professional staff in a searchable database. The goal of such "knowledge management" is to inspire innovation by helping people make connections, but all eight firms soon discovered that these databases were essentially useless at facilitating innovation. At Hewlett-Packard, one centralized computer server contained information about every completed project, but their developers never used it.

What went wrong? These databases are good at helping solve a well-defined problem, but innovation is more likely to happen when you don't yet know what you're looking for. If your task is to install a new font on the laser printer, a database will let you search for the keywords INSTALL, FONT, and PRINTER. But a database is of little use with problem-finding creativity. If you're trying to invent a new kind of printing that doesn't use fonts, or a new kind of font that installs itself when it's needed, what would you search for? When no one knows exactly what the problem is or what question to ask, databases can't help.

There is another reason databases don't contribute to innovation: Computers don't tolerate indirectness. Hargadon discovered that in these eight companies, innovations were more likely to happen when ideas were left open to multiple interpretations. Ideas that open possibilities, which he called *equivocality,* contribute to innovation by making it easier for ideas to be reused to solve a different and unexpected problem somewhere else in the organization.

The cultures of most innovative companies emphasize equivocality. At lunch one day, Hargadon watched two IDEO engineers take apart a stainless steel napkin holder to examine the spring mechanism inside—on the off chance that someday, they could reuse one of the components of that mechanism. IDEO designers make a habit of visiting the local hardware store regularly, and they take field trips to such places as airplane junkyards and the Barbie Hall of Fame. The point is to make analogies more likely by helping designers exercise their ability to reinterpret objects so that they can perceive more equivocality. This ability allowed the engineers at Design Continuum, another legendary design firm, to help Reebok design a shoe that could beat out Nike's Air technology. The designers remembered an inflatable splint that they'd created for a medical client, and the result was the Reebok Pump Shoe, which earned more than $1 billion in revenue in its first year on the market.

GlaxoSmithKline fosters cross-fertilization with information match-makers—executives assigned to be knowledge brokers. Siemens, the German industrial company, brings together cross-functional teams of managers for a year at a time. Ispat, a London-based global steel maker, instituted a policy mandating that every general manager sit on the board of at least one other unit. BP has created an elaborate system that fosters peer groups of managers and cross-unit networks in combination with digital tools such as an online expert directory. All BP managers are expected to devote about 15 percent of their time to cross-unit knowledge-sharing activities. "The model here is an open market of ideas," says David Nagel, BP's gas business unit head in Egypt. "People develop a sense of where the real expertise lies." It's a tall order, but if large companies can successfully combine their vast and distributed expertise, they can have far more insights than smaller companies. BP managers have pooled their expertise to come up with new e-business ideas, resulting in more than a hundred new projects—such as Ocean-Connect.com, an online hub for the global shipping industry that started as a marine fuel auction, sponsored by a consortium that includes BP Amoco, Shell, Texaco, and Chevron.

Equivocality happens in hallway conversations, in good brain-storming sessions, and within informal networks—such as the colleague you play pickup basketball with or your old college classmate. Using your personal and professional network is messy, ambiguous, and random, but it allows those unexpected connections to happen. According to the management scholars Ijukiro Nonaka and Hiro-taka Takeuchi, companies that encourage such connections—such as the Japanese companies Sharp (electronics) and Kao (the leading household and chemical products maker)—are more innovative because their structures encourage multiple connections across boundaries and hierarchies. They call these companies *hypertext organizations* because they heighten equivocality and enhance the potential for creative conversation.

In good improvisational theater, equivocality is a feature of every utterance. Each actor contributes raw ideas that can be interpreted in many different ways; another member of the group might see something that the speaker didn't, or might be inspired in an unexpected new direction.

It's late on a Saturday night, and the theater in the South Chicago neighborhood of Hyde Park is packed to capacity. It's the second show of the night for one of Chicago's most popular improvisational theater groups—Off-Off-Campus. The group draws a hundred paying customers for each of three shows every weekend. The name Off-Off-Campus acknowledges an important event in theater history: On July 5, 1955, improvisational comedy was born in a bar a few blocks off the University of Chicago campus when a group of former students performed without scripts as The Compass Players. The Compass would eventually lead to the legendary Second City Theater, and then to the television show *Saturday Night Live*. Off-Off-Campus is a direct descendant of the Compass Players—they're still University of Chicago students, and they perform just down the street from the bar where it all started in 1955. I studied this group for two years; I performed as the group's pianist, and I set up my video camera on a tripod behind the piano to create a record for later analysis.

On a typical weekend night, Off-Off-Campus would improvise ten scenes, each having a different length, a different format, and bizarre "rules"—such as the Entrances and Exits game, in which the audience suggests a word for each actor; whenever that word is spoken, the actor to whom it belongs has to enter or exit the stage. On this particular Saturday night, the group started by asking the audience to suggest a

proverb. The suggestion was "Don't look a gift horse in the mouth."
When the lights came up, the scene started like this:

> (DAVE *is at stage right*, ELLEN *at stage left.* DAVE *begins gesturing to his right, talking to himself.*)

DAVE	All the little glass figurines in my menagerie,
	The store of my dreams.
	Hundreds of thousands everywhere!
	(*Turns around to admire.*)
ELLEN	(*Slowly walks toward* DAVE.)
DAVE	(*Turns and notices* ELLEN.)
	Yes, can I help you?
ELLEN	Um, I'm looking for uh, uh, a present?
	(ELLEN *is looking down like a child, with her fingers in her mouth.*)
DAVE	A gift?
ELLEN	Yeah.
DAVE	I have a little donkey?
	(DAVE *mimes the action of handing* ELLEN *a donkey from the shelf.*)
ELLEN	Ah, that's—I was looking for something a little bit bigger…
DAVE	Oh.
	(*Returns item to shelf.*)
ELLEN	It's for my dad.

These thirty seconds give the audience an immediate sense of what's going on. Dave is a storekeeper, Ellen a young girl buying a present for her dad. Because she's so young, she probably needs help. This basic scene unfolded from the creative contributions of both actors. But unlike a script, in which the scene is predetermined, improv means that at every moment something wildly different might have happened. At turn 2, Ellen might have walked in forcefully and announced, "I think I'm the perfect person for the job advertised in your store window!" At turn 3, Dave could have treated Ellen as a coworker and shouted, "You're late to work again!" When Ellen entered the scene, she couldn't know she would be a little girl looking for a present for her father. She might have been a coworker, his wife, or his daughter. Paradoxically, an improv actor doesn't decide what is created by his actions; that's a collaborative decision that unfolds from the flow of dialogue. Like indirect speech, the listener collaborates in determining the meaning.

As the scene continues, we learn that Ellen is buying her dad a present because he hasn't been feeling well; he's been exhibiting psychotic behaviors. A third actor enters the scene and enacts the character of Ellen's psychotic dad; his condition is then cured through the clever actions of the storekeeper. At any point, a branching tree of possibilities is available to the actors. These actors have elevated equivocality to an art form, and that's why improv is such a powerful model for innovation today.

An organizational culture that fosters equivocality, improvised innovation, and constant conversation—that's a recipe for group genius. But to learn how to make it happen, we have to look beyond the group and examine creative organizations, and that's the challenge of the next chapter.

PART III

The Collaborative Organization

CHAPTER 8

....

Organizing for Improvisation

IMAGINE A FACTORY without shifts, without the lunch whistle, without a time clock, where three thousand employees set their own working hours. There are no official rules and no hierarchy; structures and procedures emerge from the bottom up. Imagine that even the lowest-ranked worker can examine the company's books at any time. The company provides free courses to teach the workers how to read balance sheets and cash flow statements; that's because key corporate decisions are voted on by all three thousand employees.

This workers' paradise actually exists, and not in the United States or Japan, but in Brazil—a country known more for paternalism and rigid family control. Semco is named after Antonio Curt Semler, the Viennese immigrant who founded the company in his São Paulo apartment in 1952. You might expect this sort of improvised organization to work best in knowledge-intensive, white-collar companies. But Semco is a manu-facturer: Its factories produce marine pumps, digital scanners, industrial mixers, and commercial dishwashers that can scrub more than four thousand plates an hour. Semco is a knowledge-age company in an industrial-age business. It may be the world's largest collaborative organization.

In 1980, when Ricardo Semler took over the company from his father, it had only a hundred employees and $4 million in revenues. It was a traditionally hierarchical company, and a shelf of binders specified rules and procedures for every possible circumstance. As the son of the founder, Semler could easily have continued running the company in the traditional way. But Semco was on the verge of bankruptcy, barely holding on with short-term bank loans, and Semler knew he had to do something radical. He began by firing most of the old-style senior managers on his first day on the job. Soon after Semco took on its new fluid organizational structure, it began to grow—faster than almost every other Brazilian company. By 2003, Semco's annual revenue had risen from $4 million to $212 million.

In most companies, bureaucracy prevents innovation from emerging. At Semco, the solution was to get rid of the bureaucracy. Semco improvises its way and intentionally avoids long-term planning, never looking ahead more than six months. In 2003, the company threw a party to celebrate the tenth anniversary of the last time that CEO Ricardo Semler made a decision.

Just like the W. L. Gore & Associates, Semco teams form and reform, their structure emerging improvisationally from the bottom up, and membership is largely self-selected. "That's not a lack of structure, that's just a lack of structure imposed from above," Semler points out. Although no boss is looking over shoulders, the peer pressure to perform is intense: If you don't have the respect of your coworkers, you won't be selected to serve on any of the teams, and you're on your way out of the company.

Semler came to the same conclusions as his American counterpart, Bill Gore—he recognized that once a collaborative organization gets too big, it stops working. Whenever a group exceeds 150 people, Gore erects a new building in the Delaware countryside. Semco follows the same philosophy; once, Semler split a three-hundred-person factory into three separate plants. Of course, this decision introduced ineffi-ciencies, and costs rose. But within a year, sales had doubled, inventory days dropped from 136 to 46, and innovation blossomed—eight new products were introduced.

A study of companies in Europe, Japan, and the United States found that the most innovative companies limit operating units to fewer than four hundred employees. Evolutionary experts posit that a group size of 150 people is programmed into our DNA because prehistorical bands of proto-humans did not exceed that number. It's no coincidence that Gore and Semler have committed themselves to the same maxi-mum group size that was typical at the dawn of civilization.

Many companies say they believe in empowering their employees through participation, but most of them don't look like Semco. Too often, "participation" is little more than a strategy to increase employee job satisfaction or to get their buy-in for senior management decisions. Semco is what real participatory management looks like: collaborative, improvisational, emerging from the bottom up. It's a radical rethink-ing of the organization, and most companies aren't willing to go there just yet. But as innovation becomes ever more important, there won't be any other choice.

Innovation Labs

Innovation today isn't a sudden break with the past, a brilliant insight that one lone outsider pushes through to save the company. Just the opposite: Innovation today is a continuous process of small and con-stant change, and it's built into the culture of successful companies. When I ask creators where their ideas come from, they always tell sto-ries about collaboration and connection, about innovations that emerge from a creative space that spreads out across the entire company—and sometimes beyond its boundaries. For example, when John Reed was CEO of Citibank, he spoke every month with many political and business leaders because he'd learned from experience that ideas often emerged from such conversations.

The culture of the collaborative organization is based on flexibility, connection, and conversation; improvised innovation is standard business practice. Such a culture seems unnatural to many managers because improvisation seems to imply that you didn't plan ahead. Many organizational theories have their roots in the 1960s and 1970s, a time when adaptability and innovation weren't as important as they are today. Those theories are best at explaining companies and markets with stable structures that rarely change—think of AT&T before the Bell system divestiture, or the U.S. air industry before deregulation. But such theories can't help us in today's rapidly changing economy because protected monopolies are becoming increasingly rare and new technologies are opening up formerly stable industries to radical new competition.

Although planning and structure have been the dominant trend in organization theory, there's always been a countertrend. Back in 1969, in his classic book *The Social Psychology of Organizing,* the management guru Karl Weick argued that smaller, "loosely coupled" organizations—formed of autonomous building blocks that can be brought together, disconnected, or re-formed with relatively little disturbance—are more innovative than carefully planned organizations. Decades later, the success of loosely coupled companies has shown that Weick was right. In the 1980s, legendary scholars such as Peter Drucker and Rosabeth Moss Kanter extended this insight and showed that when companies used smaller teams and fewer hierarchical levels, they were more innovative. In 1996, two professors at the University of Maryland reviewed the previous ten years of studies of organizational design; their conclusion was that team-based companies performed better than traditional bureaucratic firms.

Since 1996, more evidence in support of this collaborative countertrend has emerged. Many studies show that cross-functional, collaborative groups called "innovation labs"—made up of people from different corporate functions representing all stages of product development, including purchasing, manufacturing, marketing, engineering, service, and finance—result in quicker product development times.

The business press is filled with stories of companies that have created innovation labs.

Motorola's best-selling Razr phone was created in downtown Chicago on the twenty-sixth floor of an office building that was once occupied by an Internet start-up. Called Moto City, it features open spaces and waist-high cubicle walls, even for senior management. This design fostered teamwork and communication; for example, Razr developers used their many connections to work around a standard Motorola practice of showing all new product ideas to regional managers around the world.

Procter & Gamble recently created the Clay Street Project, a remodeled, five-story, brick-walled loft building in a gritty Cincinnati neighborhood where cross-functional teams spend ten weeks creating new brands.

Sony creates collaborations among designers, engineers, and marketers to develop products such as the new flash-based players in the Network Walkman product line (Sony's answer to Apple's iPod). Sony turned to the collaborative model after its first digital music player, developed two years before Apple's iPod, failed because an old-fashioned "silo" system prevented adequate discussion between engineers and designers.

Mattel's Project Platypus identifies from twelve to twenty employees from different departments and then moves them for three months to a new temporary office filled with movable furniture, toys, and raw materials. Their task: to conceive and develop a new brand, complete with business plan, product, and packaging. The first team effort resulted in a successful new product: the Ello Creation System, a construction set for girls, released in 2003.

Fisher-Price, Mattel's preschool toy unit, has created the Cave, a space complete with beanbag chairs and mood lighting. Crossfunctional teams bring together marketing, engineering, design, and child psychology. Only three years in operation, the team scored a hit in 2004 with its Laugh and Learn Learning Home, a $65 model home made of plastic.

Ivy Ross, formerly Mattel's senior vice president, is the executive who created Project Platypus; she explained it this way: "We're really collaborating and building ideas together as opposed to the old model where everyone works in silos." Other companies that use innovation labs include Steelcase, Wrigley, and Boeing.

Beyond Linear Innovation

What's so new about innovation labs? After all, one of the oldest strategies for increasing innovation is to separate out everyday business activities from innovative activities. Famous innovations in the past have come from isolated groups, including Xerox PARC; GM's Saturn division; IBM's PC division in Boca Raton; the small Apple groups that developed the Macintosh, the PowerBook, and the multimedia Quick-Time software; and Lockheed's "Skunk Works," the famous World War II jet fighter design team that many isolated research and development groups are named after today. But the difference is that the older model was based on linear innovation: The separate group comes up with ideas; the rest of the company selects the best ones and executes them. Over decades of use, this linear model has been rigidly codified by product development experts into linear stages, and "gates" control the transition from one stage to the next.

If innovation is linear, the idea stage can be separated out and placed in a more creative unit of the organization, and the execution can still take place in a more traditional bureaucratic structure. But although separation can be good for short-term creativity, it interferes with long-term innovation: An isolated "skunk works" usually has trouble communicating with the rest of the organization because innovation requires collaboration across the company. For example, in 1970, the Xerox Corporation, based in Rochester, New York, went all the way across the country to create a research unit in Palo Alto, California, known as PARC, the Palo Alto Research Center. Xerox hired top thinkers from the leading research labs, and by 1973 the company had already built the Alto computer, the first computer to feature overlapping windows, menus, screen icons, and a mouse to control the screen cursor. But Xerox was never successfully able to market a product based on it, in part because the visionary culture at PARC didn't interface well with the practical engineers in the rest of the company. In frustration, many of PARC's top researchers went down the street to Apple and used these ideas to design the Macintosh.

The skunk works model places all its hopes on one big flash of inspiration that must come from a select group of special people. But we've seen that even the most transformative new products and systems emerge from many small sparks of insight. Successful innovative companies keep these small sparks coming from individuals throughout the organization, each spark inspiring the next one. Innovation labs are a completely different animal—they contain people from all across the organization; they visit temporarily, and then return home; and they continue to collaborate and connect while they're at the lab. P&G's Clay Street Project and Mattel's Project Platypus bring together people from every part of the organization, including not only designers and scientists but also manufacturing and marketing staff; and at the end of a few months, they take these new insights and connections back with them.

The Ten Secrets of the Collaborative Organization

Innovation labs are just the beginning; the real benefit comes when you scale up the creative power of collaboration throughout the organization. The most innovative companies do ten things that foster collaboration and innovation.

1. Keep Many Irons in the Fire

During the 1980s, I worked for two very different Boston-area start-ups: the video game design company, General Computer Corporation, and a management consulting firm, Kenan Systems, which specialized in custom software development. After I moved to Chicago in 1990 to begin studying creativity, both companies continued to be very successful; but by 1995, neither was doing what it had been when I worked there. Because they were collaborative organizations, they were able to adapt in response to market shifts and continue growing.

In 1984, the video game industry suffered a severe slump, and GCC almost went out of business. In response, the company started several small, exploratory projects. Also in 1984, Apple released the Macintosh computer. It's hard to remember this now, but the first Macintosh didn't have an internal hard disk drive. GCC was the first company to figure out how to install an internal disk drive, and even though it had nothing to do with video games, this exploratory project went on to save the company. A few years later, when Apple released a Mac with the hard drive already installed, GCC needed another transformation. Again, an exploratory project eventually grew into a successful laser printer business.

When Kenan Systems was sold to Lucent Technologies in January 1999 for $1.48 billion, it was the largest software company in Massachusetts. But it was no longer doing custom software; Kenan Systems was valuable because one of its small projects, a system for fixing billing errors called ARBOR that I developed in the mid-1980s, had grown over time to become a stand-alone billing system. The timing for ARBOR was perfect: Just when Kenan Systems was ready to sell the billing system, the telecommunications industry was booming; companies everywhere were selling cell phones, pagers, and band-width. ARBOR was one of the only products available that allowed these new companies to bill for their services.

In 1997, Shona Brown of McKinsey and Company, working with Kathleen Eisenhardt of Stanford University's business school, com-pared three collaborative organizations with three organizations that didn't innovate. The collaborative organizations constantly experi-mented, and they always had several different low-cost projects in the works. But instead of a grand plan that organized all the projects, they responded to what emerged. The contrast with the noninnovative companies couldn't have been more stark—those companies didn't have any experimental projects under way. And their managers dealt with the future by *planning* the future—spending months on elaborate strategy and product development plans. The problem was that if the future didn't unfold according to plan, they were doomed to fail.

Cisco encourages employees to put together pilot projects and invest a few months to try them out; as we've learned, 3M, Gore, and Google reserve from 10 to 20 percent of each employee's time for innovative new projects. Such companies emphasize the quick development of prototypes to test ideas. For example, at Boeing, the Operations Tech-nology Center stays open late at night so the engineers can build proto-types with the shop floor machine when the mechanics are sleeping. IDEO staff are constantly sculpting new designs from foam core. Pixar's animators develop short films; some grow into feature films; and others test new techniques that are later adapted and inserted into an ongoing feature film project. One short film, called *Geri's Game,* never became a feature, but it used a new technique for displaying cloth surfaces that looked better than anything else. The technique was adapted and used in the feature film *A Bug's Life*. These strategies allow ideas to be tested quickly, permit less promising projects to be terminated early, and make all the new sparks visible so that other teams can adapt and use them.

Creative professionals in Hollywood know that the best way to great success is to generate a lot of ideas and then select the best one. Successful Nobel Prize–winning scientists tell us they do the same thing: They keep multiple projects on the back burner. In collaborative organizations, many projects are active at once. When the business environment changes, the best-selling product might become obsolete, but one of the back-burner ideas may suddenly emerge as the next new thing.

2. Create a Department of Surprise

At Thomas Edison's lab, when one team was testing a new way to make the underwater Atlantic telegraph cable work better, they discovered some formerly unknown conductive properties of carbon. This led to a new low-cost microphone design that was used by Edison's telephone design team: It became the key to making the telephone commercially feasible.

In the collaborative organization, sparks that fail at their original purpose are often picked up and used elsewhere. In jazz, mistakes are woven into the ongoing improvisation in a way that retrospectively shows them not to have been mistakes at all. In 1899, when the sales of electric automobiles were increasing, Edison became convinced that the gasoline engine would disappear and that future automobiles would all be electric. We know today that this was a mistake, but at the time the gasoline engine hadn't been perfected and the future wasn't at all obvious. Edison directed his lab to begin working on an improved alkaline storage battery. But immense problems faced the battery-powered car: The rough roads of the day damaged the battery's plates, and the cars were so heavy that the batteries drained quickly. By 1909, when Edison was ready to mass-produce his car batteries, the gasoline engine had been perfected and had put electric cars out of business. But Edison's battery was useful in heavy-duty factory applications—an innovation that Edison had never intended.

When you have a lot of irons in the fire, a danger is that the really good idea can get lost in the mix. A collaborative organization is good at recognizing when that one great collaboration happens. Even though you can't plan for innovation, you can put structures in place that make this recognition more likely. Anita Roddick of The Body Shop once said she should create a Department of Surprises—a group of people devoted to expecting surprises and looking for them to emerge.

One way that collaborative organizations recognize emergent ideas is with "idea marketplaces," autonomous teams that identify radical innovations. These "departments of surprises" search for ideas throughout the company and are responsible for commercializing them. Royal Dutch/Shell has been using such teams, called GameChangers, since 1999. The six teams, each composed of about six members, are based in Houston and Rijswijk, the Netherlands, and have the authority to allocate up to $20 million to try out game-changing ideas. Other employees e-mail their new ideas to one of the teams, and the teams meet weekly to sift through the messages. Those teams have created more than half of the company's innovations, including a new idea for how to use laser sensors to find new oil deposits.

Most new ideas will never pan out. That's why failure is a fact of life in the collaborative organization. But it's a law of innovation that successes can't go up unless failures go up, too. And because we won't have the successes without the failures, we need to create organizational cultures that cherish failure. If nine out of ten people work on projects that don't go anywhere, you need to make sure that these employees don't become demoralized. In a way, they need more support and positive reinforcement than the people who worked on the one successful project. Even the projects that fail result in powerful knowledge that can potentially be reused in a later project.

3. Build Spaces for Creative Conversation

When I graduated from MIT in 1982, the beginning of the first information technology venture capital boom, I took a job designing video games at a small company called General Computer Corporation (GCC). GCC was founded by two MIT undergraduates who made money after class by installing arcade games in dormitory basements. Then they figured out a way to hack into these games and reprogram them to make them more interesting, and they started selling these upgrade kits to arcade owners around the country. The business took off so fast that they dropped out of MIT to run it. I joined twelve other employees in the basement of a renovated nineteenth-century building down the street from MIT in east Cambridge; its high ceilings and wide-open spaces were originally designed to hold the printing machines of the Atheneum Press.

After GCC scored its first big hit with Ms. Pacman, the company had enough money to design its own space upstairs in the building. Rather than fill the space with cubicles, GCC chose an open floor layout on two floors that were connected by a large stairway atrium. The crowning element of the design was a working fire pole that employees used to get downstairs when the stairs just weren't fast enough. All the design workstations were in the same open space; everyone could see everyone else, and other designers were constantly walking by. If they saw something interesting on your game screen, they'd stop to talk about it. If you wanted some quick feedback, you didn't even have to stand up to call the others. This was the company that designed almost all of Atari's classic home cartridges, including Centipede, Ms. Pacman, and Pole Position. I designed three games there, including the Food Fight home cartridge. But though I was the designer, I didn't create everything myself—other designers were constantly walking by, playing the game, and providing feedback.

The open floor design has become more common today; it's found not only in trendy design firms but increasingly in such places as the BMW factory that opened in Leipzig in May 2005, which has an open layout designed to inspire spontaneous conversations and dense social networks. Open spaces feed into the natural flow of collaborative innovation—helping ideas to move from one area to another, allowing spontaneous conversations to emerge, and strengthening informal information-sharing networks.

These radical new offices often feature coffee bars and game rooms. In BP's Houston office, workers are separated by no more than waist-high furniture and clustered into neighborhoods around each café. To increase the likelihood of unplanned conversations, the office is designed so that employees have to walk through the cafés to get from one neighborhood to another. Steelcase and Herman Miller now make "scootable" furniture—desks, file cabinets, and conference tables that have rolling wheels so that furniture can be quickly reconfigured to match emergent collaborative patterns. Google's Silicon Valley campus features a massive wooden staircase equipped with electric outlets all the way up; programmers are thus encouraged to sit and work right on the stairs, again increasing the potential of chance encounters.

Office furniture companies have worked hard to stay on top of this trend; Steelcase and Herman Miller have both responded by designing workplaces that balance the power of collaboration with the need for private concentration time. In 2006, Herman Miller released a new glass-paneled workstation; it features large panels on the outside and small panels on the sides that slide open to allow neighbors to talk. At BP's new Westlake office building in Houston, designed by Herman Miller, if one person needs quiet time, he or she can work in a tented, partially enclosed space. At McCann-Erickson, a Los Angeles advertising agency, the managers work in central spaces surrounded by wooden louver walls that can be quickly opened or closed.

4. Allow Time for Ideas to Emerge

Many people say that they work better under pressure. At some companies, tight deadlines and long hours are a semiofficial part of the company's philosophy. But the Harvard researcher Teresa Amabile has found that this management tactic usually kills creativity. Yes, it makes people work harder, but it makes them less creative. In a study of 177 employees in seven U.S. companies—all working in teams where creativity was critical to the success of the group—days that were more hectic were less likely to result in creative thinking. But, paradoxically, the employees reported that they *felt* more creative when time pressure was high. Amabile discovered the real story by analyzing daily work diaries written over a six-month period. The people felt creative, but the diaries showed that creativity on high-pressure days happened less than half as often as it did on low-pressure days. And creativity remained depressed for at least two days after a high-pressure day.

Low-pressure situations allow for collaborative conversations to unfold, and that's where innovations emerge. Here are the kinds of things people wrote in their work diaries on low-pressure, high-creativity days:

In my meeting with Seth to discuss the imaging model, several ideas he mentioned meshed with ideas I had, and I came away with a better and more detailed model.

Wendy brought in her samples of the ILP films and presented them to me in a way that really made sense and triggered a lot of good ideas on my end.

You can't rush creativity. And the psychological research we've seen throughout this book tells us why: Creativity requires that we encounter and internalize previous sparks of insight, and it requires incubation time for those sparks to combine in the mind. Collaborative teams need time for group genius to unfold. AT&T's legendary Bell Labs, responsible for world-changing inventions such as the transistor and the laser, had it right with their official corporate philosophy: "Big ideas take time."

5. Manage the Risks of Improvisation

Managers have good reason to be nervous about improvisation; after all, improvisation can be risky. The first risk is that when people are improvising, they must take time away from planned projects that have been carefully analyzed. The key is to create just the right balance of planning and improvisation.

The second risk is that the improvisation can make it impossible to sustain a central vision and long-term strategy. Improvisation works best in small teams, or in groups no larger than a few hundred. The Gore Corporation has many buildings scattered throughout the Delaware countryside, and more than a hundred products in several different industries; as a result, it's hard to identify what the central unifying vision of the company is. Ricardo Semler points out that

Semco's factories are in "cellular manufacturing"—small outfits that deliver high quality at a high price—and that his system might not work for large factories that build ships or automobiles.

A third risk is that too many new ideas might bubble up. One employee at an improvising company said, "The company was jumping the gun on every new opportunity, and anybody who had an idea for something immediately started pursuing it. We split resources quite a bit, and also we lost focus somewhat from the core business." Multiple improvisations of product features that are individually attractive can easily lead to "feature creep," resulting in a product that no longer meets the needs of the market. Feature creep is a widely acknowledged issue with open-source software, such as Linux—in theory, any programmer can add whatever cool feature he or she thinks the software should have. Manufacturing and finance tend to want designs frozen; marketing and engineering see improvisation as a powerful tool for flexibility and adaptability. This difference in cultures often causes high-level organizational conflict. To be successful, the collaborative organization must deftly manage these risks.

6. Improvise at the Edge of Chaos

Improv theater groups that do "long-form" improvisation—thirty- to sixty-minute performances—almost always prepare a loose structure in advance. Some are specific (the Annoyance Theater's improvised parodies of film noir, for example, which use elaborate costumes and sets, and actors trained in detective-book dialogue); others are more general (the Improv Olympic's *Harold,* in which the actors first develop three separate plotlines, then weave them together later).

Shona Brown, then at McKinsey and Company, and Kathleen Eisenhardt of Stanford University studied the computer industry between 1993 and 1995, when telecommunications were beginning to converge with consumer electronics, when multimedia applications were emerging, and when the Internet was new. They examined nine strategic business units across nine computer companies: six U.S., two European, and one Asian; four in hardware and five in software. They focused on three companies that were very innovative, and three that were not. They conducted more than eighty interviews and ended up with almost two hundred hours of taped conversation.

The successful innovators used limited structures that Brown and Eisenhardt called "semistructures." The researchers concluded that the critical balance for innovation is at "the edge of chaos": not too rigid to prevent emergent innovation, but not too loose to result in total chaos. The successful company that they called Cruising had well-defined managerial responsibilities and explicit project priorities. The roles of marketing and engineering were clearly specified. The company also prioritized projects by market potential. But Cruising combined these structures with a culture of cross-project communication; as one engineer said: "Everybody's borrowing everybody's stuff." A second successful company, Titan, had built coffee bars throughout the development areas just so that people from different teams would talk during breaks. And, most important of all, at both Cruising and Titan, the design process itself was not structured; developers had almost complete freedom to improvise as the work demanded. One developer said, "We fiddle right up until the very end." The most effective structures are those that support what the cognitive scientist Barbara Hayes-Roth calls *opportunistic planning:* The plan provides you with a general outline of how to proceed, but it leaves enough flexibility to change in response to unexpected developments without throwing out all the advance planning.

In contrast, a looser company they called NewWave had a complete lack of structure and a culture of rule breaking. Even though the company had a stereotypical Silicon Valley culture, this was one of the least innovative companies of the nine. The other uncreative companies were at the other extreme; they had an extremely structured development process that broke projects into subtasks; there were constant checkpoints, and official specs and procedures to consider every step of the way. Managers were pretty happy with this system because it resulted in an efficient development process. But it made it impossible to adapt in mid-project if the market changed, or if a new technology became available. One of the managers said, "By the time we figure out that there is a problem, it's already too late."

The collaborative organization is no anarchy; it's filled with structuring and ordering features. The jazz bassist Charles Mingus famously said, "You can't improvise on nothing, man, you've gotta improvise on something." Within the jazz community, some songs become "standards" that are improvised on for decades because they provide good frameworks for improvisation. Other songs don't work as well as shells for improvisation. It's not a question of how good a song it is; some cheesy pop songs work for jamming, and some great compositions don't. At first, each company may need to experiment with different structures while closely watching what emerges and tuning in to the edge of chaos.

7. Manage Knowledge for Innovation

Good jazz improvisers have years of experience. Through years of practicing alone and playing with others, they build a repertoire of phrases, overall forms, and memories of other musicians' famous solos and recordings. When master musicians improvise, they draw on this large repertoire of existing material, but they never simply insert past material directly; they always modify and embellish the past to fit the unique demands of the night's performance.

The collaborative organization excels at transferring to other groups the ideas that emerge from good improvisations. This is difficult because improvisations are ephemeral and memory fades away quickly when they're over. Successful innovative organizations use procedures that select the good improvisations and then spread them throughout the organization, systems that are known today as *knowledge management.*

Franchise retail chains are often more innovative than the local mom-and-pop stores that they compete against, and they win by scaling up collaborative innovation throughout the organization. Linda Argote of Carnegie Mellon University studied a chain of thirty-six pizza stores, and during her research a new fad swept the country: the Chicago-style deep-dish pizza. The thirty-six stores quickly discovered a problem with the pepperoni deep-dish pizzas: In traditional pizza, the pepperoni pieces were scattered evenly across the cheese before cooking; but when they prepared the deep-dish pizzas this way, the extra cheese moved around like a pool of water and caused the pepperoni slices to bunch up in the middle of the pizza.

One of the stores found a solution: If you arrange the slices of pepperoni in lines from the center, like the spokes of a wheel, in the oven they magically redistributed themselves in the perfect way. That store passed the solution on to headquarters, and within weeks all thirty-six stores had adopted the innovation.

Another technique to manage knowledge for innovation is to define jobs as broadly as possible. When people have a broader range of skills, new connections and greater communication are possible. The more that jobs are formalized, the less likely innovation becomes. In one study, half of the innovations were stimulated by new job assignments or broad job assignments; in another study, innovations were rarely associated with a person's formal job description. Frequent reassignment of staff—such as rotating them through an innovation lab in three-month stints—diffuses tacit knowledge more effectively than written reports and computer databases.

8. Build Dense Networks

You might be thinking that coffee bars and open spaces work only for small intimate start-ups. Are there ways that a large company can remain collaborative? One solution is that of Gore and Semco: Keep every location smaller than two hundred people. But is there a way to create a collaborative organization that's bigger than two hundred people, that involves every member of a large organization?

That's exactly what Cisco, the leading supplier of networking equipment, is trying to do—by using the power of electronic networks to bring people together. In many companies today, e-mail supports constant collaboration by allowing the conversation to continue long after the meeting has ended. Cisco has turned the common practice of electronic connection into an art form. For example, Cisco's online directory is used about four million times each month, and even CEO John Chambers's record in the directory gives his e-mail address and a link that, with one click, will beep his electronic pager. An online scheduling system allows any employee to schedule a meeting with anyone else, including senior managers. Cisco employees have access to thousands of internal discussion lists that allow expertise to be shared broadly.

Pete Solvik, Cisco's chief information officer, says, "In a lot of companies, information is power. At Cisco, information is empowerment." Of course, some information is limited; salespeople have access to more customer information than everyone else, and managers have additional information about their employees, such as how much money they make. But apart from these few examples, information is available to every employee. In this environment, information overload is always a risk, so Cisco has structures in place to reduce that problem—special intranet sites called "dashboards" that are designed for managers, human resources, and engineers; and special applications, such as the one used by customer service to search product information.

The traditional bureaucratic structure was designed to make sure that only the right person saw the right information. Even if a company tries to shift to a culture of openness, if it still has a bureaucratic structure it'll be paddling upstream. Semco's management proves that it's truly committed to the open flow of information by allowing every employee to see the most important corporate information. Cisco provides sophisticated information systems that scale up the power of collaboration to the entire organization. Connectivity enables collaboration, and as Mary de Wysocki, a senior manager, points out, "Teams generate innovation at Cisco."

New technology helps, but it won't make an organization collaborative without the right culture and values in place. Hasbro, for example, frequently schedules unstructured meetings with top management. Managers hold regular weekly office hours during which anyone can come in without an appointment. At Pixar University, employees are trained to constantly share their ideas and seek out the ideas of others. The training helps staff members overcome the embarrassment of sharing an idea before they've spent a lot of time perfecting it; instead, the goal is to share right away.

When information is shared through collaboration, and decision making is decentralized, there's no need for a hierarchy to gather and channel information to a single decision maker, as in the 1950s bureaucratic company. Instead, the manager is a catalyst and facilitator, acting as a connector between groups, a cross-pollinator and carrier of knowledge.

In creative conversations, knowledge is represented equivocally, lending itself to multiple interpretations, new combinations, and reuse. Improv actors create lines of dialogue that have multiple possible interpretations, knowing that the later flow of the group's dialogue will use their line to collectively create something great. The collaborative organization's expertise is in the form of equivocal "riffs" that can easily be recombined—like the stock phrases that jazz musicians use over and over in different solos. Organizations that successfully manage improvisation have group riffs that are known throughout the organization, the same way that a jazz quartet develops emergent patterns over years of playing together.

9. Ditch the Organizational Chart

In the mid-1980s, when I was consulting for Kenan Systems, one of our biggest clients was U.S. West, one of the eight regional phone companies created in 1984 when AT&T split up. U.S. West didn't exist as a part of the old Ma Bell. It was an uncomfortable shotgun marriage of what had been three separate operating companies within AT&T: Mountain Bell, based in Denver, was the biggest one, and because of that U.S. West's new headquarters were in Denver; Northwestern Bell, based in Omaha; and Pacific Northwest Bell, based in Seattle.

AT&T was a protected monopoly that had, overnight, been forced to play ball in a new kind of marketplace. For decades, the company's organization had remained stable—along with its mission-critical computer systems, such as billing and customer service. Everything in U.S. West was duplicated three times, once for each operating company. But even though every computer system had been originally designed at Bell Labs, over the decades three separate teams of engineers had made layers and layers of customizations. These inefficiencies and incompatibilities had to be worked out of the system before U.S. West could become competitive.

During the mid-1980s, U.S. West was famous for undertaking a major reorganization every eighteen months or so. In the 1980s, a lot of major corporations hired management consulting firms to realign their business models. But these expensive and wrenching corporate reorganizations rarely resulted in increased innovation; because they were driven from the top, they resulted in what engineers call "brittle" systems, systems that break easily when the environment moves out of their design range.

In the 1980s, managers became familiar with research that showed that more interconnection led to greater innovation. Matrix structures—in which each employee reports to more than one boss, for example, one boss for the Midwestern region and one boss for the accounting division—were one early response to these findings, and U.S. West tried that, too. The problem is that the matrix doesn't go far enough toward the collaborative organization. Philips, the Dutch electrical giant, was an early advocate of matrix structures, but a few years ago it began to shift its emphasis to flexibility and connectivity. Philips now rewards employees for collaborating outside their own units, and it no longer allows employees to stay in the same region or product area for their entire careers. Finally, Weick's 1969 vision of the "loosely coupled" organization is becoming a reality.

10. Measure the Right Things

How do you know when you've successfully created an innovative company? Is there a way to measure corporate innovation? The oldest and most popular way is to measure the total amount spent on research and development. A 2005 study by Booz Allen Hamilton analyzed the world's one thousand biggest corporate spenders on R&D. The surprising result? There's no relationship at all between the amount of R&D spending and the usual measures of performance: sales growth, gross profit, operating profit, total shareholder return. The same study found no relationship between the number of patents issued to a company and its business results. To take just one high-profile example, in the last few years Microsoft has spent something like $5 billion a year on research, but most software innovations have come from other companies. At the top of the magazine article in which the results of the study were reported is a picture that says it all: a glum-faced manager wearing a T-shirt emblazoned with this statement: "We spent $2 billion on R&D and all we got was this lousy T-shirt."

From the perspective of the collaborative organization, this isn't so surprising. The problem is with the very *concept* of R&D spending. If a company expects all new ideas to come from a separate group called "research and development," they're still using the old linear model of creativity. But in the collaborative organization, innovation is diffused throughout the company—not boxed up in a separate department. Collaborative organizations are creative in all divisions and at all levels; they don't expect creativity to emerge from a separate division. That's why R&D spending is most effective when it's spread out across the organization—in areas with cross-functional collaboration, such as innovation labs, where the boundaries come down between engineering, marketing, sales, service, and manufacturing. Collaboration makes every step of the innovation process work better: selecting the most promising new ideas, adapting projects during development, and transitioning from design to manufacturing. Toyota is the leading innovator in the automobile industry, but it's only the third highest spender on R&D. By focusing on creating new types of innovation processes, the company now has the shortest development cycle in the industry.

A second way to measure innovation is to count the number of patents; IBM is often the leader, with 3,415 patents awarded in 2003. But as we've learned, patents aren't the same thing as innovation. Few patents actually translate directly into successful products—the rare examples include designer drugs such as Viagra and Celebrex, and genetically engineered seeds such as Monsanto's Roundup Ready line. But most successful innovations are complex combinations of many separate ideas. The patents are less important than the collaborative systems that bring them together.

The best measure of an organization's innovation potential is how successfully it has created a collaborative organization. That's why a new tool called *social network analysis* is catching on in Procter & Gamble, Merck, and Capital One; it provides quantitative measures of all the connections within an organization—particularly those informal interactions that don't show up on the organizational chart. In November 2005, the Boston Consulting Group released a new software program that tracks innovation through the coauthorships of patents and research papers, allowing them to map internal and external networks. Solvay, a Belgian pharmaceutical company, maps its scientists' internal and external networks, both before and after two-day innovation sessions that include outside university researchers. Kate Erlich, a researcher studying collaboration at IBM, explains that the tool is powerful because "making the collaboration visible makes it much easier to talk about." With the map, everyone can see where collaboration should be happening but isn't, and how teams work together and share information.

In addition to the connectivity of the social network, a second key feature of the collaborative organization is the way it manages information. Innovation is driven by representations of knowledge that can be reinterpreted and reused in new contexts, and by tools that allow access to that information in flexible and unexpected ways. But as we learned in the last chapter, there are several problems with knowledge management as traditionally conceived. The main problem is that computer databases designed to store a company's knowledge can only capture rigidly codified and exact information, but innovation emerges from the exchange of tacit, unwritten information. It's extremely difficult to measure these properties of organizational knowledge, but organizations need to start.

The first nine key features of the collaborative organization suggest a few more ways that a company can measure its innovation potential.

....

CHAPTER 9

The Collaborative Web

IN 1879, Henry George published a book that inspired fear in the hearts of property owners. The book, *Progress and Poverty,* became a best-seller. The *San Francisco Chronicle* called it "the book of this half-century." Alfred Russell Wallace, Darwin's codiscoverer of evolution, called it "the most remarkable and important book of the present century." Selling more than three million copies, it remains one of the best-selling economics books of all time.

The radical idea that frightened property owners so much was this: George argued that rents on land and housing were not only immoral but also bad for the economy. Rents robbed the workingman of his wages and contributed to poverty. George's solution was a single tax on land that would replace all rents, and no taxes on wages. He believed that a single tax would eventually lead to collective ownership of all land, and his followers became known as "Single Taxers." But the Single Taxers were opposed by powerful forces, and the movement went nowhere.

However, one woman, a Virginia Quaker named Lizzie J. Magie, latched on to the idea and propelled it into history, though not in the way that George would have expected. In 1903, six years after George's death, Magie invented a board game to teach the virtues of the single tax system; she called it "The Landlord's Game."

The players start on the upper right corner, called "Mother Earth." They take laps on a track around the edges of the board, and draw cards with names like "Beggarman's Court" and "Easy Street." With properties like the "Soakum Lighting System," it was no secret that this game demonstrated the evils of capitalism. The original patent included two sets of rules: one for the capitalist version, and one for playing with a single tax (all rent is paid into the public treasury and used to increase everyone's wages; railroads and utilities are free; Lord Blueblood's Estate is converted into a free public college). Magie took the game to Parker Brothers; they rejected it. So she decided to share it among her Quaker friends. Many Quakers were dedicated Single Taxers, and the game gradually became popular in Quaker communities around the country. By 1910, it even found its way to the Wharton School of Finance when a socialist professor of economics named Scott Nearing used it to teach his students.

The game spread, through students and Quakers, to almost every major city. Because there was no manufacturer, everyone had to make his or her own copy of the game by drawing with crayon on linen or oilcloth. For playing pieces, people used whatever objects they had lying around the house. Each new group of players modified the board and changed the rules. For example, when the game first reached a new city, the names of all the spaces were changed to major streets of that city. When Ruth Hoskins moved to Atlantic City, New Jersey, to teach at the Quaker Friends School, she brought the game with her—and there, just as in every other city, the local players made their own boards, and they named the spaces after streets in Atlantic City.

By 1930, the game had evolved many features not in Magie's original 1903 version. The spaces were named for local streets; the properties appeared in groups of three so that a "monopoly" could be purchased; "Community Chest" cards were invented. Magie's original "Mother Earth" space was renamed "Go." Along the way, the name of the game changed to Monopoly.

In 1933, with the Great Depression raging, an unemployed radiator repairman named Charles Darrow, living in Germantown, Pennsylvania, played the Atlantic City version of Monopoly with some Quaker friends. Darrow thought the game had potential; he took out a patent by claiming to be the game's inventor, and in December 1934 he sold the patent to Parker Brothers. Within three months, it became the fastest-selling board game in the country. The pieces that Parker Brothers created—iron, hat, shoe, thimble—reflected the Quaker tradition of using everyday household objects for game pieces.

Darrow made up a false insight story about how he got the idea for the game: He said it happened while he was reading a book about a boy who was kicked out of prep school and sent to a commercial school that taught practical business. In the book, business instruction was taught by handing students scraps of paper and allowing them to purchase stock with the play money. Parker Brothers marketed this fake story as a way of increasing publicity for the game. The real story didn't come out until the 1970s, when Parker Brothers sued Ralph Anspach, an economics professor, for selling his game Anti-Monopoly. Anspach fought the lawsuit all the way to the Supreme Court. In 1983, after a long string of very old Quakers had testified about the real story, the Supreme Court invalidated Parker Brothers' patent.

The game of Monopoly that we know and love today was created over many decades—with contributions from Quakers, fraternity boys, economics professors, and one radiator repairman. It unfolded in cities from Indianapolis to Philadelphia. Monopoly emerged from a collaborative web, a diffuse and informal network of people dedicated to the game. Each group of players modified the rules as they saw fit, but no one ever owned anything. The ideas spread around freely, and those that worked best survived. Parker Brothers contributed by spotting the potential, and by packaging and marketing it to success. And even after Parker Brothers printed the official rules, players continued to make up their own rules, a tradition that continues today. Every year, a new variation of Monopoly is published somewhere—among them have been Target's Michael Graves Design Monopoly and the infamous Ghettopoly of 2003. In a small way, we're all players in the collaborative web.

The Miracle at the 1939 World's Fair

The fake story about how Darrow got the idea for Monopoly caught on because it's exactly how most people think innovation works. First, a "creative person" has a moment of insight and creates an invention based on that inspiration (while Darrow is reading a book about paper money at a commercial school, he realizes a way to turn the activity into a game). Second, executives and managers decide to select that invention for development (Parker Brothers sifts through hundreds of game ideas and picks the one with potential). Third, teams of experts develop the invention into a workable product and then release it to the market.

But Darrow didn't think of the idea; it emerged from the collaborative web. Parker Brothers didn't do a great job of selection, either; the company not only rejected Lizzie Magie's version back in 1903 but also rejected Darrow's Monopoly when he first presented it; he was told there were fifty-two design errors and that the rules were "too complicated." Parker Brothers relented only after Darrow paid a printer to make five thousand copies and sold them all at Wanamaker's department store in Philadelphia.

Every other linear story of innovation is just as false as the Monopoly myth—such as the story about how television was invented. The myth: At the age of fourteen, Philo T. Farnsworth had a flash of insight. It was the summer of 1920, and the precocious teenager was farming a potato field in Idaho. As he looked out at the long, parallel lines created by the plow, he realized that a picture could be sent electronically by having a camera break an image down into very tiny lines, sending the lines one by one over a wire, and then reassembling those lines at the other end of the wire. With his high school physics teacher, he worked out the details: The camera would scan the image from left to right; then it would jump down a tiny, imperceptible amount and scan a parallel line just underneath; the procedure would continue over and over to the bottom of the screen. Furrows in the field became scan lines on a television screen.

The problem is that this gets you a still photo. To transmit a moving picture, Farnsworth realized that the system had to scan the entire screen in less than a tenth of a second—the length of time that the human eye retains an image—and send a new picture at least ten times per second. Voila, television!

At the age of nineteen, Farnsworth dropped out of college, convinced two rich investors to fund his idea, and constructed a lab to turn his potato field insight into reality. By 1927, he'd built a camera and a screen, connected by a wire. On September 7, with his brother-in-law operating the camera in the next room, Farnsworth yelled out to him to place an image of a thick black line in front of the camera. Sure enough, the line appeared on Farnsworth's screen. "Turn the slide a quarter turn," Farnsworth then instructed. The line on Farnsworth's screen turned. Farnsworth looked up and said, "That's it, folks, we've done it—there you have electronic television."

The real story, however, is very different from this myth of linear creativity by a solitary genius. Farnsworth was no solitary inventor;

with a host of other key players, he was deeply embedded in a collaborative web. Four years before, in 1923, Charles Francis Jenkins of Washington, D.C., had transmitted a picture of President Warren G. Harding over the radio from Washington to Philadelphia, impressing a group of top navy officials. In 1923, Vladimir Kosma Zworykin, a wealthy refugee from the Russian Revolution of 1917, filed a patent for electronic television through his employer, RCA. At about the same time, other televisions were patented by teams in Germany, Hungary, Canada, and Japan.

All these teams built on a string of important inventions extending back for decades. The first key step was made in 1872, when Joseph May and Willoughby Smith discovered that the brightness of a light could be translated into electrical current. The second step occurred in 1880 when the French engineer Maurice LeBlanc realized that, because the eye retains an image for a tenth of a second, an image could be scanned line by line; as long as the lines were transmitted and reassembled in time, the human eye would think it was seeing the whole picture at once. At that point, everyone realized that the trick was to figure out how to scan and transmit an image in one-tenth of a second, and an international team of engineers worked on the problem from 1880 through the 1920s. In 1908, the British engineer A. A. Campbell Swinton used a cathode ray to scan the image; the 1920s televisions of Farnsworth, Jenkins, and Zworykin were all extensions of this historical chain of ideas.

By the late 1920s, everyone knew about all these television systems—they were widely reported in the press—and all the engineers working on television agreed that none could be made into a commercially viable product. But David Sarnoff, president of RCA, didn't give up. It took more than ten years and $50 million, but at the end of it all, RCA unveiled the first commercial television at the 1939 World's Fair in New York City.

The key to understanding innovation is to realize that *collaborative webs are more important than creative people*. Of course, creative people play an important role as the active elements of collaborative webs. But in today's economy, most of the action is in the web, where everyone's creative power increases so that the whole is greater than the sum of the parts. From a board game to a complex electronic invention, from the mountain bike to the telegraph to the theory of evolution, every innovation emerges from a collaborative web. To realize your full creative potential, you must move beyond the linear creativity mindset and tap into the power of collaborative webs.

Clusters

The stories of Monopoly and of television are almost a century old, but they teach us how innovation works today, even in the most advanced technological industries. Here's a tale of two cities from the recent past.

In the 1970s, Boston was suffering. The entire northeastern region of the country had for decades been on a downward spiral as the industrial base of the economy declined in importance. The region became known as "the rust belt," an unflattering term referring to the shuttered factories and the poorly maintained bridges and infrastructure. But the late 1970s held one ray of hope for Boston: The new computer industry that stretched out along Boston's ring road, Route 128, and was fueled by the Massachusetts Institute of Technology. Businesses were eagerly buying computers, and their prices and sizes were dropping dramatically. By the early 1980s, Boston had emerged as the center of the newest thing in computers—"minicomputers," which were beginning to challenge IBM's big mainframe computers.

But the success story of Route 128 does not have a happy ending. By 1990, Boston's biggest computer companies had either gone bankrupt or were on life support—Wang, maker of word processors; Apollo and Prime, makers of once-popular minicomputers; and Digital Equipment Corporation and Data General, the biggest of them all.

Stanford University had also spawned a cluster of computer companies, in the Santa Clara Valley south of San Francisco. People started calling the area "Silicon Valley," and in the 1980s Silicon Valley boomed with venture capital, just as Route 128 did. But in the 1990s, when Route 128 declined, Silicon Valley kept going strong. How did Boston lose out?

The culture of Silicon Valley encouraged collaborative webs. In the bars where everyone in the semiconductor industry hung out, such as the legendary Wagon Wheel Restaurant and Casino in Mountain View, engineers asked each other questions and shared ideas. CEOs thought nothing of calling up a competitor's CEO on the phone and asking for help with a problem. Route 128 companies, in contrast, did not permit their employees to hang out and share information with people from other companies; indeed, current and former employees alike knew they would be sued if they shared information. Official corporate policy also discouraged workers from joining trade associations. Route 128 was lined with large companies that did everything in-house; Silicon Valley was a network of smaller companies that fostered dense relationships of subcontracts and partnerships. Route 128 companies worked hard to enforce noncompete clauses when employees left; in Silicon Valley, people changed companies often, and the companies were so small that the joke was you could change companies without changing parking lots.

In Massachusetts, all the companies suffered from the mindset of possessiveness. But in Silicon Valley, the vibrant collaborative webs resulted in collective learning and systemic adaptation, both of which made everyone in the web stronger. Silicon Valley shows the power of local collaborative webs that economists call *clusters*. During the height of American industrial prowess, Attleboro, Massachusetts, was known as the jewelry capital; St. Louis, Missouri, was the shoe capital. And, of course, there are the famous examples of Detroit (automobiles), Nashville (country music), Hollywood (movies), and Hartford, Connecticut (insurance). Outside of the United States, famous clusters include the fashion leather cluster in northern Italy (which contains the shoe companies Ferragamo and Gucci along with specialized suppliers of shoe components, machinery, and leather), the Dutch flower cluster, and consumer electronics in Japan.

Clustering is a bit counterintuitive. Wouldn't it make more sense for each jewelry or shoe company to open in a separate city rather than right next door to the competition? Businesses cluster because it makes each of them more successful; they can all tap into the power of the collaborative web. Some of the most important strengths of a collaborative web are the least visible—local bars where employees hang out together, networks of alumni from the same university, people who change jobs frequently.

These clusters are webs in which information flows freely and efficiently, making all the companies more successful. From the perspective of any one company, information that flows away is lost. But for the web as a whole, information that flows multiplies its total innovation. Even a failed company can ultimately lead to increased and faster success somewhere else; this is because the entire web learns from the failure and the employees find new work at other firms within the web.

In the nineteenth century, the English economist Alfred Marshall was the first to study clustering. His case study was the group of iron and steel companies that formed in southern Lancashire. But that was before the Internet, jet flight, television, and telephone. Information technology was supposed to make location irrelevant, but local clusters are just as important today as they were during the industrial revolution. Hewlett-Packard is based in Silicon Valley, but it moved its medical equipment business to Massachusetts, a state that has a huge concentration of research hospitals and medical instruments companies. Nestlé is based in Switzerland but it moved its candy business to York, England, because there's a strong food web there.

The Web Always Wins

Early in the 1980s, there were two competing computer network standards. IBM backed Token Ring; a group of smaller companies sponsored Ethernet, including DEC, Intel, and Xerox. Although Token Ring was technically superior at first, Ethernet won out because its supporters invited new companies into the collaborative web, among them 3Com and Bridge Communications. IBM actively prevented the formation of a web by making it difficult for other companies to participate in Token Ring. Since IBM wanted to be the primary equipment provider, the company didn't fully share information about how other equipment could interface with its own. By 1989, there were about twenty Token Ring companies and more than two hundred Ethernet companies. By the early 1990s, when new companies such as Cisco developed improved technologies for Ethernet, this larger collaborative web propelled Ethernet past Token Ring in technical quality. The collaborative web, with its hundreds of small companies, was more innovative than IBM with its powerhouse research labs. Today, everyone uses Ethernet; Token Ring is history.

Sony created and sold the first successful videotape recorder, the Betamax, in 1975. In 1976, Sony's rival, JVC, introduced a competing format called VHS, widely believed to be of inferior quality. The standard story is that VHS won out because it was cheaper and because JVC was better at marketing. But the real story is that JVC made a key strategic decision in 1976: They would openly share their technology with other companies and allow a collaborative web to emerge. In contrast, Sony, believing it would make more money by retaining control, took a more proprietary approach. Again, the web beat the proprietary approach. By 1984, forty companies used the VHS standard; only twelve used Betamax. By 1988, Sony gave in and switched to the VHS standard.

Collaborative webs didn't suddenly become important as a result of new technology. Just about every historical innovation emerged from a collaborative web—but the myths that we tell tend to leave that out. In the first chapter, I described how Wilbur and Orville Wright built the first working airplane. They didn't get a patent for "flight"; they were granted a patent for their key innovation, a lateral control mechanism that steered by warping the entire wings forward or backward. The first flight, in 1903, shows us the power of collaboration, and explains how that collaboration built on a history of prior invention. But after the first flight, the brothers tried to own the web, and that almost killed the U.S. airplane industry.

Instead of showing off their new invention, they holed up in Dayton, refused to do press interviews, and wouldn't let photographers near the farm field where they tested small improvements. During this time, they focused on getting contracts, primarily with the military.

On September 30, 1907, Alexander Graham Bell—famous for inventing the telephone—donated $20,000 to found the Aerial Experiment Association (AEA), a group of aviation enthusiasts whose goal was to build a practical airplane. Their intention was to win *Scientific American* magazine's prize for the first plane that could fly a kilometer—a little more than half a mile—in a straight line. Their first plane, the *Red Wing,* designed by Lieutenant Thomas Selfridge, was tested on March 12, 1908, in Hammondsport, New York. It looked a lot like the Wrights' plane, but to avoid infringing on the Wrights' patent, it didn't use wing warping for lateral control; instead, it used a system of trusses to curve the whole wing up or down. Casey Baldwin, an AEA member, designed the next plane, called the *White Wing*. It added wheels, and for lateral control it used ailerons—small pivoting surfaces at the trailing edge of the wing.

The third AEA project was Glenn Curtiss's *June Bug*. On July 4, 1908, Curtiss flew the *June Bug* more than a mile and won the *Scientific American* trophy. The Wrights couldn't even enter the competition because their plane didn't have wheels (they launched their planes from a special railroad track) and couldn't take off from the field. After Curtiss started flying his plane in front of paying viewers in 1909, the Wrights filed a patent infringement lawsuit. They claimed that their patent covered all lateral steering mechanisms; if true, then no plane could ever fly without infringing that patent. Curtiss fought back, arguing that his aileron design wasn't covered by the Wrights' wing-warping patent.

In 1913, a year after Wilbur died of typhoid fever, a federal court sided with Orville and ordered Curtiss to cease making airplanes using ailerons. Curtiss then built a different plane, based on an 1899 design by Samuel Pierpont Langley. It turns out that Langley had been very close, and Curtiss had the expertise to work out the kinks and make it fly. Now Curtiss was able to claim priority of invention, and, with another lawyer, the case dragged on into World War I.

During this time collaborative webs had formed in Europe. The British, French, and German airplane industries were booming, and constant innovations were leaving the Americans behind. For example, BMW was founded in 1913 as an airplane engine company; the familiar blue-and-white "roundel" logo represents a spinning propeller. The nine years of court battles finally stopped when the United States entered World War I in 1917; the Wright and Curtiss companies were then strongly encouraged to form a patent pool, with open sharing of inventions and ideas.

Curtiss and his inventor's collaborative, the AEA, were a collaborative web, and their approach soon overtook the Wrights' original design. Curtiss was the first to sell an airplane to another person, the first to fly from one city to another, and the first to obtain a pilot's license. The aileron is used on every plane flying today—it's far superior to the Wrights' wing-warping design. Curtiss's planes were the first to use retractable landing gear and pontoons for water landings. Unlike the Wrights, Curtiss shared his inventions with the entire aviation community. The evolution of the airplane happened in a collaborative web, a worldwide web that included the Wrights, of course, but then extended from the United States to Europe; a web that grew for twenty years before and after the Wright's flight, and that continues today.

The Five Key Features of Collaborative Webs

Monopoly, television, computer software: Each emerged from the power of collaborative webs. These examples show us the five key features of these webs:

1. Each Innovation Builds Incrementally on a Long History of Prior Innovations

The creative products that are successful in the market rarely spring to life full-grown. The consumer rarely sees the long historical path of small sparks that accumulate to result in the emergence of the final synergy. We learn that Eli Whitney invented the cotton gin; but his creation built on a centuries-old string of cotton gins that had been used from India to Italy before being brought to the American South. We learn that James Watt invented the steam engine, but his creation was but one version in a long chain of steam engines; the Newcomen engine had been in use throughout the world long before Watt's birth.

2. A Successful Innovation Is a Combination of Many Small Sparks

Aspects of Monopoly that we think of as central today emerged at different times and from different people, including the "Go to Jail" space and even the idea of grouping properties into a monopoly. It's the synergy of all of these ideas together that resulted in the best-selling board game of all time.

3. In Collaborative Webs, There Is Frequent Interaction Among Teams

Most of the people who played Monopoly were Quakers, and they often visited other cities and passed on their local variants of the game. In Silicon Valley, members of each team saw what other teams were doing, and key employees frequently transferred allegiances, taking their expertise from one team to another. At Hewlett-Packard, it was company policy to move engineers between projects every few years rather than have each project manager hire and fire individually.

4. In Collaborative Webs, Multiple Discovery Is Common

"Innovation is inefficient": These words were written by Nicholas Negroponte, the MIT Media Lab cofounder. From a big-picture perspective, it's a waste of resources when two companies develop two competing standards (Beta and VHS). In the 1920s, numerous teams invented television in parallel. And now that Ethernet is the dominant

Internet standard, all that work on Token Ring is lost to history. But without multiple efforts and frequent failure, there's no innovation.

5. No One Company Can Own the Web

The key characteristic of the most creative webs is a shift away from an ownership mentality to a collaborative approach. Companies that try to build the entire web themselves will end up losing everything. Sony had to give up Betamax; IBM had to give up Token Ring. Some companies still try to own it all; they wait for the web to innovate and then buy up all the products that emerge. After Parker Brothers got rich selling Monopoly, the company bought the rights to all the local variations. But even though Parker Brothers owned the products that had emerged from the web, it could never own the web itself—nor the later innovations that emerged from players around the globe. It's the difference between owning the goose and owning the golden eggs.

Managers have to allow innovation to emerge from a web that includes their company, their customers, their suppliers, and even their competitors. For much of the twentieth century, innovation was dominated by large corporations equipped with big research laboratories, but that era is over. Successful companies still invest heavily in R&D, but they increasingly collaborate with others in collaborative webs—particularly with small companies and venture-capital start-ups.

The lesson for managers is to position the company within a web for maximum innovation. To be successful, first know the lay of the land; learn everything you can about the web you want to participate in; then, identify its unoccupied niches. The success of eBay created a niche: strip-mall stores where you can take something you want to sell and have them sell it for you on eBay for a small fee. The niche is so large that several franchise chains have emerged to occupy it: iSold It,

The Online Outpost, and QuikDrop. eBay doesn't own these chains, but it benefits from them because they're part of the same web.

Ray Tomlinson's Hack

When the Department of Defense (DOD) funded the ARPANET in the 1960s and 1970s—the network that we all now know as the Internet—the purpose in networking the large mainframe computers at the fifty or so DOD research sites was to allow resources to be shared. In the 1960s, computers were huge and expensive, and had to be installed in rooms that required expensive climate-control systems. Each computer supported as many as fifty users at once, all logged in from teletype terminals that had to be hard-wired from each office to the computer room.

The DOD reasoned it could buy fewer computers if users at each location could run programs on less busy computers at other locations. For example, suppose that one semester, professors at Stanford happened to teach mostly on Mondays and Wednesdays, and their colleagues at MIT on Tuesdays and Thursdays. Stanford's computers would be sitting idle on Monday afternoons; but with the ARPANET, MIT professors could split the load and send half their work to Stanford, and return the favor on Tuesday. To do this, they would somehow have to connect their terminals in Cambridge, Massachusetts, to the computer room in Palo Alto, California, and vice versa.

Another goal was for researchers to be able to send data and programs electronically, with lightning speed. In the early 1970s, researchers were experimenting with different file transfer programs, and they eventually settled on one standard, the File Transfer Protocol (FTP). FTP allowed researchers at different locations to send files to each other instantly. For text documents, such as letters and scientific articles, FTP was of course faster than the U.S. mail. But the real leap forward was transferring computer programs; before FTP, the only way to transfer them to another computer was to record them on magnetic tapes and ship the tapes through the mail.

One of the many programmers involved in the early ARPANET was Ray Tomlinson. Tomlinson worked at Bolt, Beranek and Newman, a consulting firm in Cambridge, Massachusetts. BBN was founded as an acoustics company, but it had diversified into networks and computers; in the 1970s, it was one of the largest and most important ARPANET contractors. Tomlinson had been working on a new computer operating system that allowed everyone using the same computer to send messages to each other; that local mail program was called SNDMSG. He was also experimenting with an early file transfer program called CPYNET, and he had an idea: If he wanted to send a quick note to a researcher at another ARPANET computer, he could modify the SNDMSG program so that it could send a message to another computer, using CPYNET. However, he had to add one small feature: Senders needed a way to indicate which computer the recipient was associated with. On the spur of the moment, Tomlinson decided to use the "@" sign. He wrote the program while off duty and unofficially shared it with a few colleagues in late 1971. He didn't think much of it; after all, it was just a hack, a term that programmers used for quick, inelegant solutions.

Tomlinson's hack caught on like wildfire. In 1972, it was added to the operating system so that every ARPANET computer had a version installed. Soon after, Tomlinson's original hack was replaced by an FTP-based version, with dedicated mail features written by other programmers. By 1973—less than two years after the "@" symbol first took on its new meaning—75 percent of all network traffic was electronic mail.

This was a complete surprise to the experts who had planned and funded the ARPANET in the late 1960s. They hadn't even included e-mail in their original design for the network, and Tomlinson's program wasn't an officially authorized project. In fact, through most of the 1970s the DOD viewed e-mail as an illegitimate use of expensive computer resources; after all, the ARPANET was supposed to be used only for official government business, and it was no secret that many of the e-mails were about music, gossip, philosophy, social get-togethers, and so forth. But e-mail was tolerated because it led more research sites to join the network.

So who created e-mail? It would have been impossible without the ARPANET, but the network's designers didn't create it. And although Tomlinson took an important step forward and invented the "@" convention that we all know today, his creation was just a combination of two existing programs. What Tomlinson did was soon superseded; the e-mail programs that we use today are no longer built on top of SNDMSG and CPYNET because, once the concept was proven, other programmers built more efficient mail delivery programs. And none of this would have been possible if the ARPANET hadn't been invented and built in the first place. The web brought all these complementary inventions together, and then the Internet took off.

Even after Morse's Baltimore-to-D.C. telegraph demonstration, he couldn't find any customers. A lot of complementary inventions had to occur before the telegraph would succeed: a system for billing, a way of training operators, a hub-and-spoke system of central and branch offices, and an army of messengers to carry the handwritten messages from the office to the recipient (Thomas Edison and Andrew Carnegie both started out as telegraph messenger boys). Edison's system of electric lighting is another classic example of complementary invention. The light bulb was a nifty idea, but it didn't replace gas lighting until many other inventions followed, including the screw-in socket, the fuse, and the means of power generation and distribution. Each spark came from a different person or team; Edison's team gets the credit because they brought them all together into the first successful system. Innovations don't stand alone; they're successful only if a collaborative web emerges around them.

In an improvisation, if one actor tries to anticipate the response to a line and then think ahead to a response to that, he or she will always be wrong and have to backpedal. That mistake is called "writing the script in your head." Likewise, one common mistake that managers make is to predict how the web will unfold and then plan out their role within it. The inventors of the VCR thought that the machine would be used mostly for taping television shows, but its main use is playing rented movie videos. The web can't be managed, the outcome is unpredictable, and success or failure depends on the actions of many highly interconnected people and organizations.

The Power of Q

What's the ideal structure of a collaborative web? This is the question being pursued by scholars in the new science of social networks. A 2005 study by Brian Uzzi of Northwestern University and Jarrett Spiro of Stanford University answered that question by focusing on a legendary creative cluster: the twentieth-century Broadway musical industry. Each musical is created by a team of six artists—a composer, a lyricist, a librettist who writes the plot and dialogue, a choreographer, a director, and a producer—and a new team comes together for each project. Uzzi and Spiro were able to collect a complete set of data of all friendships, collaborations, and team memberships for all the musicals produced between 1945 and 1989—a golden age during which such artists as Cole Porter, Andrew Lloyd Webber, and Bob Fosse created their greatest works. Their database included 2,092 artists and 474 musicals, and in the average year, 500 artists were active.

Because most artists worked on more than one musical, there were many informal links among teams. The average number of links per artist—the number of people on other musicals that an artist had worked with within the last seven years—was twenty-nine. This results in what network researchers call a *small world network*—many densely connected small groups that are connected to each other more loosely with less strong connections. Uzzi and Spiro derived a single number, Q, that's a measure of how densely interconnected the entire musical community was. When Q is low, there aren't many links among teams, and those links aren't very strong. When Q is high, the teams are connected by more and more people who know people on the other teams. If Q is very high, then teams are connected by many members, and everyone has worked with everyone else multiple times.

The question that Uzzi and Spiro set out to answer was this: At what level of Q did the music industry generate the most creative products? With more than forty years of data to work with, they were able to compare years that had more creative musicals with other years when the industry, collectively, wasn't as innovative—with creativity measured both by critical acclaim and by financial success.

The fascinating result is that yes, more connectivity is better, but only up to a point. After that point, increasing connectivity begins to interfere with innovation. At low levels of Q, when teams are isolated and their artists don't work with other teams, the industry isn't as innovative as at higher levels of Q. At the ideal Q of 2.6, a musical's probability of being a hit is 2.5 times greater than if Q is at its lowest value of about 1.4, and the probability that a show will be critically acclaimed is 3 times greater. Above this ideal Q, the likelihood of success decreases—too much interconnection reduces innovation. It's still better than *no* connectivity, but the maximum creativity of a web comes with an intermediate value of Q—teams that are connected, but not too strongly.

Connections expose a team to new sources of creative material. But if the network is totally connected, there is less diversity of ideas and the web risks falling into a rut of conventional styles. Recall the research showing that brainstorming groups often fall into groupthink and become less innovative than solitary workers. The most creative web is the one in which good connections exist among the teams, but the teams still enjoy independence and autonomy.

Open Innovation

On April 27, 1983, a computer hacker at MIT known by his login ID, "rms," circulated an e-mail message titled "Free Unix!" The message began: "Starting this Thanksgiving I am going to write a complete Unix-compatible software system called GNU (for Gnu's Not Unix), and give it away for free to everyone who can use it." Richard "rms" Stallman advocated his vision to everyone he met (he corralled me once in an elevator at MIT's artificial intelligence lab), and a loose network of idealistic programmers worked for years at creating GNU. In 1991, a Finnish programmer, Linus Torvalds, completed the final and most difficult task—programming the Unix kernel. Through an accident of history, GNU is now largely known as Linux.

Linux emerged from a collaborative web that contained many teams working independently and collaboratively, without any central control and without a guiding plan. This kind of scattershot anti-organization might sound like a horrible way to create an effective innovation; but, in fact, experts acknowledge that Linux is one of the most reliable operating systems ever built. That reliability is one of the reasons that Linux is seriously challenging Microsoft's proprietary Windows operating system; NASA supercomputers run on Linux, and more than half the world's Web servers run Linux. Versions of Linux are even in Motorola cell phones and Mitsubishi robots. In 2005, IBM had six hundred programmers working on Linux—and there's also a large group at IBM's competitor, Hewlett-Packard.

Why does IBM pay six hundred salaries for something they don't own and can't sell? Because IBM sells its network servers with Linux pre-installed, they don't have to pay another company (i.e., Microsoft) for a software license. Other companies, such as Red Hat and Novell, make money by selling user manuals, customer service, and annual subscription fees in exchange for passing on the regular updates that emerge from the international community of programmers. Software companies that develop word processors and accounting packages sell versions that run in Linux, and they can do a better job writing those applications if their programmers know the innards of the operating system. In a collaborative web, companies make money by finding a niche within the system, not by owning the system.

The business press is fascinated with Linux; Linus Torvalds appeared on the cover of *Business Week* in 2005, and books such as *Democratizing Innovation* by the MIT professor Eric von Hippel advocate this model, which has come to be known as "open source," as the driver of innovation. Other widely used open-source products include the free Internet browser, Mozilla; the free PC e-mail client, Thunderbird; the online encyclopedia *Wikipedia;* and the productivity suite OpenOffice, which has a word processor, a spreadsheet program, a presentation tool, a database, and a drawing program.

The open-source model has spread far beyond computer software. The Toyota company, repeatedly voted the most innovative auto company of the year, has developed an internal system called the Toyota Production System that's also a self-organizing web. When an early-morning fire destroyed the Kariya Number 1 plant of one of Toyota's most important suppliers—the Aisin Seiki company—Toyota could no longer make cars. The plant supplied 99 percent of all of the brake fluid valves used in Toyota's Japanese plants, and Toyota had only a day's worth of inventory.

The solution emerged from the bottom up. Just hours after the fire, engineers from Toyota and Aisin started collaborating. Aisin sent blueprints for its valves to other suppliers, and also gave Toyota whatever undamaged specialized tools and raw materials that could be salvaged. Aisin and Toyota engineers worked together to improvise temporary production lines at sixty-two locations, including boarded-up old machine shops and a sewing machine shop owned by the Brother corporation. Another of Toyota's largest suppliers, Denso, volunteered to collect all these valves, send them to Aisin engineers for inspection, and then send them on to Toyota's plants. Within two weeks, this distributed and improvised network had attained the pre-fire level of production.

Collaborative webs have a lot in common with open-source communities, but the open-source model is not the ideal web for innovation. Often forgotten is that Linux began as a copy of an already existing operating system, Unix. The OpenOffice word processor, called Writer, is similar to Microsoft Word. Being able to reverse engineer an existing product and develop a copy isn't what most of us mean when we talk about innovation. Krzysztof Klincewicz, a management professor at the Tokyo Institute of Technology, analyzed the five hundred top open-source projects, and found that only five—1 percent—were examples of radical innovation. Another fifty-nine demonstrated incremental innovation; the majority of these were taking a product that existed on one operating system, such as Windows, and reprogramming it for another, such as the Mac. Almost 90 percent demonstrated no innovation whatsoever.

So how can you create a collaborative web that generates real innovation? How can open source turn into open innovation? Most of the examples I've given are of collaborative webs that emerge independently of any one company, webs that no company could create or control. But there's one place that companies can take action to foster a collaborative web—with the people the company already has a connection with, its customers. With many products, customers independently form themselves into informal communities with user groups, Web sites, and Internet discussion lists. Customer webs are where real innovation comes from. Every company should be working hard to collaborate with these naturally forming organic webs, which we'll explore in the next chapter.

···

CHAPTER 10

Collaborating with Customers

Picture yourself living in a science fiction future. You're flying your personal hovercraft over Manhattan, looking for a good bagel. You dive down into the skyscraper canyon of Broadway and then start heading uptown. Fortunately for you, there's no traffic today (remember, this is science *fiction*) and you can move as fast as you like. It's easy to spot each bagel place; they have signs out front—but you're looking for the best bagel. You're in luck, because in this imaginary future, right next to its sign each bagel store has placed a billboard displaying its customers' opinions about its bagels.

This imaginary future already exists—if you've installed Google Earth on your personal computer. Of course, there's no hovercraft, but Google Earth lets you fly through a 3-D image of Manhattan's skyscraper canyons. You can search for the best pizza by the slice, or for men's restrooms that have diaper-changing tables. You can look for the nearest bar or find a good jogging route.

But Google didn't hire an army of expensive graphic designers and programmers to provide these features—instead, the company nurtured a collaborative web by sharing its new mapping technology with its users. If you're a fan of good affordable wine, you can start your own Web site about your favorite wine stores and Google will let you use its satellite photos and its technology. These joint efforts are called "mash-ups" because they combine Google's mapping technology with a customer's own applications.

Why would Google give away expensive cutting-edge technology? Why not hoard it and grab all that web traffic as its own? Google decided instead to trust that group genius would emerge from a collaborative web of thousands of volunteer workers. After all, Google's famous search algorithm is based on group genius—it aggregates the collective wisdom of everyone who uses the Web by ranking a Web page higher when other pages connect to it. No one at Google decides which pages will result from a search; we all make it collectively.

Trusting the collaborative web is standard business practice at Google. To take another example, Google hosted four Code Jam competitions in 2006, giving developers around the world an opportunity to work on its most difficult technical problems. Thousands participated, and the one hundred finalists flew to Google's headquarters in Mountain View, California, even though the top prize was only $10,000.

Google is not alone in its strategy of building collaborative webs with its customers. IBM has hosted internal idea jams since 1998; in 2006, they decided to expand the collaborative web and invited their customers to join in their first Innovation Jam. The online bookseller Amazon.com opened its servers to business partners several years ago; if you put a link to Amazon.com on your Web site, and a buyer clicks through and buys a book, Amazon sends you a cut of the sale. The online auction site eBay is legendary for trusting the collective mind of its users. In 2005, more than seven hundred thousand Americans reported that eBay selling is a primary or secondary source of income. Thirty thousand developers are registered with eBay and have access to the inner workings of the eBay Web site; they've created more than two thousand enhancements to it.

Many video games today allow players to modify the rules of the game to suit their own tastes—it's called "modding." The hit video game Quake sold a lot more copies after it allowed players to create new scenery. Valve, the company that sells the video game Half-Life, built in even more sophisticated support for modding. Epic Games and Digital Extremes, the companies that created the Unreal Tournament computer game, have sponsored a $1 million contest in which players are rewarded for creating new weapons, characters, and fantasy worlds. To teach users how to create their own game content, Epic Games put one hundred hours of free video training on its Web site. When you buy the game, you also get sophisticated design tools. Some modders do such a good job that the company hires them; two Half-Life modders did such original work that Valve used the modifications as the basis for a new game, Counter-strike, which went on to sell more than four million copies.

These games were first designed by a company, and only later opened to users. But some of today's most significant innovations are completely created by them. *Wikipedia* is a free online encyclopedia, its entries created and edited by its users. At more than 1.5 million entries, it has far surpassed the 120,000 articles in the online *Encyclopedia Britannica*. A second example is YouTube, the free video-sharing site where users film, edit, and post their own videos. In July 2006, a hundred thousand clips were viewed daily, and sixty-five thousand new videos were uploaded in every twenty-four-hour period. Just about everything on YouTube is created by amateurs, yet in October 2006, the big players were lining up to join in this collaborative web: NBC, CBS, Warner Music Group, and Sony BMG Music had all announced partnerships with YouTube.

These are the latest high-profile examples of customer-driven collaborative webs. But customers have always driven innovation. During World War I, there was a shortage of cotton, an essential commodity in battlefield surgery. To respond to the demand, army surgeons started buying a substitute made from wood pulp: an absorbent material called Cellucotton. Huge amounts were delivered to wartime hospitals and to front-line troops.

At the end of the war, Cellucotton's maker Kimberly-Clark had a problem: It still had warehouses of the stuff, and a peacetime use was needed. The company thought up Kleenex Kerchiefs, the "Sanitary Cold Cream Remover," and marketed the product as a disposable substitute for the cloth facial towels that women used each night to remove makeup. Kimberly-Clark developed an advertising campaign featuring Hollywood and Broadway stars, and the glamorous associations worked—sales took off.

But something unexpected happened. Mail started arriving at Kimberly-Clark from men who were using Kleenex—not to remove makeup, but to blow their noses. These letters offered a suggestion: Why not market Kleenex this way? They had to use this "feminine" product in secret, but an ad campaign targeted at men would reduce the stigma. But Kimberly-Clark's management, thinking the idea a little odd, ignored the letters.

In 1921, Andrew Olson, the Chicago inventor, invented the pop-up tissue box. The tissues were folded together just as we know them today: When one was removed another one popped out, easy to reach. Kimberly-Clark marketed this as Serv-a-Tissue. But the unintended side effect of this additional spark was that even more people started using Kleenex to blow their noses—the easy accessibility made it particularly handy for unpredictable sneezes.

It wasn't until 1930 that the company's management decided to test-market the idea of selling Kleenex as a handkerchief. The response was overwhelming; 61 percent of customers wanted Kleenex for their noses instead of for their faces. A new ad campaign was introduced and by 1936 the use of Kleenex as a cold-cream tissue was fading fast.

You can find hundreds of examples of new products that emerge from customers in the same way. Here's another example: In the 1970s, when health and exercise became a fad, some people began to mix their wine with soda water to lower the drink's calorie count. Soft drink makers responded by making ready-to-drink wine coolers. In another example, lots of people like to dip their chips into sour cream mixed with onion soup mix. The practice became so widespread that most sales of onion soup mix were for dip, and the companies that sold the onion soup mix responded by marketing the product as a dip mix. Later, chip makers responded by putting the dip flavoring directly onto the chips—now you can buy chips already flavored with sour cream and onion.

Customer innovation isn't limited to consumer products and snack foods; back in 1969, a widely cited National Science Foundation study of five hundred innovations found that four out of five of them origi-nated in user suggestions or were actually invented by the users. In 1981, another study by Eric von Hippel, an MIT professor of manage-ment, found similar percentages across industries: Users came up with 81 percent of the innovations in scientific instruments, 60 percent in process machinery. Between 10 percent and 40 percent of all users modify the products they buy. These are the so-called "lead users," and their ideas often filter throughout the collaborative web. The Lego Corporation still sells literally tons of its famous interlocking blocks every year. But it's also known today for technology innovation because of its wildfire 1998 hit called Lego Mindstorms—a robot construction kit built around Lego bricks with microchips, motors, and sensors. Version 2.0, released in 2001, sold forty thousand kits a year with no advertising; it's Lego's best-selling product ever.

When the Lego corporation realized in 2005 that it needed to update Mindstorms with a new release, it tapped into the collaborative web; by participating in online discussion forums, the company discovered who were the most respected users. These four—Steve Hassenplug, John Barnes, David Schilling, and Ralph Hempel—were legendary among the cult-like fans of Mindstorms for their skill and artistry in designing amazing robots with Lego bricks. Parents buy the kits for their young tinkerers, but it's so complex to use that more than half of its customers are adults who have the technical skills to tap its incredible potential— building robots that can solve Rubik's Cubes or pick blue M&Ms out of a multicolored pile.

Lego didn't wait until a prototype was ready to tap into the web; instead, they wanted its wisdom right from the beginning. These four fans were so loyal that Lego didn't even have to pay them; the company just gave them free Legos. Hassenplug put it this way: "They're going to talk to us about Legos, and they're going to pay us with Legos? It doesn't get much better than that." Later, the insider group grew from four to fourteen, and Lego invited a hundred more devoted customers to test the prototype.

Lego was receptive to the collaborative web because of its experience with version 1.0 back in 1998. Within weeks of 1.0's release, a Stanford graduate student, Kekoa Proudfoot, had reverse engineered the microchips in the bricks and had posted detailed information online. Other engineers downloaded the info and started to design their own Mindstorms tools—including a completely new operating system and a programming language to replace the one Lego had used. At first, Lego was worried about this loss of intellectual property; but after a few months, the company realized that this emerging collaborative web increased customer loyalty, enhanced the creativity of the product, and, most important, was a source of free innovation. After all, the user community had extended Mindstorms far beyond anything Lego had envisioned for the product; it had built new sensors that interfaced with the Lego products and created such amazing things as soda machines and card dealers.

"Listen to your customers and give them what they want" is just about the oldest business advice in the book. But in today's innovation economy, that advice is no more than an unhelpful truism. After all, how are you supposed to understand the customers' needs? Sometimes we don't even know what we need, and even when we do, we can't always put it into words. And in many businesses, customers have different specialized needs; you can't "listen" to millions of people at the same time. The solution: Create webs where the company improvises collaboratively *with* the customer. As we've learned, innovation today doesn't always originate in the old "linear" fashion; instead, it emerges from collaborative webs. Once a company truly realizes this, it needs to modify the way it operates, to redesign itself to link into the collaborative web. A study at 3M shows what companies could be leaving on the table if they don't do this: Annual sales of products that emerged from users were eight times the annual sales of products developed in-house in the traditional linear way—$146 million as opposed to $18 million.

Customer innovation has increased dramatically, and two technological developments will continue the increase: The Internet and e-mail support the dense networks of communication that allow the frequent sharing of small sparks, and new software tools that support design—such as computer-aided design tools and visually oriented programming environments—make it easier than ever for a customer to contribute a spark to the web. The companies that succeed will be the ones that seek collaboration with their customers, the ones that lead collaborative webs extending beyond their company's boundaries.

The way to collaborate with customers is to foster links up and down the organization—not to channel customers through a sales contact or the customer service desk. Cisco customers, on average, know twenty people within the company. Businesses generally frown on so much contact, thinking that it might confuse the customer and potentially send mixed messages; customers are thought to want one person to call. "That's totally wrong," says Yves Morieux of the Boston Consulting Group. "Because all these people connect with each other in a very effective way, they're able to collectively reconstruct the real customer." We've already learned how Cisco builds dense information networks; Cisco gives customers and suppliers access to much of this same information—customers can download daily bug fixes anytime, without waiting for a new release, and suppliers can access sales data to help them plan their inventory.

SAS Institute is another company that uses customer webs to drive innovation. It's the largest privately held software company in the world, and it's famous among corporate leaders for its enterprise management software—a product that keeps the entire company running. Its home is Cary, North Carolina, where there's no local cluster of software companies. But creativity flourishes because SAS has nourished a collaborative web with its customers. Like a lot of companies, SAS pays close attention to customer complaints and suggestions—every one is categorized and entered into a database, and they're tracked to make sure nothing falls between the cracks. Like many customer-focused companies, SAS hosts an annual users' conference; but this one has been compared to a Grateful Dead show because of its creative energy and the active participation of the audience. Even the members of the technical support staff collaborate with customers to innovate. As at Cisco, customers can contact anyone in the company, even the software's developers. Because of what we've learned about group genius, we know why this works for SAS and Cisco: The most innovative collaborative webs have complex and multiple links, not fully understood or controlled by anyone.

Extreme Innovation

In the 1970s, a few sailboarders had discovered that if they sailed over the top of a wave at high speed, they would become airborne; they called it "jumping." The problem was that the rider's feet would rise up off the sailboard in midair, and even if the rider was lucky enough to land back on the board, the impact was bone-jarring.

Years before, a group of top sailboarders, including Larry Stanley and Mike Horgan, had built a board equipped with foot straps, but at that time no one had discovered jumping and the straps didn't seem very useful. At the first Hawaiian World Cup in 1978, Stanley remembered the foot straps, thought they might help with jumping, and added some to his board. When he went on the water, he discovered something he hadn't expected: With his feet in the two foot straps, he could actually change the direction of the board in midair. Stanley reported what happened next: "There were about ten of us who sailed all the time together and within one or two days there were various boards out there that had foot straps of various kinds on them, and we were all going fast and jumping waves and stuff. It just kind of snowballed from there." Today, the majority of sailboards sold have manufacturer-designed foot straps.

Extreme sports are a common source of user innovations because the participants form a dedicated and tight-knit community. For example, the collaborative web of inveterate tinkerers that developed the mountain bike in the 1970s didn't stop innovating just because big companies entered the business. A 2002 study found that 38 percent of the 287 mountain bikers interviewed had an idea for how to improve their bikes, and almost 50 percent of those ideas had been implemented by the bikers themselves. A panel of ten mountain biking experts determined that about 30 percent of these ideas had market potential. One such idea involved stunt riding. Stunt riders often take their feet off the pedals while up in the air. The problem is that the pedals spin around, so that when riders try to put their feet back down, the pedal isn't flat. This rider's solution was to add a foam ring between the pedal axle and the pedal, providing just enough friction to stop the spinning but still allowing him to pedal after landing.

Many of today's most successful innovations started out as youth fads. Common wisdom has it that this is a recent phenomenon, but it goes back farther than one might think—because wherever young people come together, the conditions are ripe for a collaborative web to form. The Frisbee flying disk is a good example. Arthur "Spud" Melin, the founder and president of the Wham-O toy company, was said to be the creator of the Frisbee. And indeed, Wham-O held the patent for the plastic flying disk. But Melin didn't invent the Frisbee.

The Frisbee that we all know and love originated in the Frisbie Pie, made in Bridgeport, Connecticut, from 1871 to 1958 at a bakery not far from Yale University. Yale students apparently ate a lot of Frisbie pies in the first half of the twentieth century, and afterwards, they tossed around the empty metal tins using the now-familiar flick of the wrist.

In 1947, two Californians whose bottled-gas business was a bit slow dreamed up a side business. Fred Morrison and Warren Franscioni figured that if the pie tins were made of the new material known as plastic, they might fly better. The famous Roswell incident of June 1947—when a UFO crash site was supposedly discovered and then covered up by the military—inspired a flying saucer craze, so they marketed their idea as the Flyin' Saucer. Morrison later redesigned the disk and sold it as the Pluto Platter for a couple of years before selling it to Melin at Wham-O. Wham-O began production in 1957, but didn't have much success at first; it was a hit on California beaches, but didn't catch on elsewhere. Sometime just before 1960, Richard Knerr, Wham-O's cofounder, went on a promotional tour with his UFOs to college campuses in the eastern United States; he was surprised to find that students were still throwing pie tins to each other, and were calling the sport "Frisbie-ing." Knerr changed the name to Frisbee, and this superficial change was enough for the flying platter to piggyback on the existing college fad.

So who invented the Frisbee? Not Knerr, who only changed the name. Not Melin, who bought Morrison's patent. Not Morrison, because he simply co-opted a fad that had emerged from a group of students. And not William Russell Frisbie, who just wanted to make pies. The Frisbee wasn't created in a sudden burst of genius; it emerged from a collaborative web.

Like the Frisbee, many products today are clever appropriations of fads that emerge from youth culture. In the summer of 2005, the Anheuser-Busch corporation released a new game called Bud Pong. The game is played with Ping-Pong balls and tables; with free balls and glasses bearing the Bud logo featured prominently, A-B promoted Bud Pong tournaments at bars around the country. Everyone seems to ignore the official rule that calls for putting water in the glasses.

In Bud Pong, two teams face off across a Ping-Pong table with the net removed, and each team sets up a triangle of six cups partially filled with beer (er, water). The goal is to bounce the ball once off the table and into one of the other team's glasses at the other end of the table. If the ball goes in, the other team has to drink what's in that cup. Paradoxically, perhaps, the losers drink more.

Anyone who's been to college recently knows that Anheuser-Busch didn't invent Bud Pong; it's that company's adaptation of a game that's been played on campuses for more than a decade that's called either beer pong or, sometimes, Beirut (for unclear reasons). The 2006 World Beer Cup Tournament in Nevada drew more than one hundred players from California to New York. And like modded video games or YouTube videos, there are as many versions of beer pong as there are fraternities. One variation has the empty glasses removed from the table; another has them put back and imposes a penalty for sinking a ball in an empty cup. Another common variation is to shoot two balls at once, and there are many rules about what happens if both balls are sunk. Many fraternities use complex rules about "redemption" and "returns" that you are likely to understand only after the buzz that comes from losing a few games.

Anheuser-Busch isn't the only company trying to make money from this emergent phenomenon; Urban Outfitters carries a beer pong kit called Bombed. A company called Bing Bong sells a portable folding table that's narrower than a Ping-Pong table but still the right length.

Drinking games emerge from a collaborative web; like old folk songs, no one knows where they originate. As I write this, college students are also playing a card game called Asshole, and a variation of the classic drinking game Quarters called Moose, where players try to bounce the quarters into an ice tray. But these games come and go. The hippie game Cosmic Wimpout, associated with the Grateful Dead, was big in the 1970s and 1980s, but has faded in popularity. It was originally played with five ordinary dice and was called the Bong Game on many campuses. Then a small Massachusetts company designed a special set of five dice and sold them along with tiny stickers that began to appear in elevators and phone booths everywhere the Dead performed. All such games feature a dizzying array of bizarre rules for special situations, combined in ways that lend themselves to local variation. These game variations aren't due to alcohol only; after all, Monopoly's infinite variations were created by Quakers, and many of them were active in the temperance movement.

Idea Marketplaces

Innovative companies reach out to their customers, and they also reach out to other businesses—even their competitors—to build collaborative relationships that lead to innovation. Research In Motion (RIM), the company that makes the legendary BlackBerry PDA, decided to share its proprietary software in 2002. The first fruit of this decision was a licensing arrangement in November of that year with Nokia that allowed Nokia cell phones to run BlackBerry e-mail software. But wait a minute—until 2002, only BlackBerry's own devices would work with its corporate servers; wouldn't the Nokia deal cut into its sales? Just the opposite happened—in the following years, when RIM also extended licenses to Siemens, Motorola, and others, the company's stock rose 800 percent. What was going on?

These collaborations worked for RIM because they were selling more than just a phone. They sold the entire system—the corporate servers that handled the e-mail, the network of standards, the wireless bandwidth. Techies call this "middleware," and when you occupy the middle position of the web, everyone has to work with you. By partnering with other cell phone providers, they made sure that their system was the market standard. Companies were more likely to buy the RIM system if all their customers could connect to it, using whatever device they owned. Ultimately, RIM got to have its cake and eat it, too: Sales of BlackBerrys have been increasing from 50 to 100 percent each year.

Perhaps the one company that has invested the most in collaborative webs is Procter & Gamble, the consumer-goods maker based in Cincinnati, Ohio. Larry Huston, P&G's vice president for innovation and knowledge, calls this strategy "connect and develop" to contrast it with the older "research and develop" model of innovation. Connect and develop has already resulted in the Swiffer Duster, the Mr. Clean Magic

Eraser, and Pringles Prints—the chips with jokes and odd factoids printed on them in brightly colored edible dye. Thirty-five percent of P&G's new products today were invented outside and are licensed; A. G. Lafley, P&G's CEO, wants to get that up to 50 percent. P&G has created a proprietary network around the world of seventy "technology entrepreneurs" whose full-time job is to scour the literature, meet with university researchers, and nurture networks of suppliers.

P&G has accelerated the growth of collaborative webs by creating Internet sites that bring together needs and solutions. They call these Web sites "idea marketplaces." Several other large corporations, including IBM and Eli Lilly, are also strong supporters of these idea marketplaces:

NineSigma (created by P&G) links companies that have technology problems with scientists in universities that can develop solutions. For example, P&G wanted to create a soap that could wash even in cold water. NineSigma created a technology brief describing the problem, and it was instantly delivered to thousands of solution providers. P&G has sent briefs to more than seven hundred thousand people and has completed more than one hundred projects based on these outsider solutions.

InnoCentive (created by Eli Lilly) connects companies to research scientists around the world. How it works: An interested company signs up with InnoCentive and receives permission to post anonymous "challenges" to the Web site; these contain detailed descriptions of the requirements, a deadline, and an award amount. Scientists scan the challenges; if they have an answer, they submit a solution.

TechEx, www.techex.com, (started at Yale University) links buyers and sellers of biomedical technology. More than seven hundred companies are registered as buyers, and thousands of universities and researchers are sellers.

YourEncore (created by P&G) connects about eight hundred top retired scientists and engineers with businesses. A company can use
YourEncore to contact a retired expert for a short-term assign-
ment. This allows a company to bring in another disciplinary perspective without having to make the commitment to hiring a
full-time expert.

Yet2.com (created by a group of Fortune 100 companies, including
P&G) is an online marketplace for intellectual property. Inventors
post ideas for licensing or purchase; needy companies post problems they want solved. P&G used Yet2.com to license a low-cost
microneedle technology for drug delivery.

In 2003, the consulting firm Accenture studied innovation in forty
global companies in five industries and found that, on average, 45 percent of innovation came from external sources. At some retail companies the number was as high as 90 percent. One of the lowest
percentages of outside innovation in 2003 was the pharmaceutical industry, at 30 percent. But the pharmaceutical companies are catching
up fast; in 2006—only three years later—more than 50 percent of pharmaceutical innovation came from outside the big players.

The key to innovation is to find just the right way to guide and
shape the collaborative web. Companies can nourish the web by giving
public credit for the ideas that emerge—even the ones that they don't
use—and by creating idea marketplaces that allow them to identify the
good ideas that emerge. Group genius happens when you relinquish
control and defer to the web.

Creativity today is everywhere. We all contribute to collaborative
webs, even when we don't realize it—just by doing our chores, working at the office, or taking a break with our favorite hobby. But if
that's true, then how come we're not making any money from our

creative contributions? The profits go to the company that owns the innovation—even if the innovation emerges from a collaborative web, the company holds the patent or the copyright. But if everyone in the web could make some money from their participation, wouldn't that drive greater innovation? We'll explore those questions in the next chapter.

···

CHAPTER 11

Creating the Collaborative Economy

THE COLLABORATIVE WEB is a conversation writ large, a conversation that spans the company, its customers, the industry, even the globe. Group genius is, ultimately, the genius of all humanity. Our success in solving the most critical problems and needs that we face, today and in the future, depends on our ability to tap into the creative power of collaboration.

Still, it takes a person to have an idea, and people should be financially rewarded for their ideas. That's why we have patents. Abraham Lincoln—the only U.S. president to hold a patent—once said that the U.S. patent laws were one of "the three most important events in the world's history" (the other two were the invention of the printing press and the discovery of America).

But if ideas are always collaborative, one person should never have complete ownership. History is filled with stories of how patent holders block innovation, hurting themselves as much as they hurt everyone else. We've already seen how the Wrights' possessiveness held back the U.S. airplane industry ten years. In another famous example, after Edison was successful with his New York City lighting system, he inhibited innovation by fighting against a superior technology, alternating current (AC), developed by Nikola Tesla and used by his competitor, Westinghouse. Edison bet wrong when he chose to use direct current (DC); direct current could be transmitted only a few blocks from the power station, but AC could last for miles. Edison carried out a vicious public-relations campaign to prove that AC was less safe than DC—one of his more extreme moves was to use AC to electrocute stray cats and then claim that they'd been "Westinghoused." But AC was a superior technology, and in spite of Edison's campaign, AC is the technology that homes use today. (DC lives on in battery-powered devices.)

The challenge society faces is to reward individuals and still nurture the collaboration that allows the next innovation to emerge. Finding the right balance is essential because creativity is the most important feature of today's economy, and it's becoming more important every year. The economist Richard Florida has argued that our economy is powered by human creativity; 30 percent of American workers participate in the creative economy—they have jobs that regularly require them to be creative—and 12 percent represent a *super-creative core,* people who work in directly creative activity in science, technology, and the arts. By comparison, the traditional blue-collar working class represents 25 percent of the workforce.

Companies that can't transform themselves into collaborative organizations will suffer in today's innovation economy. For one thing, repetitive tasks that don't require creativity can be automated—and then you're just one step away from being in a commodities business, competing to be the lowest-cost provider. But, more important, jobs that don't require creativity can be performed by an uneducated workforce, and that means they can be outsourced. The competitive advantage in the United States today is the ability to out-innovate global competition. But the United States can't rest easy; from Singapore to Finland, governments are investing heavily in education for creativity.

Countries need legal systems in place that balance the rights of individual creators without blocking the collaborative webs that give them inspiration. In recent years, U.S. copyright and patent law has shifted toward the greater protection of individual ownership of ideas. This recent shift is ironic because, at the same time, innovation has become more and more dependent on collaborative webs. The science of innovation has shown us the power of collaboration, but U.S. government policy remains based on the myth of the solitary genius.

To release the innovation potential of society, we need to modify seven aspects of our legal system to create a closer match to the natural behavior of collaborative webs.

1. Reduce Copyright Terms

We should reduce the number of years of copyright protection at least to what it was when the law was first passed in 1790: fourteen years, with an option to renew for fourteen more if the creator is still alive. Innovation happens more rapidly today than it did in 1790; why should an idea be protected for even longer when the innovation cycle is shorter? Congress has been running in the opposite direction; since 1962, it has extended copyright terms eleven times, and it's now ninety-five years. This has happened not because it's consistent with the way innovation works but because the corporate owners of those copyrights have used their influence to make it so.

2. Reward Small Sparks

Current policy favors linear, centralized innovation and blocks the natural rhythm of the collaborative web. First, large corporations often use their R&D labs to create "patent thickets"—many related patents that aren't quite usable (because the complementary innovations haven't appeared) but that give the company a strong defensive position: the ability to sue anyone else who innovates, even if that idea fills in one of the gaps in the thicket. But in collaborative webs, each person or company has only a subset of the ideas needed for innovation.

The open-source community thrives because programmers share their sparks without charge—for intangible benefits such as recognition, and also in exchange for receiving the sparks from others. Creators of small sparks could get a patent; but that takes effort and money, and current patent protections aren't designed to reward small sparks of innovation. With very small innovations, a patent holder rarely receives income from licensing—it's often easy for a large R&D lab to get around one small patent by inventing a slightly different solution. We should consider new government policies that would provide additional incentives for sharing small sparks; these policies could expand the number and size of collaborative webs dramatically.

3. Legalize Modding

In many areas—such as mountain biking, video-game modding, and music sampling—many people create modifications for their own use and never share them. There are thousands of people like the extreme bike jumper who invented a way to keep his pedals from spinning. One reason they don't share is that those modifications are often illegal. The U.S. Digital Millennium Copyright Act—designed to prevent users from making illegal copies of software, music, and movies—has the side effect of making it impossible to modify the products consumers purchase. If a dedicated video-gamer hacks into a game's code and changes the way the game plays, that person is breaking the law. LEGO could have sued the engineers who hacked into Mindstorms and then wrote a new operating system. But they realized that constant modification by many people in a collaborative web is what drives innovation.

4. Free the Employees

Another way that government policy can support the emergence of collaborative webs is to make employee noncompete clauses illegal and to allow the free flow of employees—and in all but a few limited cases, the free flow of whatever knowledge those employees have. In most states in the United States, it's legal for an employer to prevent an employee from working for a similar company for one or two years after leaving. The motivation seems reasonable: You don't want your key employee taking all your best ideas to your main competitor. But the story of how Route 128 companies fizzled while the more open culture of Silicon Valley thrived shows that proprietary mindsets and lawsuits against former employees are self-defeating. The economy as a whole will be more innovative if companies are restricted in imposing noncompete clauses; the result will be more vibrant collaborative webs. Individual companies will be more innovative if they all shift away from a possessiveness mindset.

5. Mandatory Licensing

Today, patent owners can license their technology to others, and copyright holders can license the reuse of their media content. But they're not required to do this, and the licensing fees aren't regulated.

If a movie producer or an actor wants to charge an arm and a leg, you have to forget about using that film clip. And even when the owners are willing to license reuse, it can take a year or more to contact everyone who holds an ownership right, find out how much money each person wants, and sign all the release forms. As the Stanford law professor Lawrence Lessig puts it: "The cost of complying with the law is impossibly high." Patent owners should be required to license their technology, and pricing for the license should be removed from the patent owner to prevent the excessively high pricing that would interfere with the flow of ideas. Government law could specify a fixed rate (Lessig suggests 1 percent of revenues), or perhaps an auction-like system would allow the true market for the idea to set the value of the license.

6. Pool Patents

One historically successful way to foster a collaborative web has been to pool patents. With both the airplane and the sewing machine industries, once the competitors got out of the courtroom and pooled their patents, innovation took off. With pooled patents, every company shares in the collective benefits of participating in the web. New laws could encourage the formation of such patent pools—and that would require open access and nondiscriminatory membership arrangements.

7. Encourage Industry-Wide Standards

Complex mechanical devices like typewriters, accordions, and adding machines never had a cross-industry standard. The Underwood typewriter had a different mechanism from the Remington, and innovations in one mechanism didn't transfer to the others. As a result, innovation was extremely slow. One of the main reasons that technical innovation has proceeded so rapidly during the last forty years is the spread of industry-wide standards. With universal and shared standards in place, modular innovation takes off: Anyone can attach a new innovation to the rest of the system. Proprietary ownership of a standard almost always reduces innovation. Ethernet won out over Token Ring because it was a more open standard; VHS won out over Betamax because Sony tried to retain control of the collaborative web.

Innovation is the key to a better future for our planet. Without a good understanding of how innovation works for all of us, government policies have often responded to the interests of the corporations that hold existing patents and copyrights. Unfortunately, established corporations often have the most to lose from the onset of radical new innovations, and the temptation is great to use their power to block the emergence of collaborative webs. Now that we know the true story of how innovation works, we can respond as a society by changing the rules to foster group genius.

When I speak to audiences about my research on creativity, and emphasize the key role of collaboration, I always hear the same questions: Aren't most creative people mentally ill, or at the very least, nonconformists? Aren't there people who will be creative no matter what they choose to do? Doesn't brain imaging show that creative people's brains are different? These questions reveal the amazing power and persistence of the myth of the lone genius.

This myth isn't only wrong; it's also dangerous because it ultimately has the effect of reducing creativity. If you believe that creativity is reserved for special geniuses, you're more likely to think that you can't be creative. If you believe that creativity is an unexplainable gift that happens in a magical flash of insight, you won't invest the hard and sustained work that it takes to generate a long string of small sparks. If you believe that creativity happens to nonconforming, solo operators, you won't work together with others to build group genius.

This is why understanding the science of group genius is so important. To build the kinds of organizations that generate innovation, we have to move beyond these myths and tap into the creative power of collaboration. To attain our true creative potential as a society, we need to embrace the real truth about creativity. I hope this book contributes, as one small spark, to helping humanity attain its true creative potential.

ACKNOWLEDGMENTS

All science is collaborative; the science of creativity is no different, and over the years, I've learned a great deal from my collaborations with other creativity scientists. First, and most important, Mihaly Csikszentmihalyi was my professor when I was pursuing my PhD at the University of Chicago; he first introduced me to the scientific field of creativity research, and has remained a close colleague. Other colleagues whom I've collaborated or coauthored with include David Henry Feldman, Howard Gardner, Vera John-Steiner, and Robert Sternberg. I'm deeply grateful to these brilliant scientists for our conversations and collaborations.

My collaborative web includes many researchers whom I've not yet met but with whom I have collaborated through the written word—I have read and occasionally reviewed their books and scientific articles, and they have read and commented on mine. These invisible collaborations are too many for me to name here, although most of the writings that I've drawn on are named in the notes. Many creativity scientists have their own theories about collaborative webs and group genius that are similar to mine, although each of us uses slightly different terms and emphasizes slightly different aspects of these webs. This intellectual convergence increases my confidence that we're going down the right path. I'm grateful for the inspiring and important work that has been published previously by my colleagues.

As I wrote *Group Genius*, I benefited immensely from the comments and corrections of my fellow researchers. I'm particularly grateful to two good friends who offered comments on multiple chapters: Allen Orr and Alphonse DeSena. Many colleagues read and commented on specific sections of the book: Larry Barsalou, David Bearison, Mike Csikszentmihalyi, Kevin Dunbar, Michael P. Farrell, Bill Fischer, Ray Gibbs, James Hampton, Ed Hutchins, Jason Jimerson, Vera John-Steiner, Giovan Francesco Lanzara, Janet Metcalfe, Paul B. Paulus, David Perkins, Ryan Quinn, John Reed, Dan Schwartz, Dean Keith Simonton, Steven P. Smith,

Wolfgang Stroebe, Jyrki Suomala, Brian Uzzi, Ruth Wageman, Robert W. Weisberg, Edward Wisniewski. Of course, any errors that remain are my fault.

A special thanks goes to my two closest collaborators on this book: my literary agent, Esmond Harmsworth, who went far beyond the call of duty in closely reading my drafts at every stage and offered insightful suggestions that I accepted gratefully; and my editor at Basic Books, Jo Ann Miller, who more than lived up to her stellar reputation and worked with me at every stage to clarify the focus and vision of the book, reconceptualize its overall flow, and dramatically reshape most of the chapters at least twice. Although my name is the only one that appears on the cover, this book is the result of a deeply collaborative process.

Most of all, I'd like to thank my wife, Barb, my son, Graham, and my stepdaughter, Nina, who have created for me a happy and fulfilling life that gives me the emotional strength to undertake the sustained effort required to write a book.

Writing this book has confirmed my belief in the creative power of collaboration. The hidden roots of my ideas in the works of past scientists, the frequent conversations I had with other scientists while writing the book, and the immediate and deep collaborations with Esmond and Jo Ann: All are part of the collaborative web that resulted in *Group Genius*. The book you hold isn't the one I originally planned to write, and it couldn't have been predicted when I started a year ago. That's the nature of group genius.

NOTES

Chapter 1

3 **The Wright brothers:** One competitor was Samuel Pierpont Langley, who received $50,000 from the U.S. Army (a fortune in today's dollars) to spend several years working on his Aerodrome. His final flight attempt crashed into the Potomac River in December 1903, just days before the Wright brothers' success. My sources include L. Wescott and P. Degen, *Wind and Sand: The Story of the Wright Brothers at Kitty Hawk* (Ft. Washington, PA: Eastern National, 1999), and S. Shulman, *Unlocking the Sky: Glenn Hammond Curtiss and the Race to Invent the Airplane* (New York: HarperCollins, 2002). The Wilbur Wright quotation is from page 19 of Wescott and Degen.

5 **The mountain bike:** For the early history, see Amici Design, *Fat Tire: A Celebration of the Mountain Bike* (San Francisco: Chronicle Books, 1999). Many histories of the mountain bike appear on the Web; see http://www.mtnbikehalloffame.com/history.cfm. The open-source nature of today's mountain bike evolution is analyzed in C. Lüthje, C. Herstatt, and E. von Hippel, "The Dominant Role of Local Information in User Innovation: The Case of Mountain Biking" (working paper, MIT Sloan School of Management, Cambridge, MA, 2002), http://userinnovation.mit.edu/papers/6.pdf.

8 **The history of creativity research:** See chapters 2, 3, and 4 of R. K. Sawyer, *Explaining Creativity: The Science of Human Innovation* (New York: Oxford, 2006).

8 **Freud, Monet, Renoir, and Einstein:** An analysis of the creative circles they worked in is found in M. P. Farrell, *Collaborative Circles: Friendship Dynamics and Creative Work* (Chicago: University of Chicago Press, 2001).

8   **On Freud's collaborations:** See P. Kirchner, *Freud's Dream: A Complete Interdisciplinary Science of Mind* (Cambridge, MA: MIT Press, 1992). Einstein worked closely with the mathematician Marcel Grossman; the collaborative emergence of quantum physics is documented in W. Heisenberg, *Physics and Beyond* (New York: Harper and Row, 1971), and G. Gamow, *Thirty Years That Shook Physics: The Story of Quantum Theory* (New York: Dover Publications, 1966).

9   **Jazz Freddy and improv theater:** R. K. Sawyer, *Improvised Dialogues: Emergence and Creativity in Conversation* (Westport, CT: Greenwood, 2003). "Freddy" doesn't mean anything; Chicago improv groups have a tradition of creating meaningless non sequiturs as names. To take some other examples, two other groups I studied were the Punk Mahonies and the Lost Yetis.

13   **Steelcase:** P. B. Brown, "What I Know Now," *Fast Company,* June 2005, 100.

13   **Target:** D. Sacks, "Be Cooler by Design," *Fast Company,* June 2005, 91–92. Quotation is on page 91.

13   **Whole Foods:** J. Pfeffer, "Putting People First," *Stanford Social Innovation Review* (Spring 2005): 27–33. Quotation is on page 28.

13   **The black box of collaboration:** Research that focuses on team composition is reviewed in several recent articles, and these reviews don't cite any research that analyzes the interactional dynamics of collaboration. Two examples are S. E. Jackson and A. Joshi, "Research on Domestic and International Diversity in Organizations: A Merger That Works," in vol. 2, *Handbook of Industrial, Work and Organizational Psychology,* ed. N. Anderson et al., 206–231 (Thousand Oaks, CA: Sage, 2002), and S. W. J. Kozlowski and B. S. Bell, "Work Groups and Teams in Organizations," in vol. 12, *Handbook of Psychology: Industrial and Organizational Psychology,* ed. W. C. Borman, D. R. Ilgen, and R. J. Klimoski, 333–375 (New York: Wiley, 2003).

13   **Interaction analysis:** R. K. Sawyer, "Analyzing Collaborative Discourse," in *Cambridge Handbook of the Learning Sciences,* ed. R. K. Sawyer, 187–204 (New York: Cambridge University Press, 2006).

14   **The improvisational team:** Many businesses have discovered the importance of improvisation. Second City and iO, the two best-known Chicago improv theater companies, each have a thriving side business facilitating workshops for executives. John Kao's 1996 book *Jamming* described jazz ensembles and used musical metaphors to provide advice to business teams. The management guru Karl Weick has been using improvisation as a metaphor for modern organizations for more than a decade. J. Kao,

Jamming: The Art and Discipline of Business Creativity (New York: Harper-Collins, 1996); K. E. Weick, *Making Sense of the Organization* (London: Blackwell, 2001).

17   **IDEO:** Much has been written about this company; my main sources include a book by general manager Tom Kelley and an academic journal article by two Stanford professors: T. Kelley, *The Art of Innovation: Lessons in Creativity from IDEO, America's Leading Design Firm* (New York: Doubleday, 2001); R. I. Sutton and A. B. Hargadon, "Brainstorming Groups in Context: Effectiveness in a Product Design Firm," *Administrative Science Quarterly* 41 (1996): 685–718.

18   **Gore:** A. Deutschman, "The Fabric of Creativity," *Fast Company,* December 2004, 54–62.

Chapter 2

21   **1980 southern Italian earthquake:** The improvised response following the Naples earthquake is reported in G. F. Lanzara, "Ephemeral Organizations in Extreme Environments: Emergence, Strategy, Extinction," *Journal of Management Studies* 20, no. 1 (1983): 71–95.

A similar analysis of the Hurricane Katrina response appears in T. Wachtendorf and J. M. Kendra, "Improvising Disaster in the City of Jazz: Organizational Response to Hurricane Katrina," in *Understanding Katrina: Perspectives from the Social Sciences* (New York: Social Science Research Council, 2005). A Web resource is provided by the Social Science Research Council at http://understandingkatrina.ssrc.org.

A broader overview of emergent responses to disasters can be found in T. E. Drabek, and D. A. McEntire, "Emergent Phenomena and Multiorganizational Coordination in Disasters: Lessons from the Research Literature," *International Journal of Mass Emergencies and Disasters* 20, no. 2 (2002): 197–224.

23   **Jazz Freddy:** I conducted a variety of research studies of improvised dialogues that are published in R. K. Sawyer, *Improvised Dialogues: Emergence and Creativity in Conversation* (Westport, CT: Greenwood, 2003).

23   **Script-think:** Psychologists and philosophers alike believe that this is a natural human tendency; see William James, as quoted and elaborated on page 123 of J. Dewey, *Art as Experience* (New York: Perigee Books, 1934).

G. H. Mead also wrote about how often we erroneously think we can predict the present by what came before; see G. H. Mead, *The Philosophy of the Present* (Chicago: University of Chicago Press, 1932).

23   **Honda motorcycles in the United States:** A 1996 article brings together articles by the key players, including BCG consultants, Pascale, and others: H. Mintzberg et al., "The 'Honda Effect' Revisited," *California Management Review* 38, no. 4 (1996): 78–117.

Pascale's original article: R. T. Pascale, "Perspectives on Strategy: The Real Story Behind Honda's Success," *California Management Review* 26, no. 3 (1984): 47–72.

25   **The USS *Palau*:** The name "Palau" is a pseudonym. See E. Hutchins, "Organizing Work by Adaptation," *Organization Science* 2, no. 1 (1991): 14–39.

28   **The Stanford product development study:** K. M. Eisenhardt and B. N. Tabrizi, "Accelerating Adaptive Processes: Product Innovation in the Global Computer Industry," *Administrative Science Quarterly* 40 (1995): 84–110.

29   **On-time projects earn 50 percent more:** In 1991, Joseph Vesey showed that high-technology products entering the market only six months late earn 33 percent less than products that are on time. Even if the late projects stay within budget, they still earn less than on-time projects that are 50 percent over budget: J. T. Vesey, "The New Competitors: They Think in Terms of Speed to Market," *Academy of Management Executive* 5, no. 2 (1991): 23–33.

29   **Children's game creation study:** D. J. Bearison and B. Dorval, *Collaborative Cognition: Children Negotiating Ways of Knowing* (Westport, CT: Albex, 2001).

30   **The OC school and playcrafting:** J. Baker-Sennett, E. Matusov, and B. Rogoff, "Sociocultural Processes of Creative Planning in Children's Playcrafting," in *Context and Cognition: Ways of Learning and Knowing,* ed. P. Light and G. Butterworth, 93–114 (Hillsdale, NJ: Lawrence Erlbaum Associates, 1992).

31   **FastTrack improvisations:** A. S. Miner, P. Bassoff, and C. Moorman, "Organizational Improvisation and Learning: A Field Study," *Administrative Science Quarterly* 46 (2001): 304–337.

33   **Improvisational teams are associated with technical innovation:** Research showing this includes A. T. Belasen, *Leading the Learning Organization: Communication and Competencies for Managing Change* (Albany, NY: SUNY Press, 2000); C. Moorman and A. S. Miner, "The Convergence of Planning and Execution: Improvisation in New Product Development," *Journal of Marketing* 62 (1998): 1–20; and K. E. Weick, *Making Sense of the Organization* (London: Blackwell, 2001).

34   **Self-managing teams are more adaptable:** See pages 325–336 of R. A. Guzzo and M. W. Dickson, "Teams in Organizations: Recent Research on

Performance and Effectiveness," *Annual Review of Psychology* 47 (1996): 307–338.

34   **Orpheus Chamber Orchestra:** I used two sources for this story: H. Seifter and P. Economy, *Leadership Ensemble: Lessons in Collaborative Management from the World's Only Conductorless Orchestra* (New York: Henry Holt, 2001). The story about the musician who stands up while they're playing is in Hackman's foreword to that book.

The quotations are all taken from J. Traub, "Passing the Baton: What CEOs Could Learn from the Orpheus Chamber Orchestra," *New Yorker,* August 26 and September 2, 1996, 100–105.

36   **Peter F. Drucker's new organization:** P. F. Drucker, "The Coming of the New Organization," *Harvard Business Review* 66, no. 1 (1988): 45–53.

36   **John Kao and jamming:** J. Kao, *Jamming: The Art and Discipline of Business Creativity* (New York: HarperCollins, 1996).

36   **Organizational theorists using the improvisation metaphor:** Influential publications include D. T. Bastien and T. J. Hostager, "Cooperation as Communicative Accomplishment: A Symbolic Interaction Analysis of an Improvised Jazz Concert," *Communication Studies* 43 (1992): 92–104; M. M. Crossan et al., "The Improvising Organization: Where Planning Meets Opportunity," *Organizational Dynamics* 24, no. 4 (1996): 20–35; M. Crossan and M. Sorrenti, "Making Sense of Improvisation," in vol. 14 of *Advances in Strategic Management,* ed. J. P. Walsh and A. Huff, 155–180 (Greenwich, CT: JAI Press, 1997); E. M. Eisenberg, "Jamming: Transcendence Through Organizing," *Communication Research* 17, no. 2 (1990): 139–164; M. J. Hatch, "Exploring the Empty Spaces of Organization: How Improvisational Jazz Helps Redescribe Organizational Structure," *Organizational Studies* 20, no. 1 (1999): 75–100; A. S. Miner, P. Bassoff, and C. Moorman, "Organizational Improvisation and Learning: A Field Study," *Administrative Science Quarterly* 46 (2001): 304–337; C. Moorman and A. S. Miner, "The Convergence of Planning and Execution: Improvisation in New Product Development," *Journal of Marketing* 62 (1998): 1–20; L. T. Perry, "Strategic Improvising: How to Formulate and Implement Competitive Strategies in Concert," *Organizational Dynamics* 19, no. 4 (1991): 51–64; and K. E. Weick, *Making Sense of the Organization* (London: Blackwell, 2001).

Chapter 3

39   **The Waukegan YMCA:** The story about Alan and Pip is told in J. B. Jimerson, "Interpersonal Flow in Pickup Basketball" (unpublished manuscript, Indiana University, Bloomington, 1999).

40   **Lincoln Park in Santa Monica:** See E. M. Eisenberg, "Jamming: Transcendence Through Organizing," *Communication Research* 17, no. 2 (1990): 139–164.

40   **West Fourth Street:** Two excellent sources are W. Martindale Jr., *Inside the Cage: A Season at West 4th Street's Legendary Tournament* (New York: Simon Spotlight Entertainment, 2006), and C. Ballard, *Hoops Nation: A Guide to America's Best Pickup Basketball* (Lincoln: University of Nebraska Press, 2004).

40   **Pickup basketball:** Two good books about New York City pickup basketball are P. Axthelm, *The City Game: Basketball from the Garden to the Playgrounds* (Lincoln: University of Nebraska Press, 1999), and R. Telander, *Heaven Is a Playground* (Lincoln: University of Nebraska Press, 1995).

This excellent anthology has wonderful articles about pickup basketball: D. Rudman, *Take It to the Hoop: A Basketball Anthology* (Richmond, CA: North Atlantic Books, 1980).

40   **Bill Russell:** The block quotation is from pages 155–157 of B. Russell and T. Branch, *Second Wind: The Memoirs of an Opinionated Man* (New York: Random House, 1979).

41   **"I was guarding Paul . . .":** Jimerson tells this story on page 14 of his "Interpersonal Flow in Pickup Basketball."

41   **Mihaly Csikszentmihalyi and flow:** M. Csikszentmihalyi, *Beyond Boredom and Anxiety* (San Francisco: Jossey-Bass, 1975). The quotation "a unified flowing . . ." is on page 43.

42   **Flow and work:** See two books by M. Csikszentmihalyi: *Good Business: Leadership, Flow, and the Making of Meaning* (New York: Viking, 2003), and *Flow: The Psychology of Optimal Experience* (New York: HarperCollins, 1990).

42   **Teresa Amabile found that flow fosters insight:** T. M. Amabile et al., "Affect and Creativity at Work," *Administrative Science Quarterly* 50 (2005): 367–403. Note that this is in contrast to the popular myth that mentally ill, depressed individuals are more likely to be creative.

43   **Flow happens in conversation:** Csikszentmihalyi, *Flow.*

43   **Managers get in flow while in conversation:** See page 818 of M. Csikszentmihalyi and J. LeFevre, "Optimal Experience in Work and Leisure," *Journal of Personality and Social Psychology* 56, no. 5 (1989): 815–822.

43   **Group flow participants are the highest performers:** R. Cross and A. Parker, "Charged Up: Creating Energy in Organizations," *Journal of Organizational Excellence* (2004): 3–14.

44   **Problem-finding and problem-solving creativity:** This distinction was first noted in the 1960s and has been widely studied by Mihaly Csikszentmihalyi

and others. See J. W. Getzels and M. Csikszentmihalyi, *The Creative Vision* (New York: Wiley, 1976).

44   **The biggest barrier to team performance is unclear objectives:** H. J. Thamhain and D. L. Wilemon, "Building High Performance Engineering Project Teams," *IEEE Transactions on Engineering Management* 34, no. 3 (1987): 130–137.

45   **3M's Post-it notes:** See pages 38–40 of 3M's official history, *A Century of Innovation*, which is available on the web at http://solutions.3m.com/wps/portal/3M/en_US/our/company/information/history/

45   **BMW and team competition:** G. Edmondson, "BMW's Dream Factory," *Business Week,* October 16, 2006, 70–80.

45   **Jeffrey Sweet on great Chicago improv:** J. Sweet, *Something Wonderful Right Away: An Oral History of the Second City & the Compass Players* (New York: Avon Books, 1978), xxxix.

46   **Curtis Fuller quotation:** P. Berliner, *Thinking in Jazz: The Infinite Art of Improvisation* (Chicago: University of Chicago Press, 1994), 389.

47   **Quotation about the energizing manager:** Page 10 of R. Cross and A. Parker, "Charged Up: Creating Energy in Organizations," *Journal of Organizational Excellence* (2004): 3–14.

47   **People who listen closely are energizing:** R. Cross, W. Baker, and A. Parker, "What Creates Energy in Organizations?" *MIT Sloan Management Review* 44, no. 4 (2003): 51–56.

47   **Csikszentmihalyi basketball player quotation:** Csikszentmihalyi, *Beyond Boredom and Anxiety,* 40.

47   **High-pressure deadlines block flow:** T. Amabile, C. N. Hadley, and S. J. Kramer, "Creativity Under the Gun," *Harvard Business Review* 80, no. 8 (2002): 52–61.

48   **IDEO and T-shirts:** Page 96 of T. Kelley, *The Art of Innovation: Lessons in Creativity from IDEO, America's Leading Design Firm* (New York: Doubleday, 2001).

48   **The downside of complete concentration, at SeeFoods and FastTrack:** Pages 321–324 of A. S. Miner, P. Bassoff, and C. Moorman, "Organizational Improvisation and Learning: A Field Study," *Administrative Science Quarterly* 46 (2001): 304–337.

49   **Patagonia and Michael Crooke:** A. Marsh, "The Art of Work," *Fast Company,* August 2005, 76.

49   **Patagonia and Yves Chouinard:** Csikszentmihalyi, *Good Business.*

49   **Autonomy contributes to group flow:** R. W. Quinn and J. E. Dutton, "Coordination as Energy-in-Conversation," *Academy of Management Review* 30, no. 1 (2005): 36–57.

49   **Team autonomy predicts performance:** One of many studies with this finding is M. Jabri, "Job-Team: Its Dimensionality and Importance in the Management of R & D Teams" (PhD diss., Manchester Business School, Manchester, England, 1985).

50   **David Byrne quotation:** Page 49 of R. F. Thompson, "David Byrne: The Rolling Stone Interview," *Rolling Stone,* April 21, 1988, 42–52, 116.

50   **"He is animated and engaged with you" quotation:** Page 54 of R. Cross, W. Baker, and A. Parker, "What Creates Energy in Organizations?" *MIT Sloan Management Review* 44, no. 4 (2003): 51–56.

50   **"We had been working like crazy on this project" quotation:** Page 11 of R. Cross and A. Parker, "Charged Up: Creating Energy in Organizations," *Journal of Organizational Excellence* (2004): 3–14.

51   **Social network analysis, managers, and flow:** Both the petrochemical organization and the government agency are described in, Cross and Parker, "Charged Up," 3–14.

51   **"You gotta know how to play with them":** Jimerson, "Interpersonal Flow in Pickup Basketball," 24.

51   **Shared understandings and team effectiveness:** In the social psychological literature this is sometimes referred to as team coherence; see page 347 of S. W. J. Kozlowski and B. S. Bell, "Work Groups and Teams in Organizations," in vol. 12, *Handbook of Psychology: Industrial and Organizational Psychology,* ed. W. C. Borman, D. R. Ilgen, and R. J. Klimoski (New York: Wiley, 2003) 333–375.

   Also see R. W. Quinn, "Flow in Knowledge Work: Performance Experience in the Design of National Security Technology," *Administrative Science Quarterly* 50 (2005): 610–641.

51   **Tacit knowledge and team effectiveness:** See D. Leonard and S. Sensiper, "The Role of Tacit Knowledge in Group Innovation," *California Management Review* 40, no. 3 (1998): 112–132.

52   **Group flow fades after a few years:** Page 376 of K. E. Weick and K. H. Roberts, "Collective Mind in Organizations: Heedful Interrelating on Flight Decks," *Administrative Science Quarterly* 38 (1993): 357–381.

52   **Familiarity and effectiveness:** This research is summarized in two review articles: R. A. Guzzo and M. W. Dickson, "Teams in Organizations: Recent Research on Performance and Effectiveness," *Annual Review of Psychology* 47 (1996): 307–338, and Kozlowski and Bell, "Work Groups and Teams in Organizations."

53   **Balancing the nature of the goal and the degree of shared knowledge:** I elaborate this balance in R. K. Sawyer, *Group Creativity: Music, Theater, Collaboration* (Mahwah, NJ: Erlbaum, 2003).

53 **Stefan Falk at Ericsson:** A. Marsh, "The Art of Work," *Fast Company,* August 2005, 76.

54 **FastTrack's unreliable part:** Miner, Bassoff, and Moorman, "Organizational Improvisation and Learning," 312.

54 **Franklin Gordon quotation:** Berliner, *Thinking in Jazz,* 388.

55 **Jimmy Robinson quotation:** Ibid., page 357.

55 **Deliberate practice:** K. A. Ericsson, R. T. Krampe, and C. Tesch-Römer, "The Role of Deliberate Practice in the Acquisition of Expert Performance," *Psychological Review* 100, no. 3 (1993): 273–305.

56 **Sid Caesar and *Your Show of Shows*:** B. Fischer and A. Boynton, "Virtuoso Teams," *Harvard Business Review* 83, no. 4 (2005): 117–123. Also see A. Boynton and B. Fischer, *Virtuoso Teams: Lessons from Teams That Changed Their Worlds* (Harlow, England: Pearson Education Limited, 2005).

57 **Mel Brooks quotation:** Page 26 of T. Sennett, *Your Show of Shows* (New York: Macmillan, 1977).

57 **The global war for talent:** A. Wooldridge, "The Battle for Brainpower" (survey), *Economist,* October 7, 2006.

Chapter 4

59 **Osborn's brainstorming:** A. F. Osborn, *Applied Imagination: Principles and Procedures of Creative Problem Solving,* 3rd ed. (Buffalo, NY: Creative Education Foundation Press, 1963). (The first edition of the book was published in 1953.)

60 **IDEO and brainstorming:** There are two good sources; the second one is by IDEO's general manager Tom Kelley: R. I. Sutton and A. B. Hargadon, "Brainstorming Groups in Context: Effectiveness in a Product Design Firm," *Administrative Science Quarterly* 41 (1996): 685–718, and T. Kelley, *The Art of Innovation: Lessons in Creativity from IDEO, America's Leading Design Firm* (New York: Doubleday, 2001).

60 **Groups led by a trained facilitator perform better:** A. K. Offner, T. J. Kramer, and J. P. Winter, "The Effects of Facilitation, Recording, and Pauses on Group Brainstorming," *Small Group Research* 27, no. 2 (1996): 283–298; N. L. Oxley, M. T. Dzindolet, and P. B. Paulus, "The Effects of Facilitators on the Performance of Brainstorming Groups," *Journal of Social Behavior and Personality* 11, no. 4 (1996): 633–646.

61 **The first study of Osborn's technique:** D. W. Taylor, P. C. Berry, and C. H. Block, "Does Group Participation When Using Brainstorming Facilitate or Inhibit Creative Thinking?" *Administrative Science Quarterly* 3, no. 1 (1958): 23–47.

61   **Replication of Taylor study findings:** Two good reviews of the history of brainstorming research were authored by M. Diehl and W. Stroebe: "Productivity Loss in Brainstorming Groups: Toward the Solution of a Riddle," *Journal of Personality and Social Psychology* 53, no. 3 (1987): 497–509, and "Why Groups Are Less Effective Than Their Members: On Productivity Losses in Idea-Generating Groups," *European Review of Social Psychology* 5 (1994): 271–303.

62   **Another set of instructions that works even better:** V. S. Gerlach et al., "Effects of Variations in Test Directions on Originality Test Response," *Journal of Educational Psychology* 55, no. 2 (1964): 79–83. Similar results were reported in D. M. Johnson, G. L. Parrott, and R. P. Stratton, "Production and Judgment of Solutions to Five Problems," *Journal of Educational Psychology* 59, no. 6 (1968): 1–21 (part 2, monograph supplement).

63   **1961 Purdue study:** E. Weisskopf-Joelson and T. S. Eliseo, "An Experimental Study of the Effectiveness of Brainstorming," *Journal of Applied Psychology* 45, no. 1 (1961): 45–49.

63   **Groups are better at evaluating ideas:** T. S. Larey, "Convergent and Divergent Thinking, Group Composition, and Creativity in Brainstorming Groups" (PhD diss., University of Texas, 1994). A more recent study also underlined the importance of evaluation: E. F. Rietzschel, B. A. Nijstad, and W. Stroebe, "Productivity Is Not Enough: A Comparison of Interactive and Nominal Brainstorming Groups on Idea Generation and Selection," *Journal of Experimental Social Psychology* 42 (2006): 244–251.

64   **Study of brainstorming in a company with a strong team culture:** P. B. Paulus, T. S. Larey, and A. H. Ortega, "Performance and Perceptions of Brainstormers in an Organizational Setting," *Basic and Applied Social Psychology* 17 (1995): 249–265.

64   **Productivity loss is greater in larger groups:** T. J. Bouchard and M. Hare, "Size, Performance, and Potential in Brainstorming Groups," *Journal of Applied Psychology* 54, no. 1 (1970): 51–55.

65   **Groups get fixated faster:** T. S. Larey and P. B. Paulus, "Group Preference and Convergent Tendencies in Small Groups: A Content Analysis of Group Brainstorming Performance," *Creativity Research Journal* 12, no. 3 (1999): 175–184.

65   **Electronic brainstorming:** A. R. Dennis and J. S. Valacich, "Computer Brainstorms: More Heads Are Better Than One," *Journal of Applied Psychology* 78, no. 4 (1993): 531–537. Also see the citations on page 687 of Sutton and Hargadon, "Brainstorming Groups in Context."

65   **Social inhibition and social loafing:** See M. Diehl and W. Stroebe, "Productivity Loss in Idea-Generating Groups: Tracking Down the Blocking Effect," *Journal of Personality and Social Psychology* 61 (1991): 392–403; also

Diehl and Stroebe, "Productivity Loss in Brainstorming Groups," 497–509.

65   **Presence of an expert increases productivity loss:** P. A. Collaros and L. R. Anderson, "Effect of Perceived Expertness upon Creativity of Members of Brainstorming Groups," *Journal of Applied Psychology* 53 (1969): 159–163.

66   **Individual assessment increases productivity and quality:** Diehl and Stroebe, "Productivity Loss in Brainstorming Groups," 497–509.

66   **The illusion of group effectiveness:** Paulus, Larey, and Ortega, "Performance and Perceptions," 249–265. Brainstorming groups are more likely to be in flow: See citations on page 687 of Sutton and Hargadon, "Brainstorming Groups in Context." Brainstormers don't think they're being inhibited or blocked: P. B. Paulus, T. S. Larey, and M. T. Dzindolet, "Creativity in Groups and Teams," in *Groups at Work: Theory and Research,* ed. M. Turner (Mahwah, NJ: Erlbaum, 2001), 319–338.

66   **Groupthink:** I. L. Janis, *Victims of Groupthink: A Psychological Study of Foreign-Policy Decisions and Fiascos* (Boston: Houghton Mifflin, 1972). The group of smokers story is on page 8.

69   **Gear problem learning:** D. L. Schwartz, "The Emergence of Abstract Representations in Dyad Problem Solving," *Journal of the Learning Sciences* 4, no. 3 (1995): 321–354. Schwartz believes that groups will always perform worse than individuals unless there is some collaborative creation of a visual representation (page 350).

69   **IDEO's new rules:** The "be visual" rule is in A. Boynton and B. Fischer, *Virtuoso Teams: Lessons from Teams That Changed Their Worlds* (Harlow, England: Pearson Education Limited, 2005); the other two are in Kelley, *The Art of Innovation.*

71   **Diverse groups perform better:** Two literature reviews survey the research on this topic: S. E. Jackson, K. E. May, and K. Whitney, "Understanding the Dynamics of Diversity in Decision-Making Teams," in *Team Effectiveness and Decision Making in Organizations,* ed. R. A. Guzzo and E. Salas (San Francisco: Jossey-Bass, 1995), 204–261, and R. A. Guzzo and M. W. Dickson, "Teams in Organizations: Recent Research on Performance and Effectiveness," *Annual Review of Psychology* 47 (1996): 307–338.

An unpublished study by Diehl from 1992 is described in W. Stroebe and M. Diehl, "Why Groups Are Less Effective Than Their Members: On Productivity Losses in Idea-Generating Groups," *European Review of Social Psychology* 5 (1994): 271–303.

71   **Innovative banks have diverse management teams:** K. A. Bantel and S. E. Jackson, "Top Management and Innovations in Banking: Does the Composition of the Top Team Make a Difference? *Strategic Management Journal* 1 (1989): 107–124.

71   **Friction, conflict, and team creativity:** Several studies showing that diversity results in greater creativity are cited in T. R. Kurtzberg and T. Amabile, "From Guilford to Creative Synergy: Opening the Black Box of Team-Level Creativity," *Creativity Research Journal* 13, nos. 3 and 4 (2000–2001): 285–294. Other studies, however, suggest that the conflict can reduce productivity: F. Milliken and L. Martins, "Searching for Common Threads: Understanding the Multiple Effects of Diversity in Organizational Groups," *Academy of Management Review* 21 (1996): 402–433.

71   **Conflict can increase performance:** Page 116 of D. Leonard and S. Straus, "Putting Your Company's Brain to Work," *Harvard Business Review* 75, no. 5 (1997): 110–121. The benefits of conflict are a key theme in these two business books: D. Leonard and W. C. Swap, *When Sparks Fly: Igniting Creativity in Groups* (Boston: Harvard Business School Press, 1999), and W. Bennis and P. W. Biederman, *Organizing Genius: The Secrets of Creative Collaboration* (Reading, MA: Addison-Wesley, 1997).

71   **John Seely Brown quotation:** Pages 169–170 of M. Stefik and B. Stefik, *Breakthrough: Stories and Strategies of Radical Innovation* (Cambridge, MA: MIT Press, 2004).

71   **Effective diversity requires a collective team identity:** G. S. Van der Vegt and J. S. Bunderson, "Learning and Performance in Multidisciplinary Teams: The Importance of Collective Team Identification," *Academy of Management Journal* 48, no. 3 (2005): 532–547; M. Landsberg and M. Pfau, "Developing Diversity: Lessons from Top Teams," *Strategy+Business* (Winter 2005): 10–11.

71   **The Medici Effect:** F. Johansson, *The Medici Effect: Breakthrough Insights at the Intersection of Ideas, Concepts, and Cultures* (Boston: Harvard Business School Press, 2004).

71   **Paul Saffo quotation:** Stefik and Stefik, *Breakthrough,* 168.

72   **Ruth Wageman study of group rewards:** The study was of the U.S. Customer Service division, with twelve thousand people who repair machines, working in teams of three to nine people. R. Wageman, "Interdependence and Group Effectiveness," *Administrative Science Quarterly* 40 (1995): 145–180.

72   **No evidence of social loafing:** Ruth Wageman, personal communication.

73   **Task interdependence and rewards:** This research is reviewed in J. S. DeMatteo, L. T. Eby, and E. Sundstrom, "Team-Based Rewards: Current Empirical Evidence and Directions for Future Research," *Research in Organizational Behavior* 20 (1998): 141–183.

73   **French sociologist Gustave Le Bon:** This classic work on groups is G. Le Bon, *The Crowd: A Study of the Popular Mind* (London: T. Fisher Unwin

Ltd., 1895/1896). Originally published as *Psychologie des foules* (Paris: Alcan, 1895).

73   **Take frequent breaks:** Taking brief five-minute pauses enhances productivity, as demonstrated in an unpublished study by E. M. Horn, 1993, described on page 325 of Paulus, Larey, and Dzindolet, "Creativity in Groups and Teams," 319–338.

73   **Low social anxiety increases group performance:** L. M. Camacho and P. B. Paulus, "The Role of Social Anxiousness in Group Brainstorming," *Journal of Personality and Social Psychology* 68 (1995): 1071–1080.

Chapter 5

77   **The Inklings:** My main source for this story is Michael Farrell's wonderful book: M. P. Farrell, *Collaborative Circles: Friendship Dynamics and Creative Work* (Chicago: University of Chicago Press, 2001).

When Tolkien and Lewis first met, Lewis had already published a book of poetry, but he didn't start writing about mythical creatures until inspired by the Inklings. Tolkien's hobby was completely secret, and Lewis encouraged him to publish. In addition to the Tuesday night pub sessions, the group regularly met on Thursday nights in Lewis's rooms. Although Oxford largely rejected Christianity, a few old Newmanites (followers of Cardinal Newman's nineteenth-century revival of English Catholicism) were still around (Farrell, personal communication).

The Tolkien quotation "vague or half-formed ideas" is from J. R. R. Tolkien, "Letter to William Luther White," in *Letters of J. R. R. Tolkien,* ed. H. Carter and C. Tolkien (London: Allen and Unwin, 1967), 387.

78   **T. S. Eliot:** For example, the original manuscripts of Eliot's "Waste Land," with extensive edits by Pound and Eliot's wife, have been published as T. S. Eliot, *The Waste Land: A Facsimile and Transcript of the Original Drafts Including the Annotations of Ezra Pound* (New York: Harcourt Brace Jovanovich, 1971).

79   **John Reed's consumer bank:** P. L. Zweig, *Wriston: Walter Wriston, Citibank and the Rise and Fall of American Financial Supremacy* (New York: Crown, 1995).

The quotation from my interview was first published in M. Csikszentmihalyi and R. K. Sawyer, "Shifting the Focus from Individual to Organizational Creativity," in *Creative Action in Organizations,* ed. C. M. Ford and D. A. Gioia, 167–173 (Thousand Oaks, CA: Sage, 1995).

80   **The cash machine:** Docutel and Don Wetzel were issued the patent for the cash machine in 1973, and are recognized as the inventors of the ATM

by the Smithsonian's National Museum of American History. But as with every other invention, there is a long sequence of prior, related inventions; these range from a 1939 version by Luther Simjian to a 1967 version by John Shepherd-Barron installed at a branch of Barclay's Bank in Enfield, near London. Docutel's was the first machine to use a card with a magnetic stripe, and the first to network the ATM to the bank's central computer. E. Florian, D. Burke, and J. Merro, "The Money Machines," *Fortune,* July 26, 2004.

81   **The stages of creativity:** R. K. Sawyer, *Explaining Creativity: The Science of Human Innovation* (New York: Oxford, 2006).

82   **Hubble space telescope:** The official NASA history is available on the Internet: J. N. Tatarewicz, "The Hubble Space Telescope Serving Mission," in *From Engineering to Big Science: The NASA History Series,* ed. P. E. Mack (Washington, DC: NASA History Office, 1998), chap. 16, http://history.nasa.gov/SP-4219/Chapter16.html. In October 2006, NASA approved a shuttle mission, to take place in 2008, to service and upgrade the Hubble telescope to extend its working life.

85   **Duncker's 1926 study:** K. Duncker, "A Qualitative (Experimental and Theoretical) Study of Productive Thinking (Solving of Comprehensive Problems)," *The Pedagogical Seminary and Journal of Genetic Psychology* 33 (1926): 642–708.

85   **The x-ray problem:** This version is taken from pages 307–308 of M. L. Gick and K. J. Holyoak, "Analogical Problem Solving," *Cognitive Psychology* 12 (1980): 306–355.

86   **Janet Metcalfe's metacognition studies:** J. Metcalfe, "Feeling of Knowing in Memory and Problem Solving," *Journal of Experimental Psychology: Learning, Memory, and Cognition* 12, no. 2 (1986): 288–294; J. Metcalfe and D. Wiebe, "Intuition in Insight and Noninsight Problem Solving," *Memory & Cognition* 15, no. 3 (1987): 238–246.

87   **Weisberg and Alba insight studies:** R. W. Weisberg and J. W. Alba, "An Examination of the Alleged Role of 'Fixation' in the Solution of Several 'Insight' Problems," *Journal of Experimental Psychology: General* 110, no. 2 (1981): 169–192.

89   **Mary Gick and solving similar problems first:** R. S. Lockhart, M. Lamon, and M. L. Gick, "Conceptual Transfer in Simple Insight Problems," *Memory & Cognition* 16, no. 1 (1988): 36–44. This finding is also explained by the theory of case-based reasoning, associated with Roger Shank and summarized in J. L. Kolodner, "Case-Based Reasoning," in *The Cambridge Handbook of the Learning Sciences,* ed. R. K. Sawyer (New York: Cambridge University Press, 2006), 225–242.

91   **Coleridge and Kubla Khan:** J. L. Lowes, *The Road to Xanadu: A Study in the Ways of the Imagination* (Boston: Houghton Mifflin, 1927); E. Schneider, *Coleridge, Opium, and Kubla Khan* (Chicago: University of Chicago Press, 1953).

92   **Norman Maier's two-rope problem:** N. R. F. Maier, "Reasoning in Humans, II: The Solution of a Problem and Its Appearance in Consciousness," *Journal of Comparative Psychology* 12 (1931): 181–194.

93   **Confabulation:** Confabulation is based on "a priori, implicit causal theories," according to R. E. Nisbett and T. D. Wilson, "Telling More Than We Can Know: Verbal Reports on Mental Processes," *Psychological Review* 84, no. 3 (1977): 231–259.

93   **Schunn and Dunbar study of biology problems:** C. D. Schunn and K. Dunbar, "Priming and Awareness in Complex Reasoning," *Memory & Cognition* 24 (1996): 271–284.

95   **Remote Associates Test:** S. A. Mednick, "The Associative Basis of the Creative Process," *Psychological Review* 69, no. 3 (1962): 220–232.

96   **Kenneth Bowers and the fifteen-word task:** K. Bowers et al., "Intuition in the Context of Discovery," *Cognitive Psychology* 22 (1990): 72–110.

Chapter 6

99   **Morse and the telegraph:** T. Standage, *The Victorian Internet: The Remarkable Story of the Telegraph and the Nineteenth Century's On-Line Pioneers* (New York: Walker and Company, 1998).

103   **Anne Lamott's writing style:** A. Lamott, *Bird by Bird: Some Instructions on Writing and Life* (New York: Pantheon Books), 38.

103   **Charles Darwin and evolution by natural selection:** H. E. Gruber, *Darwin on Man: A Psychological Study of Scientific Creativity* (Chicago: University of Chicago Press, 1974); L. Eiseley, *Darwin's Century: Evolution and the Men Who Discovered It* (Garden City, NJ: Doubleday, 1958).

105   **Morse's dead ends:** T. Standage, *The Victorian Internet: The Remarkable Story of the Telegraph and the Nineteenth Century's On-Line Pioneers* (New York: Walker and Company, 1998).

106   **Darwin's dead ends:** H. E. Gruber, *Darwin on Man: A Psychological Study of Scientific Creativity* (Chicago: University of Chicago Press, 1974).

107   **Simonton and historiometry:** D. K. Simonton, "Creative Productivity: A Predictive and Explanatory Model of Career Trajectories and Landmarks," *Psychological Review* 104, no. 1 (1997): 66–89; D. K. Simonton, "Creativity from a Historiometric Perspective," in *The Handbook of Creativity,* ed. R. J. Sternberg (New York: Cambridge University Press, 1999),

116–133. The data for the graph on p. 108 are for papers published in the journal *Econometrica* and were reported in H. A. Simon, *Models of Man, Social and Rational* (New York: Wiley, 1957).

109   **Sir Harold Kroto quotation:** *All Our Futures: Creativity, Culture and Education* (London: National Advisory Committee on Creative and Cultural Education, 1999), 34, http://www.dfes.gov.uk/naccce/naccce.pdf.

109   **Intel's Mary Murphy-Hoye quotation:** Interview with Robert Sutton by P. LaBarre, "Fresh Start 2002: Weird Ideas That Work," *Fast Company,* January 2002, 68.

109   **Product Development and Management Association 2004 survey:** http://www.pdma.org/cpas.php.

109   **Alessi's failures:** I. Wylie, "Failure Is Glorious," *Fast Company,* October 2001, 35.

110   **Edison's light bulb sockets:** R. Friedel and P. Israel, *Edison's Electric Light: Biography of an Invention* (New Brunswick, NJ: Rutgers University Press, 1986). Also see R. Corot, *A Streak of Luck* (New York: Seaview Books, 1979), 187.

110   **James Fitch and the steamboat:** H. Evans, *They Made America* (New York: Little, Brown, 2004).

111   **Gick and Holyoak study of the x-ray problem:** M. L. Gick and K. J. Holyoak, "Analogical Problem Solving," *Cognitive Psychology* 12 (1980): 306–355.

114   **James Hampton and concept pairs:** J. A. Hampton, "Emergent Attributes in Combined Concepts," in *Creative Thought: An Investigation of Conceptual Structures and Processes,* ed. T. B. Ward, S. M. Smith, and J. Vaid (Washington, DC: American Psychological Association, 1997), 83–110.

114   **Edward Wisniewski and Dedre Gentner studies of combination:** E. J. Wisniewski and D. Gentner, "On the Combinatorial Semantics of Noun Pairs: Minor and Major Adjustments to Meaning," in *Understanding Word and Sentence,* ed. G. B. Simpson, 241–284 (New York: Elsevier, 1991).

115   **Connections between distant concepts are more creative:** A recent neuroimaging study presented subjects with either three related words (magician, trick, rabbit) or three unrelated words (flea, sing, sword), and asked them to create a simple story using all three words. The stories that were made with the unrelated words were judged to be about 50 percent more creative, on average. P. A. Howard-Jones et al., "Semantic Divergence and Creative Story Generation: An fMRI Investigation," *Cognitive Brain Research* 25 (2005): 240–250.

115   **For many concepts, properties interact:** D. L. Medin and E. J. Shoben, "Context and Structure in Conceptual Combination," *Cognitive Psychology* 20 (1988): 158–190.

116   **Arm & Hammer Baking Soda:** The official company history is available at http://www.churchdwight.com/Company/corp_history.asp. Additional details of the 1972 decision can be found in D. C. Minton, "Facts, Fables, and Our Environment" (1998), http://www.uwyo.edu/enr/ienr/DistinguishedSpeakers/MintonApr98.asp.

117   **Thomas Ward's studies of extraterrestrials:** T. B. Ward, "Structured Imagination: The Role of Category Structure in Exemplar Generation," *Cognitive Psychology* 2 (1994): 1–40.

118   **Morphological analysis with board games:** This table is adapted from a talk given by Jeff Stamp at Syracuse University in 2004.

119   **Ad-hoc concepts:** L. W. Barsalou, "Ad Hoc Categories," *Memory & Cognition* 11, no. 3 (1983): 211–227.

120   **Ad-hoc concepts have graded structure:** L. W. Barsalou, "Ideals, Central Tendency, and Frequency of Instantiation as Determinants of Graded Structure in Categories," *Journal of Experimental Psychology: Learning, Memory, and Cognition* 11, no. 4 (1985): 629–654.

120   **Visual imagery:** R. Finke, *Creative Imagery: Discoveries and Inventions in Visualization* (Hillsdale, NJ: Erlbaum, 1990). The Invention Exercise on p. 121 is adapted from page 41 (© 1990 Lawrence Erlbaum Associates, Inc.; reprinted by permission).

124   **The ten-year rule:** H. Gardner, *Creating Minds* (New York: Basic Books, 1993); K. A. Ericsson, "Attaining Excellence Through Deliberate Practice: Insights from the Study of Expert Performance," in *The Pursuit of Excellence in Education,* ed. M. Ferrari (Hillsdale, NJ: Erlbaum, 2002), 21–55.

Chapter 7

127   **Dunbar's studies of lab conversations:** K. Dunbar, "How Scientists Think: On-Line Creativity and Conceptual Change in Science," in *Creative Thought: An Investigation of Conceptual Structures and Processes,* ed. T. B. Ward, S. M. Smith, and J. Vaid (Washington, DC: American Psychological Association, 1997), 461–493.

129   **Synectics:** Transcript is from W. J. J. Gordon, *Synectics: The Development of Creative Capacity* (New York: Harper, 1961), 41–42. The method is still practiced by Synectics, which is still based in Cambridge, MA: www.synecticsworld.com.

131   **Art Markman's study of LEGO spaceship models:** A. B. Markman, T. Yamauchi, and V. S. Makin, "The Creation of New Concepts: A Multifaceted Approach to Category Learning," in *Creative Thought: An Investigation of*

Conceptual Structures and Processes, ed. T. B. Ward, S. M. Smith, and J. Vaid (Washington, DC: American Psychological Association, 1997), 179–208.

132   **Vera John-Steiner and creative collaboration:** V. John-Steiner, *Creative Collaboration* (New York: Oxford University Press, 2000). The Kaplan and Rose quotation is on page 97; the Ochs and Schieffelin quotation is on page 110.

133   **Monet and the circle of impressionists:** M. P. Farrell, *Collaborative Circles: Friendship Dynamics and Creative Work* (Chicago: University of Chicago Press, 2001), 44. The story about how Monet and Renoir couldn't remember who painted what is on page 40.

133   **Quotation from Picasso's biographer:** J. Richardson, *A Life of Picasso: Volume 1, 1881–1906* (New York: Random House, 1991, 1996), 334.

134   **Picasso on Braque:** F. Gilot and C. Lake, *Life with Picasso* (New York: McGraw-Hill, 1964), 76.

134   **Picasso and Braque both signed the back:** J. Richardson, *A Life of Picasso: Volume 2, 1907–1917* (New York: Random House, 1991, 1996), 238.

134   **Ronald Carter's CANCODE corpus:** R. Carter, *Language and Creativity: The Art of Common Talk* (New York: Routledge, 2004). The transcript is from pages 104–105.

136   **Theresa and Tony's conversation:** This originally appeared on page 40 of R. W. Quinn and J. E. Dutton, "Coordination as Energy-in-Conversation," *Academy of Management Journal* 30, no. 1 (2005): 36–57.

138   **Computer Motion's AESOP:** J. Suomala et al., "Chance Discovery as a First Step to Economic Innovation" (paper presented at the CogSci 2006, Vancouver, BC, Canada, July 26–29, 2006).

139   **Cartoon Network conversation:** A. Wilkinson, "Moody Toons: The King of the Cartoon Network," *New Yorker,* May 27, 2002, 76–81.

140   **Indexical speech:** S. C. Levinson, *Pragmatics* (New York: Cambridge University Press, 1983). The 90 percent estimate appears in Y. Bar-Hillel, "Indexical Expressions," *Mind* 63, no. 251 (1954): 359–379.

142   **Michael Silverstein's study:** M. Silverstein, "Indexical Order and the Dialectics of Sociolinguistic Life" (paper presented at the SALSA III, Austin, TX, 1954).

143   **Japan and indirect speech:** Y. Yokochi and B. J. Hall, "Exploring the Communication/Culture Connection," in *Constituting Cultural Differences Through Discourse,* ed. M. J. Collier (Thousand Oaks, CA: Sage, 2001), 189–214. The transcript is on page 202.

144   **Andrew Hargadon's study of equivocality:** A. B. Hargadon, "Firms as Knowledge Brokers: Lessons in Pursuing Continuous Innovation," *California Management Review* 40, no. 3 (1998): 209–227. The Reebok pump shoe story is on page 215.

146   **GlaxoSmithKline, Siemens, Ispat, and BP:** M. T. Hansen and B. V. Oetinger, "Introducing T-Shaped Managers," *Harvard Business Review* 79, no. 3 (2001): 106–116. The David Nagel quotation is on page 6.

146   **OceanConnect.com:** A case study is available at http://www.boozallen .com/about/article/658434.

146   **Hypertext organizations:** I. Nonaka and H. Takeuchi, *The Knowledge-Creating Company: How Japanese Companies Create the Dynamics of Innovation* (New York: Oxford University Press, 1995).

Chapter 8

153   **Semco:** The best sources for Semco are both by R. Semler: *Maverick: The Success Story Behind the World's Most Unusual Workplace* (New York: Warner Business Books, 1993), and "Managing Without Managers," *Harvard Business Review* 67, no. 5 (1989): 76–84. Also see S. Caulkin, "Who's in Charge Here? No One," *Observer* (London), Sunday, April 27, 2003. The $212 million 2003 revenue figure is from R. Semler, *The Seven Day Weekend: Changing the Way Work Works* (New York: Portfolio, 2004). The quotation "That's not a lack of structure . . ." is on page 7 of the 1989 *HBR* article.

155   **Limit operating units to fewer than four hundred employees:** J. B. Quinn, "Managing Innovation: Controlled Chaos," *Harvard Business Review* 63, no. 3 (1985): 73–80. Hewlett-Packard has long insisted on keeping all units smaller than one thousand people; page 19 of M. Jelinek and C. B. Schoonhoven, *The Innovation Marathon: Lessons from High Technology Firms* (Oxford: Basil Blackwell, 1990).

155   **Proto-human bands did not exceed 150 people:** R. Dunbar, *Grooming, Gossip, and the Evolution of Language* (Cambridge, MA: Harvard University Press, 1996). Dunbar's hypothesis is that this is the maximum size at which primate bands can sustain their main form of social bonding, which is grooming each other's fur.

156   **John Reed's network:** M. Csikszentmihalyi and R. K. Sawyer, "Creative Insight: The Social Dimension of a Solitary Moment," in *The Nature of Insight,* ed. R. J. Sternberg and J. E. Davidson, 329–363 (Cambridge, MA: MIT Press).

156   **Traditional organization theory emphasizes planning:** Examples include J. G. March and H. A. Simon, *Organizations* (New York: Wiley, 1958), and K. D. MacKenzie, "Virtual Positions and Power," *Management Science* 32 (1986): 622–642.

156   **Karl Weick:** K. E. Weick, *The Social Psychology of Organizing* (Reading, MA: Addison-Wesley, 1969).

156   **Flatter organizational structures:** In the 1980s, three scholars were ahead of the curve on this: Drucker, Kanter, and Mintzberg. See P. F. Drucker, "The Coming of the New Organization," *Harvard Business Review* 66, no. 1 (1988): 45–53; R. M. Kanter, *The Change Masters: Innovation and Entrepreneurship in the American Corporation* (New York: Simon & Schuster, 1983); and H. Mintzberg, *Structure in Fives: Designing Effective Organizations* (Englewood Cliffs, NJ: Prentice-Hall, 1983).

156   **Team-based companies perform better than bureaucratic firms:** Pages 326–331 of R. A. Guzzo and M. W. Dickson, "Teams in Organizations: Recent Research on Performance and Effectiveness," *Annual Review of Psychology* 47 (1996): 307–338.

157   **Innovation labs:** See T. Kelley and J. Littman, *The Ten Faces of Innovation: IDEO's Strategies for Defeating the Devil's Advocate and Driving Creativity Throughout Your Organization* (New York: Doubleday, 2005), 193–214.

157   **Multifunctional teams have quicker product development times:** K. M. Eisenhardt and B. N. Tabrizi, "Accelerating Adaptive Processes: Product Innovation in the Global Computer Industry," *Administrative Science Quarterly* 40 (1995): 84–110.

157   **Moto City, P&G's Clay Street Project, Fisher-Price and the Cave:** J. Weber, "'Mosh Pits' of Creativity," *Business Week,* November 7, 2005, 98–100.

157   **Sony's collaborations and the Network Walkman:** Interview with Ellen Glassman of Sony in J. Vilaga, "One Design Does Not Fit All," *Fast Company,* June 2005, 44, and M. Singer, "Stringer's Way: Can Sony's British C.E.O. Save an Ailing Brand?" *New Yorker,* June 5, 2006.

158   **Ivy Ross quotation:** D. Womack, "Project Platypus: Reinventing Product Development at Mattel," *Gain: Journal of Business and Design,* March 6, 2003. Note: In 2004, Ross moved to Old Navy as executive VP of product design and development.

158   **Linear innovation:** Here are two classic analyses from the 1960s: T. Burns and G. M. Stalker, *The Management of Innovation* (London: Tavistock Publications, 1961), and J. Q. Wilson, "Innovation in Organization: Notes Toward a Theory," in *Approaches to Organizational Design,* ed. J. D. Thompson, 193–218 (Pittsburgh: University of Pittsburgh Press, 1966).

159   **Xerox's invention of windows:** D. K. Smith and R. C. Alexander, *Fumbling the Future: How Xerox Invented, Then Ignored, the First Personal Computer* (New York: William Morrow, 1988). In 1969, Xerox moved its corporate headquarters from Rochester, NY, to Stamford, CT, but its engineering did not relocate.

161   **Brown and Eisenhardt study:** S. L. Brown and K. M. Eisenhardt, "The Art of Continuous Change: Linking Complexity Theory and Time-Paced Evolution in Relentlessly Shifting Organizations," *Administrative Science Quarterly* 42 (1997): 1–34.

161   **Reserving a percentage of employee time for new projects:** These numbers appear in several sources: T. Amabile, C. N. Hadley, and S. J. Kramer, "Creativity Under the Gun," *Harvard Business Review* 80, no. 8 (2002): 52–61; R. M. Kanter, *The Change Masters: Innovation and Entrepreneurship in the American Corporation* (New York: Simon & Schuster, 1983); and C. J. Nemeth, "Managing Innovation: When Less Is More," *California Management Review* 40, no. 1 (1997): 59–74.

161   **Rapid prototyping:** Michael Schrage advocates a culture of rapid prototyping in his *Serious Play: How the World's Best Companies Simulate to Innovate* (Boston: Harvard Business School Press, 2000).

161   **Boeing's Operations Technology Center:** A. B. Hargadon, "Firms as Knowledge Brokers: Lessons in Pursuing Continuous Innovation," *California Management Review* 40, no. 3 (1998): 209–227.

161   **Pixar:** C. Warren, "Innovation, Inc.," *American Way,* December 15, 2004, 92–99.

162   **Thomas Edison's Atlantic telegraph and microphone design:** Hargadon, "Firms as Knowledge Brokers," 223.

163   **Edison's car battery:** T. P. Hughes, "Edison's Method," in *Technology at the Turning Point,* ed. W. B. Pickett (San Francisco: San Francisco Press, 1977), 5–22.

163   **Anita Roddick and Department of Surprises:** Page 52 of L. T. Perry, "Strategic Improvising: How to Formulate and Implement Competitive Strategies in Concert," *Organizational Dynamics* 19, no. 4 (1991): 51–64.

163   **Idea marketplaces at Royal Dutch/Shell:** R. Stringer, "How to Manage Radical Innovation," *California Management Review* 42, no. 4 (2000): 70–88.

165   **BMW's Leipzig factory:** G. Edmondson, "BMW's Dream Factory," *Business Week,* October 16, 2006, 70–80.

165   **Steelcase:** Steelcase published two reports in 2001, available on the company's Web site: *Face to Face, Screen to Screen: Collaboration in the New Workplace,* http://www.steelcase.com/na/knowledgedesign.aspx/f=10251& c=10222, and *Hothouse Environments: Fostering Breakthrough Innovations,* http://www.steelcase.com/na/hothouse_seminar_findings_knowledgedesign .aspx?f=10119.

165   **BP, Google, and McCann Erickson:** E. Lotozo, "Tearing Down the Walls," *Philadelphia Inquirer,* November 28, 2006.

166   **On BP's Houston office:** Herman Miller, "BP WOW" (2006), http://www .hermanmiller.com/hm/content/case_studies/pdfs/CS_BPW_FUL.pdf.

166   **Working under pressure kills creativity:** Amabile, Hadley, and Kramer, "Creativity Under the Gun," 52–61. Quotations from workers are on page 58 and AT&T's philosophy is stated on page 52.

168   **"The company was jumping the gun":** Page 323 of A. S. Miner, P. Bassoff, and C. Moorman, "Organizational Improvisation and Learning: A Field Study," *Administrative Science Quarterly* 46 (2001): 304–337.

168   **Annoyance Theater and Improv Olympic:** R. K. Sawyer, *Improvised Dialogues: Emergence and Creativity in Conversation* (Westport, CT: Greenwood, 2003).

168   **Brown and Eisenhardt study:** S. L. Brown and K. M. Eisenhardt, "The Art of Continuous Change: Linking Complexity Theory and Time-Paced Evolution in Relentlessly Shifting Organizations," *Administrative Science Quarterly* 42 (1997): 1–34. Quotations are on pages 10, 11, and 14. In 2003, Shona Brown became senior vice president of business operations at Google.

169   **Opportunistic planning:** B. Hayes-Roth, "Opportunistic Control of Action in Intelligent Agents," *IEEE Transactions on Systems, Man, and Cybernetics* 23, no. 6 (1992): 1575–1587.

170   **Charles Mingus quotation:** B. Kernfeld, *What to Listen for in Jazz* (New Haven, CT: Yale University Press, 1995), 119.

171   **Deep-dish pizza story:** E. Darr, L. Argote, and D. Epple, "The Acquisition, Transfer and Depreciation of Knowledge in Service Organizations: Productivity in Franchises," *Management Science* 41 (1995): 1750–1762. Andrall Pearson, who was CEO of Pepsi (which owned Pizza Hut), points out that Pizza Hut's pan pizza went through four or five iterations before it worked properly; see page 124 of A. E. Pearson, "Tough-Minded Ways to Get Innovative," *Harvard Business Review* 80, no. 8 (2002): 117–125.

171   **Innovations stimulated by job assignments:** R. M. Kanter, *The Change Masters: Innovation and Entrepreneurship in the American Corporation* (New York: Simon & Schuster, 1983). A summary appears on page 180 of R. M. Kanter, "When a Thousand Flowers Bloom: Structural, Collective, and Social Conditions for Innovation in Organization," *Research in Organizational Behavior* 10 (1988): 169–211.

172   **Cisco and information sharing:** J. McGregor, "The Architect of a Different Kind of Organization," *Fast Company,* June 2005, 67–68.

172   **Cisco quotations:** From a case study: S. L Woerner, *Networked at Cisco* (Cambridge, MA: MIT Press, 2001).

173   **Hasbro's meetings with top management:** Page 120 of A. E. Pearson, "Tough-Minded Ways to Get Innovative," *Harvard Business Review* 80, no. 8 (2002): 117–125.

173   **Pixar university training:** President Ed Catmull quoted in an interview in Warren, "Innovation, Inc.," 92–99.

175   **1970s research showing that interconnection leads to innovation:** Page 177 of R. M. Kanter, "When a Thousand Flowers Bloom: Structural, Collective, and Social Conditions for Innovation in Organization," *Research in Organizational Behavior* 10 (1988): 169–211.

175   **Philips and matrix structures:** "The New Organization," *Economist,* January 21, 2006, 3–18. On the problems with frequent restructurings, see J. A. Oxman and B. D. Smith, "The Limits of Structural Change," *MIT Sloan Management Review* 45, no. 1 (2003): 77–82. Karl Weick advocated for an improvisational and emergent approach to organizational redesign; see K. E. Weick, *Making Sense of the Organization* (London: Blackwell, 2001). Weick noted that "design often codifies previous unplanned change rather than creates future planned change" (page 62).

175   **Booz Allen Hamilton study of R&D spending:** B. Jaruzelski, K. Dehoff, and R. Bordia, "Money Isn't Everything," *Strategy+Business* 1 (Winter 2005): 54–67.

177   **Social network analysis:** J. McGregor, "The Architect of a Different Kind of Organization," *Fast Company,* June 2005, 67–68. IBM's Erlich is quoted on page 48.

Chapter 9

179   **Henry George and the single tax:** I learned additional details about Henry George from a history written by his granddaughter, Agnes George de Mille: *Who Was Henry George?* (Henry George School of Social Science, 1979), http://www.henrygeorgeschool.org/whowashg.htm. The Henry George School of Social Science is located today in a brownstone on East Thirtieth Street, and still teaches George's single-tax philosophy.

180   **Monopoly history:** An excellent version of the story is B. H. Wolfe, "The Monopolization of Monopoly," *San Francisco Bay Guardian,* April 23, 1976, http://www.adena.com/adena/mo/. National Public Radio featured this story in the *Present at the Creation* series on November 25, 2002, www.npr.org/programs/morning/features/patc/monopoly/. Another account of the story appears in P. E. Orbanes, *The Game Makers: The Story of Parker Brothers from Tiddledy-Winks to Trivial Pursuit* (Boston: Harvard Business School Press, 2004). Ralph Anspach, the inventor of Anti-Monopoly, has self-published his own history as G. Anspach, *The Billion Dollar Monopoly Swindle* (Redwood City, CA: R. Anspach, 2000). I found the original rules from Magie's patent at http://tt.tf/gamehist/games/lg-1910/lg-1910_egc-rules.html.

183   **Philo T. Farnsworth and the invention of television:** Two recent books tell this history: E. I. Schwartz, *The Last Lone Inventor: A Tale of Genius,*

Deceit, and the Birth of Television (New York: HarperCollins, 2002), and D. Stashower, *The Boy Genius and the Mogul: The Untold Story of Television* (New York: Broadway Books, 2002). Farnsworth's quotation "That's it, folks" appears on page 112.

185   **The rise and decline of Route 128:** This is the theme of A. Saxenian, *Regional Advantage: Culture and Competition in Silicon Valley and Route 128* (Cambridge, MA: Harvard University Press, 1996).

187   **Famous clusters:** Famous clusters are described and analyzed in M. E. Porter, "Clusters and the New Economics of Competition," *Harvard Business Review* 76, no. 6 (1998): 77–90.

187   **Alfred Marshall and clusters:** *Principle of Economics,* first edition published in 1890 by Macmillan. Richard Florida has recently made a new argument for the importance of location to innovation: R. Florida, *The Rise of the Creative Class and How It's Transforming Work, Life, Community and Everyday Life* (New York: Basic Books, 2002).

188   **Token Ring and Ethernet:** U. von Burg and M. Kenney, "Sponsors, Communities and Standards: Winning in the Local Area Networking Business" (working paper no. 154, Berkeley Roundtable on the International Economy, Berkeley, CA, 2003).

189   **Glenn Curtiss and the AEA:** S. Shulman, *Unlocking the Sky: Glenn Hammond Curtiss and the Race to Invent the Airplane* (New York: HarperCollins, 2002).

191   **Eli Whitney and the cotton gin; James Watt and the steam engine:** For both, the real story appears in an excellent and influential book that tells many unknown incremental histories of famous inventions: G. Basalla, *The Evolution of Technology* (New York: Cambridge University Press, 1988).

192   **Hewlett Packard reassigns its engineers:** L. Fleming, "Finding the Organizational Sources of Technological Breakthroughs: The Story of Hewlett-Packard's Thermal Ink-Jet," *Industrial and Corporate Change* 11, no. 5 (2002): 1059–1084.

192   **Negroponte, "Innovation is inefficient":** N. Negroponte, "Creating a Culture of Ideas," *Technology Review,* February 2003, 34–35.

194   **Ray Tomlinson and e-mail:** There are many accounts of this story, most of them available on the Internet. Here I've drawn heavily on Tomlinson's own account at http://openmap.bbn.com/~tomlinso/ray/firstemailmain.html.

196   **Complementary invention:** The study of complementarities and complementary inventions is associated with Nathan Rosenberg, an economics professor at Stanford University. Rosenberg's works include *Inside the Black Box: Technology and Economics* (Cambridge: Cambridge University

Press, 1982), and *Exploring the Black Box: Technology, Economics, and History* (Cambridge: Cambridge University Press, 1994).

197   **Uzzi and Spiro study of the Broadway musical industry:** B. Uzzi and J. Spiro, "Collaboration and Creativity: The Small World Problem," *American Journal of Sociology* 111, no. 2 (2005): 447–504.

199   **Origins of GNU/Linux:** Several technical but clearly written Web pages appear at http://www.gnu.org/.

200   **More than half the world's Web servers run Linux:** C. Ferguson, "How Linux Could Overthrow Microsoft," *Technology Review,* June 2005.

200   **Torvalds on the cover of *Business Week*:** See the issue of January 31, 2005.

200   **Eric von Hippel:** *Democratizing Innovation* (Cambridge, MA: MIT Press, 2005).

200   **Toyota Production System:** This story is taken from P. Evans and B. Wolf, "Collaboration Rules," *Harvard Business Review* 83, nos. 7–8 (2005): 96–104.

201   **Krzysztof Klincewicz study:** K. Klincewicz, "Innovativeness of Open Source Software Projects" (paper presented at the Proceedings of the First International Conference on Open Source Systems, Genova, Italy, July 2005), http://opensource.mit.edu/papers/klincewicz.pdf. Because the five hundred projects Klincewicz studied were the ones that managed to catch on among developers, he notes that it's not that there aren't novel ideas that are proposed; what happens is that novel ideas don't recruit other developers, and never diffuse throughout the community. Ilkka Tuomi also makes the point that Linux is not innovative: I. Tuomi, "The Future of Open Source," in *How Open Is the Future?* ed. M. Wynants and J. Cornelis (Brussels: VUB Brussels University Press, 2005), 429–459.

Chapter 10

204   **Google Code Jam competition:** http://www.google.com/codejam/.

204   **IBM Innovation Jam:** J. Hempel, "Big Blue Brainstorm," *Business Week,* August 7, 2006, 70.

204   **eBay statistics:** eBay press release dated July 21, 2005.

205   **Quake and Half-Life:** D. H. Freedman, "Hands On: The Secrets of Open-Source Managing," *Inc. Magazine,* December 2004, 33–37.

205   **Epic Games and Digital Extremes:** G. Hamel and G. Getz, "Funding Growth in an Age of Austerity," *Harvard Business Review* 82, nos. 7–8 (2004): 76–84.

205   **YouTube:** In the spirit of this chapter, my source for the YouTube facts is its *Wikipedia* entry.

205   **Cellucotton/Kleenex:** C. Panati, *Panati's Extraordinary Origins of Everyday Things* (New York: Perennial Library, 1987).

207   **NSF study of five hundred innovations:** D. G. Marquis and S. Myers, *Successful Industrial Innovations* (Washington, DC: National Science Foundation, 1969).

207   **Eric von Hippel's study of user innovation:** E. von Hippel, "Users as Innovators," in *Corporate Strategy and Product Innovation,* ed. R. R. Rothberg, 239–251 (New York: Free Press, 1981).

207   **From 10 to 40 percent of users modify the products they buy:** E. von Hippel, *Democratizing Innovation* (Cambridge, MA: MIT Press, 2005), 4.

207   **Lego Mindstorms 2.0:** B. I. Koerner, "Geeks in Toyland," *Wired,* February 2006, 106–111, 150.

209   **3M study of annual sales of user-originated products:** G. L. Lilien et al., "Performance Assessment of the Lead User Idea-Generation Process for New Product Development," *Management Science* 48, no. 8 (2002): 1042–1059.

210   **Boston Consulting Group Yves Morieux quotation:** Page 67 of J. McGregor, "Gospels of Failure," *Fast Company,* February 2005, 62–67.

210   **Cisco provides customers access to internal information:** S. L. Woerner, *Networked at Cisco* (Cambridge, MA: MIT Press, 2001), 10.

210   **SAS Institute:** R. Florida and J. Goodnight, "Managing for Creativity," *Harvard Business Review* 82, nos. 7–8 (2005): 125–131. Jeffrey Pfeffer of Stanford University made the comparison to the Grateful Dead show in this article.

211   **Sailboard jumping and foot straps:** E. von Hippel, *Democratizing Innovation.* The Larry Stanley quotation is on page 2.

211   **Mountain bike innovation:** C. Lüthje, C. Herstatt, and E. von Hippel, "The Dominant Role of Local Information in User Innovation: The Case of Mountain Biking" (working paper, MIT Sloan School of Management, Cambridge, MA, 2002), http://userinnovation.mit.edu/papers/6.pdf.

212   **Frisbee:** I used several sources for this story: J. McMahon, "History of the Disc" (2006), http://www.goaltimate.com/discsports.htm; Panati, *Panati's Extraordinary Origins;* and S. Shulman, "Frisbee's Marketing Wind," *Technology Review,* October 2002, 75.

213   **Drinking games:** J. Gettleman, "As Young Adults Drink to Win, Marketers Join In," *New York Times,* October 16, 2005.

214   **Cosmic Wimpout:** See http://www.cosmicwimpout.com/tales.html.

215   **Research in Motion:** A. Frankel, "The Willing Partner," *Technology Review,* July 2005, 36–38.

215 **Larry Huston's "connect and develop":** L. Huston and N. Sakkab, "Connect and Develop: Inside Procter & Gamble's New Model for Innovation," *Harvard Business Review* 84, no. 3 (2006): 58–66.

217 **2003 Accenture study of external innovation:** J. C. Linder, S. Jarvenpaa, and T. H. Davenport, "Toward an Innovation Sourcing Strategy," *MIT Sloan Management Review* 44, no. 4 (Summer 2003): 43–49.

217 **2006 external innovation in pharmaceuticals:** "The New Organization," *Economist,* January 21, 2006, 3–18 (see page 9).

Chapter 11

219 **Abraham Lincoln quotation:** E. I. Schwartz, *The Last Lone Inventor: A Tale of Genius, Deceit, and the Birth of Television* (New York: Harper-Collins, 2002), 201.

220 **Edison's battle with AC:** Many sources tell this story, including Edison's *Wikipedia* entry. Another concise version appears at http://inventors.about.com/od/hstartinventions/a/Electric_Chair.htm.

220 **Richard Florida and the creative economy:** R. Florida, *The Rise of the Creative Class and How It's Transforming Work, Life, Community and Everyday Life* (New York: Basic Books, 2002).

222 **Patent thickets:** E. von Hippel describes this strategy in his *Democratizing Innovation* (Cambridge, MA: MIT Press, 2005).

222 **The U.S. Digital Millennium Copyright Act makes it impossible to modify:** H. R. Varian, "New Chips Can Keep a Tight Rein on Consumers," *New York Times,* July 4, 2002.

224 **Lawrence Lessig:** Lessig is the most vocal advocate of modifying intellectual property law, and what I say in this chapter is partially inspired by, and completely consistent with, his 2004 book, *Free Culture: The Nature and Future of Creativity* (New York: Penguin). The quotation is on page 106, as is the 1 percent suggestion.

224 **Sewing machine industry and its patent pool:** G. R. Cooper, *The Sewing Machine: Its Invention and Development* (Washington, DC: Smithsonian Institution, 1976).

ABOUT THE AUTHOR

Keith Sawyer is an Associate Professor of Education and of Psychology at Washington University in St. Louis. He is one of the world's leading experts on creativity, and has written or edited nine books and over fifty scientific articles. He combines this scientific expertise with a strong hands-on background in real-world creativity, having designed video games for Atari and consulted for top corporations on innovative technologies. His research has been featured on *CNN, Fox News, Time* magazine, and other media. A popular speaker, he lectures to corporations, associations, and universities around the world on creativity and innovation. Sawyer lives in St. Louis, Missouri, with his wife and their two children.

Join the conversation: visit www.groupgenius.net.

INDEX